EMERGENT FEMINISMS

Through twelve chapters that historicize and re-evaluate postfeminism as a dominant framework of feminist media studies, this collection maps out new modes of feminist media analysis at both theoretical and empirical levels and offers new insights into the visibility and circulation of feminist politics in contemporary media cultures. The essays in this collection resituate feminism within current debates about postfeminism, considering how both operate as modes of political engagement and as scholarly traditions. The authors analyze a range of media texts and practices including American television shows *Being Mary Jane* and *Inside Amy Schumer*, Beyoncé's "Formation" music video, misandry memes, and Hong Kong cinema.

Jessalynn Keller is an assistant professor in Critical Media Studies at the University of Calgary, Canada.

Maureen E. Ryan is an instructor in Media and Cinema Studies at DePaul University, USA.

Routledge Research in Gender, Sexuality, and Media

Edited by Mary Celeste Kearney, University of Notre Dame

The Routledge Research in Gender, Sexuality, and Media series aims to publish original research in the areas of feminist and queer media studies, with a particular but not exclusive focus on gender and sexuality. In doing so, this series brings to the market cutting-edge critical work that refreshes, reshapes, and redirects scholarship in these related fields while contributing to a better global understanding of how gender and sexual politics operate within historical and current mediascapes.

EMERGENT FEMINISMS

Complicating a Postfeminist Media Culture

Edited by Jessalynn Keller and Maureen E. Ryan

Routledge
Taylor & Francis Group

NEW YORK AND LONDON

First published 2018
by Routledge
711 Third Avenue, New York, NY 10017

and by Routledge
2 Park Square, Milton Park, Abingdon, Oxon OX14 4RN

Routledge is an imprint of the Taylor & Francis Group, an informa business

© 2018 Taylor & Francis

Library of Congress Cataloging-in-Publication Data
Names: Keller, Jessalynn, 1982– editor. | Ryan, Maureen E., editor.
Title: Emergent feminisms : complicating a postfeminist media culture /
   edited by Jessalynn Keller and Maureen E. Ryan.
Description: New York, NY : Routledge, 2018. Identifiers: LCCN 2017047085 |
   ISBN 9780815386605 (hardback) | ISBN 9780815386612 (pbk.)
Subjects: LCSH: Feminism. | Feminism and mass media.
Classification: LCC HQ1155 .E495 2018 | DDC 305.42—dc23
LC record available at https://lccn.loc.gov/2017047085

ISBN: 978-0-8153-8660-5 (hbk)
ISBN: 978-0-8153-8661-2 (pbk)
ISBN: 978-1-351-17546-3 (ebk)

Typeset in Bembo
by Apex CoVantage, LLC

CONTENTS

FIGURES

CONTRIBUTORS

Jonathan Cohn is an assistant professor in the English and Film Studies Department at the University of Alberta, Canada. His research focuses on the history of digital cultures and technologies. His work has appeared in various anthologies and journals, including *Camera Obscura* and *Television & New Media*.

Emilie Lawrence is a Ph.D. candidate at University College London whose dissertation research explores the construction of and performance of feminism online. Her research interests include glamor and emotional labor, fourth-wave feminism, fat activism, body positivity discourses, and affect theories.

Gina Marchetti is an associate professor at the University of Hong Kong, where she teaches courses in film, gender and sexuality, critical theory, and cultural studies. She is the author of several books, including the most recent *The Chinese Diaspora on American Screens: Race, Sex, and Cinema* (Temple University Press 2012) and has also co-edited numerous anthologies exploring Asian cinema and film culture. Her current research interests include women filmmakers in the HKSAR, China and world cinema, and contemporary trends in Asian and Asian American film culture.

Sujata Moorti is a professor of Gender, Sexuality, and Feminist Studies at Middlebury College. She has published extensively on media representations of gender, sexuality, and diasporic formations and is currently completing a manuscript on iFeminism where she teases out the ways in which social media are altering understandings of feminism around the world. She is author of *Color of Rape: Gender, Race and Democratic Public Spheres* (SUNY Press 2002) and co-editor of

Global Bollywood: The Travels of Hindi Song and Dance (University of Minnesota Press 2008) and *Local Violence, Global Media: Feminist Analyses of Gendered Representations* (Peter Lang 2009).

Taylor Nygaard is a visiting assistant professor at the University of Denver in the Department of Media, Film, and Journalism Studies. She received a Ph.D. from the School of Cinematic Arts at the University of Southern California. Her research on gender and the media industries has been presented at conferences such as the Society for Cinema and Media Studies and Console-ing Passions and has been published in *Feminist Media Studies, Television & New Media, Spectator*, and elsewhere.

Sarah Projansky is Associate Dean for Faculty & Academic Affairs in the College of Fine Arts, as well as Professor of Film and Media Arts and of Gender Studies at the University of Utah. She is author of *Spectacular Girls: Media Fascination and Celebrity Culture* (NYU Press 2014) and *Watching Rape: Film and Television in Postfeminist Culture* (NYU Press, 2001), and co-editor of *Enterprise Zones: Critical Positions on Star Trek* (Westview Press 1996).

Bryce Renninger is the Managing Editor of Field of Vision, a documentary journalism unit started by Laura Poitras. He received his Ph.D. in Media Studies with a certificate in Women's and Gender Studies from Rutgers University.

Jessica Ringrose is a professor of Sociology of Gender and Education at the UCL Institute of Education in London, UK. Her current research explores feminist activism in school and teen's digital gender and sexual cultures. She is author of over fifty journal articles and book chapters, editor of four special issues of journals and author of four books including, *Post-Feminist Education?: Girls and the Sexual Politics of Schooling* (Routledge 2013). She is currently working on two new books, *Gender, Activism and #FeministGirl* (Routledge forthcoming) with Emma Renold, and *Digital Feminist Activism: Girls and Women Fight Back Against Rape Culture* (Oxford University Press 2018) with Kaitlynn Mendes and Jessalynn Keller.

Amanda Rossie is an adjunct professor of Women's and Gender Studies at the College of New Jersey and West Chester University. Her dissertation "New Media, New Maternities: Representations of Maternal Femininity in Postfeminist Popular Culture" maps the production of maternal femininity across new media by pinpointing how postfeminist themes of temporality, consumption, and transformation are emphasized in/by/through new media technologies. Her research is published in *Continuum: Journal of Media and Cultural Studies* and *Girls' Sexualities and Media* (Peter Lang 2013).

Cheryl Thompson is a Banting Postdoctoral Fellow (2016–2018) in the Centre for Drama, Theatre, and Performance Studies at the University of Toronto and the Department of English and Drama at the University of Toronto Mississauga. Her research aims to elucidate the system of meaning in the blackface minstrelsy's theatrical playbills, portraits, photographs, illustrations, and visual ephemera outside the traditional theatre in the spaces and places of nation-building during Canada's modern period, 1890s to 1940s. Dr. Thompson also teaches courses on feminist media studies, visual culture and identity, Black Canadian studies, and North American consumer culture. Her first book, *Beauty in a Box: Detangling the Roots of Black Beauty Culture in Canada* is forthcoming with Wilfrid Laurier Press in 2018.

Verity Trott is a Ph.D. candidate, sessional tutor, and casual lecturer at the University of Melbourne. Her interdisciplinary research focuses on digital activism, feminist theory, and big data.

Alyxandra Vesey is an assistant professor in the Department of Journalism and Creative Media at the University of Alabama. Her research focuses on the relationship between gender, music culture, and media labor. She is currently working on a manuscript investigating musicians' contributions to television industry practice during the post-network era. She also studies the ideologies of gender that circulate within merchandising in the recording industry. Her work has been published in *Television & New Media*, *Feminist Media Studies*, *Popular Music and Society*, and *Cinema Journal*.

Emilie Zaslow is an associate professor of Communication Studies at Pace University in New York City. She is author of *Feminism Inc: Coming of Age in Girl Power Media Culture* (Palgrave 2009) and *Playing with America's Doll: A Cultural Analysis of the American Girl Collection* (Palgrave 2017).

ACKNOWLEDGMENTS

This work emerged from a series of conversations we had at conferences in 2013 and 2014 about the state of feminist media studies. It later grew into several conference panels devoted to exploring emergent feminisms: the 2015 Society for Cinema and Media Studies (SCMS) Conference in Montreal and the 2016 Console-ing Passions International Conference on Television, Video, Audio, New Media, and Feminism at the University of Notre Dame. We would like to thank our original SCMS co-panelists, Carrie Rentschler and Sarah Banet-Weiser, for their early contributions to this project, as well as the attendees of both panels for the lively discussion that ensued. We would also like to thank our series editor Mary Celeste Kearney for her guidance and support, as well as our editor Erica Wetter and editorial assistant Mia Moran at Routledge. Heartfelt thanks also go to Monica Henderson for her help with photos, Peter Kersten at Getty for assisting us with the cover photo, and Murray Leeder for his work on the index. Finally, we would each like to thank one another. Working together has been an extremely rewarding pursuit—and, we would add, an example of feminist solidarity in practice.

INTRODUCTION

Mapping Emergent Feminisms

Jessalynn Keller and Maureen E. Ryan

At the 2014 MTV Video Music Awards, Beyoncé performed part of her hit song "Flawless" in front of the glowing word "FEMINIST." While she snaked her way around the stage in a glittering bodysuit, the sampled words of Nigerian author and activist Chimamanda Ngozi Adichie proclaimed a feminist to be "a person who believes in the social, political, and economic equality of the sexes." While the crowd went wild, news media was also abuzz with this moment of "feminist zeitgeist" (Valenti 2014), with print and digital news outlets debating the significance of the event. The darkened outline of Beyoncé's famous curves against the emblazoned f-word was an image that *felt different* to many, and seemed to make visible a shift in the relationships between feminism, identity, and politics in popular media culture. Yet not everyone was enthused with Beyoncé's articulation of feminism to her sexualized, commercial brand. Feminist scholar bell hooks declared her to be a "terrorist, especially in terms of [her] impact on young girls" in a lecture at the New School (Juzwiak 2014), while Scottish singer Annie Lennox, in an interview with NPR, disparaged Beyoncé's performance by saying, "Twerking is not feminism" (Leight 2014).

Considered together, these discourses surrounding the "is-she-or-isn't-she" question of Beyoncé's feminism reveal important instances of feminism's renewed *mattering* to popular culture. Perhaps unimaginable a decade earlier, Beyoncé's performance was only one example of the ways in which feminism has become increasingly visible within popular media cultures. Other celebrities such as Emma Watson and Taylor Swift have joined Beyoncé in self-proclaiming as feminists, prompting Hannah Hamad and Anthea Taylor (2015) to describe "celebrity feminism" as a significant trend in popular culture. We also see feminist politics incorporated into digital cultures, especially in the feminist blogosphere anchored by sites such as *Feministing* (feministing.com) and

Racialicious (racialicious.com) and activist campaigns such as #YesAllWomen and #BeenRapedNeverReported (Thrift 2014; Keller, Mendes and Ringrose 2016). Elsewhere, feminist politics are bubbling up through girls' and women's media production; comedians like Amy Schumer, Tina Fey, and Mindy Kaling, and teenage web editor and actress Tavi Gevinson are all provocative examples of the ways in which feminist politics are emerging in commercial media texts in ways that both converge with, and diverge from, the feminisms of previous decades (Dow 1996; Lauzen 2012; Keller 2015a).

These mediated "emergent feminisms" are the focus of this book. The word "emergent" has multiple meanings; it suggests something "arising unexpectedly," "calling for prompt action," and occurring as a "natural or logical consequence," definitions that have affective, temporal, and material implications that require careful consideration in relation to feminism (Merriam-Webster 2015). In this sense, the word embodies the characteristics we see in visible contemporary feminisms and functions as an analytic tool to help us theorize contemporary gendered subjectivities within popular media cultures. With the unexpected, and seemingly sudden, resurfacing of feminism, we are not arguing that feminism is only emerging *now* within popular cultures, as this is hardly the case. Scholars have mapped the lengthy history of feminism as a popular politics, including commercial magazines (Farrell 1998), television (Dow 1996), and film (Brunsdon 1997). This scholarship informs our approach and use of the word "emergent" as a concept that accounts for both important historical continuities *and* the unique ways in which feminisms are responding to the specificity of our current cultural moment. We do not argue for the presence of a unified, singular popular feminism that has usurped a media culture once dominated by postfeminist sensibilities. Instead, we aim to map a diverse range of emergent feminisms in popular media cultures and suggest that they require not a *rejection* of theorizing postfeminism, but an expanded theoretical lens that can offer insight into a media culture that has changed dramatically over the past decade, when many of the landmark texts about postfeminism were written. In this volume, we ask what a contemporary "feminist zeitgeist" suggests about the relationships between and among femininity, feminism, postfeminism, anti-feminism, and contemporary media culture. Which feminisms attain mediated visibility and which remain marginalized? And, what is the relationship between emergent feminisms, postfeminist sensibilities, and mediated misogyny?

Emergent Feminisms: Complicating a Postfeminist Media Culture aims to make sense of this historical moment within media cultures where emergent feminisms are increasingly visible, yet remain somewhat slippery and difficult to pin down as they pulse through musical performances, hashtags, celebrities, brands, and even business practices. The chapters in this collection contribute to developing a clearer understanding of emergent feminisms and what they do politically, culturally, and socially by addressing the diverse visibility of feminisms across mediated cultures, including in popular television programs, fashion media, celebrity culture, and YouTube videos. Indeed, it is this flourishing of feminisms across pockets of popular culture that seems to call into question the widely held assumption by feminist media scholars over the past decade that popular media culture is marked by an explicitly "postfeminist sensibility" (Gill 2007). This book explores this tension, with the goal of *resituating* postfeminism within our current moment marked by emergent feminisms, without denying its significance and ongoing importance as a framework for understanding feminized media cultures. To do so, we turn now to the foundational writing on postfeminism to evaluate its contributions to feminist media studies over the past two decades, and to highlight what it might continue to offer feminist media scholars today.

The Long Roots of Postfeminism

The term "postfeminism" originally appeared in the popular press in 1982, when *New York Times* journalist Susan Bolotin described how the young career women she interviewed were reluctant to identify as feminist, despite feeling that they were discriminated against because of their gender. Bolotin identified these women as part of a "postfeminist" generation, for their feelings that feminism put too much pressure on women—and men—to change. Other media discourses in the 1980s blamed women for "wanting it all" and prescribe a return to traditional femininity as a strategy for dealing with lingering sexism (see Hewlett 1986). Since then, popular media have continued to rely on the concept of postfeminism to describe an era *after* the feminist political activism of the 1960s and 1970s, as well as to denote more generally a feeling among women and the culture that the time of feminism is "over."

In the late 1980s and 1990s, feminist media scholars adopted this notion of postfeminism as that which is *after*, describing it as a hegemonic response to the crisis feminism presented to dominant interests. Judith Stacey (1987) defined postfeminism as "the simultaneous incorporation, revision, and depoliticization of many of the central goals of second-wave feminism" which occurred after the women's liberation movement (cited in Dow 1996, 87). For Bonnie Dow, postfeminism represents "a hegemonic negotiation of second-wave ideals, in which the presumption of equality for women in the public sphere has been retained" (1996, 87–88). Similarly, Charlotte Brunsdon (1997) considers postfeminism as a way of accommodating certain feminist ideas, such as autonomy of self and body and career options for women, within dominant structures of power. In *Screen Tastes*, Brunsdon argues that postfeminism is a concept that has purchase in the context of the late 1970s and 1980s, following the women's liberation movement, when certain aspects of feminism were repudiated while others were gaining acceptance. Employed as such, it is a historicizing concept that can help scholars identify discursive shifts in popular culture at particular points in time. Outside of such uses, Brunsdon writes, "'postfeminism' is a profoundly ahistorical concept, and in that sense misleading and not useful to the feminist political project" (85). To Brunsdon, we cannot divorce the notion of postfeminism from the historical conjuncture in which it appeared.

Scholarship on postfeminism in the 2000s built on some of these ideas, but shifted away from postfeminism as a temporal construct in response to influential writing by feminist media scholars, including Angela McRobbie (2009) and Rosalind Gill (2007), who situated postfeminism as "an object of critical analysis" in the media landscape and a historically located "sensibility," respectively. In these analyses, postfeminism functions not as a *temporal concept* or a *form of feminism*, but as a set of neoliberal cultural ideas that privilege the individual, apolitical empowerment of girls and women, who are hailed as productive feminized workers, citizens, and mothers (also see Tasker and Negra 2007; Gill 2016). Our use of the term postfeminism is aligned with this understanding of the concept, and we use the terms "postfeminism" and "postfeminist sensibilities" interchangeably throughout this project, following in the footsteps of McRobbie and Gill.

While it is beyond the scope of this introduction to fully explore McRobbie and Gill's important arguments here (although many contributors do so throughout this volume), it is crucial to our project to highlight how both scholars draw attention to the ways in which contemporary media culture circulates these postfeminist sensibilities. This includes so-called "chick lit" (Harzewski 2011), films like *Bridget Jones' Diary* (McRobbie 2004, 2009), television programs such as *What Not to Wear* (McRobbie 2009), *Gilmore Girls*, *Providence*, and *Judging Amy* (Negra 2009; Lotz 2006) and magazines like *Glamour* (Gill 2009). In other words, in twenty-first-century scholarship, postfeminism functions as a media phenomenon. Importantly, in her influential article, Gill observes that "much of what counts as feminist debate in western countries today takes place in the media rather than outside it" (2007, 161). Yet she notes that it isn't quite that "the media has somehow become feminist and has adopted an unproblematically feminist perspective. Instead it seems more accurate to argue that the media offers contradictory, but nevertheless patterned, constructions" whereby feminist notions are systematically reworked to accommodate mainstream ideas (Gill 2007, 161). Consequently, media culture is a significant space for not only postfeminist sensibilities, but also diverse feminist politics that can both align with and challenge postfeminist sensibilities, depending on the cultural ideas, debates, and tensions circulating at particular historical moments. Indeed, it is this idea that undergirds this collection, and has encouraged us to explore what we see as the feminisms emerging today.

Yet, our suggestion that we need to better account for emergent feminisms has been met with some skepticism. For example, partly in response to our call for papers for this collection, Gill (2016) cautioned scholars against abandoning postfeminism in their analyses of contemporary media cultures. In her article "Post-Postfeminism?" she writes that she:

disputes the idea that the concept of postfeminism has nothing to offer in reading the current moment and aims to show how some of the popular mediated feminism circulating is in fact distinctively postfeminist in nature. I suggest the need to make distinctions between different kinds of (mediated) feminism, arguing that the corporate/neoliberal feminism (Catherine Rottenberg 2014) of *Lean In* (Sheryl Sandberg 2013) may have little in common with—and indeed may be antithetical to—the activist feminism of those protesting budget cuts to women's services or deportation of migrants. I posit that these feminisms may in turn be remote from dominant media constructions of feminism as a youthful, stylish identity.

(2016, 612)

Frankly, we agree with Gill's assessment. Many of the media texts and practices that are circulating in popular culture today are indeed antithetical to "activist feminism" and may or may not share sentiments with a postfeminist sensibility. However, we posit that they remain part of the landscape of emergent feminisms, which includes activist feminism, but is not limited to it. In-depth discussions of some of these ambivalent—or even outright antifeminist—texts can be found in this collection in several chapters, including Cheryl Thompson's analysis of Rachel Dolezal and Beyoncé (chapter nine), and Jonathan Cohn's interrogation of the #WomenAgainstFeminism social media campaign (chapter ten). Yet we also contend that alongside these ambivalent texts, politically engaged and anti-patriarchal texts and practices are sharing space—and audiences—in the sphere of contemporary culture. Our book showcases these as well; for example, Sarah Projansky explores feminist mainstream media coverage of campus sexual violence (chapter seven), while Sujata Moorti looks at the ways in which YouTube has been used to challenge rape culture (chapter six). Indeed, our interest is in exploring how a range of feminisms are being made visible within popular media cultures and critically interrogating how they might complicate, compete with, or complement our current understandings of postfeminism.

We hope it is clear then, that in re-centering feminism within debates about postfeminism, we are not asserting that postfeminism as we've been discussing it is no longer useful; instead, we aim to return to a historically informed analysis by problematizing constructions of postfeminism as an all-encompassing and more or less permanent state of affairs, a cultural climate from which there is no escape. Gill's deployment of postfeminism as a sensibility has since been applied by scholars with disregard to historical and geographic specificity, production contexts, and audience engagement, assuming that postfeminism functions as a widespread "consciousness" amongst all young women (see Press 2012). Here then, we echo Sean Fuller and Catherine Driscoll's (2015) insistence against using postfeminism as a blanket concept to dismiss media texts like *Girls*; instead, they argue for the importance of "acknowledging a popular feminist history in which 'post-' is just the current name for feminism's long struggle to remain visibly relevant to changing conditions" (261). Fuller and Driscoll's emphasis on changing cultural conditions is foundational to our own analysis and suggests the need to approach postfeminism with a degree of caution.

An overreliance on postfeminism as the only framework to make sense of gender politics in media culture also occludes the ways in which it has been oriented around white Western women's culture (for exceptions, see Springer 2007; Butler 2013; Dosekun 2015). While scholars have rightly acknowledged that postfeminism privileges white feminine subjects through an erasure of race, racism, or racial politics (Projansky 2001), and the "disarticulation" of solidarity between diverse women (McRobbie 2009), the continued scholarly attention to white women's postfeminist culture reifies that culture's centrality and relegates the cultures of women of color to the margins. Further, this analysis leaves little leverage to understand celebrities like Beyoncé, whose visibility as a black woman with feminist and anti-racist politics sits uneasily with the white, straight, middle-class, apolitical heroine central to the writing on mediated postfeminist sensibilities. We are not the first to acknowledge this; as Kimberly Springer (2007, 249) maintains, "Studies of postfeminism have studiously noted that many of its icons are white and cited the absence of women of color, but the analysis seems to stop there." Likewise, Jess Butler (2013) argues for an "intersectional approach to postfeminism" whereby scholars attend to how women of color such as Nicki Minaj disrupt the primacy of whiteness in postfeminist popular culture. We agree with Springer and Butler's assessments, but instead propose an attention to emerging feminisms, rather than a continued reliance on postfeminism, as a way to decenter the whiteness of postfeminism and uncover the new configurations of power inherent in contemporary media culture. Here we follow in the footsteps of Sarah Projansky (2014), who argues that scholars can problematize ideas about "dominant" representations—in this case, white girls and women—by choosing to look for media texts that exist outside normative racial representations.

Addressing Contemporary Moments of Conjuncture

With these issues in mind, we turn to the deeper structural question at the heart of this project: why has feminism returned to the forefront of popular media *now*, and what forms is feminism taking? How do these iterations of feminism relate to postfeminism, as well as to earlier formations of feminist politics? An attention to feminisms within our specific historical moment will allow us to develop new analyses of gendered subjectivities in media cultures, particularly with regard to race, class, sexuality, nationality, age, and other axes of difference. In this section we explore the political, social, and cultural conjuncture of the present moment in order to think critically about what distinguishes emergent feminist forms from residual and dominant ideas about gender and feminism that still circulate today. Drawing on Antonio Gramsci, Stuart Hall (1979) describes a conjuncture as "the coming together of often distinct though related contradictions, moving according to different tempos, but condensed in the same historical moment" (14). A conjunctural analysis is attuned to historical specificities, yet problematizes history as a linear, progressive narrative. Instead, thinking about the present as a *conjuncture* allows us to examine multiple, often contradictory hegemonic and counter-hegemonic forces working at specific moments in time and negotiating resistant discourses and practices. These forces shape individual and collective experiences of political, economic, cultural, and social life.

This idea is particularly useful for our project, as it both problematizes some of the linear framings of postfeminism as a time after feminism (see Tasker and Negra 2007; Gill 2007; McRobbie 2009 for discussions of this perspective) *and* highlights the need to re-examine the hegemonic forces and the challenges that feminist politics may pose to those forces today. The work of feminist media studies has historically been to evaluate how dominant interests (including patriarchy, capitalism, and white supremacy) have shaped representations of gender and sexuality, and in so doing, we have had to contend with the confluence of economic conditions, political currents, popular sentiment, and media that are shaped by and seek to respond to all of those things. We return to this approach here, examining in more detail what political, economic, and cultural forces make up the present conjuncture to situate both emergent feminisms and postfeminist sensibilities within our current moment. While this discussion is not meant to be comprehensive, it aims to begin to stake out some of the conjunctural qualities that authors address in this collection.

Firstly, we are acknowledging a shift in the political sphere where issues of economic and social justice have arguably re-emerged as flashpoints for what Nancy Fraser calls a "redistributive" feminist politics, concerned with structural inequalities and seeking to redistribute power and access (Fraser 2013). Fraser contrasts redistributive feminist politics with what she calls "recognition" feminist politics that are rooted in a desire for recognition of identity categories, and which, according to Fraser, "dovetailed all too neatly with a rising neoliberalism that wanted nothing more than to repress all memory of social egalitarianism" (2013, 5). Yet, we aim to problematize this binary set up by Fraser by suggesting that we are now seeing not only a resurgence of redistributive politics that seeks women's economic and social equality, but also an articulation of identity politics as an integral part of economic and social justice. For example, popular feminist columnist Lindy West wrote an op-ed for the *New York Times* (2017) that argued powerfully for the connection between identity politics and economic politics in the wake of the 2016 U.S. presidential election:

> I hear from some people on the left that Donald Trump's victory was at least partially the fault of "identity politics"—of feminists pushing too hard, of Black Lives Matter being too aggressive, of trans people needing to go to the bathroom—as though the violent suppression of a movement points more toward its irrelevance than its necessity. What the Democrats need

> to do, I often hear, is to move away from issues of "identity" and toward purer, broader issues of economic equality. But there is no model of economic equality that does not reckon with "identity politics." There is no economic equality without the ability to terminate a pregnancy. There is no economic equality without the overthrow of white supremacy.

Here, West makes the case for the inextricable linkage between identity politics and economic politics forcefully and with a renewed sense of urgency. Perhaps in the Obama years, with a somewhat progressive administration in the U.S., identity politics were seen by those on the right (and many, even, on the left) as frivolous. Yet, progressives and leftists in particular have been chastened by the election of Donald Trump, which emboldened a variety of misogynist, racist, and anti-globalization voices once assumed to be relics of the past. It is in this context that feminist commentators such as West make a renewed plea for the ways in which identity politics offer vital inroads to the structures of power. Moreover, we find it significant that a discussion of the connection between identity politics and economic politics, once discussed and circulated in the academy and in gender studies classrooms, are now topics for mainstream media publications, through the work of West and other popular feminists.

In conjunction with this revitalization of identity politics, economic and redistributive politics have become more widely discussed in popular media. For example, gendered violence in the West, a problem that a postfeminist sensibility would deem "solved," has not only persisted but has gained high-profile coverage in relation to a few key events over the past five years. Sarah Projansky observes that "1990s rape coverage in the news drew on a linear historical postfeminism, not bothering with a feminist perspective at all, now that feminism was supposedly 'over'" (2001, 90). In this decade, however, we have witnessed the development of public discourse informed by feminist perspectives about the problem of "rape culture" in response to events such as the digitally documented rapes of teenage girls in Steubenville, Texas, and Nova Scotia (Oved and Kane 2013). Another is the widespread recognition of the harassment of women online, in response to such incidents as #GamerGate and the harassment of Zoe Quinn and Anita Sarkeesian (Valenti 2015). Gendered violence has become more difficult to ignore in the West, and it has also been connected to public outrage at violence against women globally, including Boko Haram's kidnapping of 200 Nigerian girls in 2014, the attempted assassination of Pakistani teenager Malala Yousafzai in 2012, and the 2012 gang rape and murder of Jyoti Singh, a young Indian woman who was returning home from a night at the movies when she was attacked.

These events and the significant news coverage they generated made the issue of violence against girls and women publicly legible. They also produced activist agendas that have been working to change laws and create initiatives to combat gendered violence in local and global contexts. It has shown that the West has not, in fact, solved the problem of violence against women, and that it remains a global issue; even the *Huffington Post* has framed violence against women in the U.S. as part of a global problem (Chemaly 2011). Further, many of these initiatives have produced new forms of solidarities between girls and women, evident in events such as SlutWalk (Ringrose and Renold 2012; Mendes 2015) and hashtags like #BeenRapedNeverReported (Keller, Mendes, and Ringrose 2016). They've also suggested the need to re-engage feminist histories, pointing towards the enduring currency of women's liberation-era concepts like "rape culture" (Sills et al. 2016) and "domestic violence," both of which have featured prominently in well-publicized news stories such as Emma Sulkowicz's 2014 "Mattress Performance" to protest the refusal of Columbia University administration to expel her alleged rapist (see Grigoriadis 2014; Projansky, this volume) and the public assaults of singer Rihanna in 2009 and Janay Palmer in 2014 by their celebrity male partners (Chris Brown and Ray Rice, respectively).

Other terms such as the "War on Women" have been revived from feminist histories and reframed to critique contemporary sexism, including Republican policies on women during the 2012 U.S. election cycle, and the multiple sexual assault allegations against President Donald Trump that emerged in 2016. These critiques focused many longstanding feminist issues, including the Republican policies on women's reproductive rights, particularly birth control and abortion services, violence against women, and workplace discrimination. In this sense, Carrie Rentschler and Samantha Thrift (2015) recognize the 2012 election as being significant in galvanizing a popular feminism rooted in "an emergent set of practices for doing feminisms online defined by craftiness, humour, timeliness, and newsworthiness" (335). Rentschler and Thrift's (2015) discussion of the "Binders Full of Women" meme as an emergent feminist practice should then be understood as one example of a larger movement where feminist identities became publicly celebrated, the production of feminist media intensified, and the recognition of institutionalized sexism became part of mainstream discourse.

Alongside these emergent gender politics, we also see the proliferation of anti-racist political protest, most notably anchored by the Black Lives Matter movement, which began in 2012 in response to the killing of black teenager Trayvon Martin by a security guard in Florida. Since then, the numerous shootings of black boys and men by white police officers in the U.S. have continued to draw attention to structural racism in policing and other public institutions. Importantly, feminist activists have complicated the focus on black boys and men by pointing out the prevalence of anti-black violence against black girls and women, especially those who are queer and transgender. Using the hashtag #SayHerName, activists highlighted how black women have been continually excluded from the dominant framing of police brutality and racism and advocated for the recognition of the intersection of gender, race, sexuality, and class identities in the lives of black women (see Towns 2016). This type of anti-racist activism extends beyond U.S. borders and can also be seen in movements like Canada's Idle No More, where Indigenous peoples have engaged in a variety of tactics to protest various government bills that suppress Indigenous sovereignty. This anti-racist activism is also part of contemporary popular media culture, including being referenced in Beyoncé's 2016 "Formation" music video, an acceptance speech by actor Jesse Williams at the 2016 Black Entertainment Television Awards, and in the Netflix television series *Orange is the New Black*. While the relationship between anti-racist protest and popular culture is of course not new, the visibility of and cultural attention to Black Lives Matter and other anti-racist activism seems to mark a shift away from the post-racial discourses that dominated popular culture in the early 2000s (Joseph 2009).

Second, there are specific economic currents that define the present conjuncture, with the continuing shift to neoliberal capitalism foremost among them. According to Nikolas Rose (1999), Lisa Duggan (2003), and David Harvey (2005), neoliberalism is an economic force that individualizes and financializes every human endeavor, including those falling within social or political life, recasting them in entrepreneurial terms. Catherine Rottenberg emphasizes the political consequences of the neoliberal turn, arguing, "Collective forms of action or well-being are eroded, and a new regime of morality comes into being, one that links moral probity even more intimately to self-reliance and efficiency, as well as to the individual's capacity to exercise his or her own autonomous choices" (2014, 421). Moreover, neoliberal policies disavow the persistence of structural inequality, placing the onus to "get ahead" squarely on the individual. Media echo this discourse, as lifestyle and makeover programs encourage individuals to engage in "entrepreneurialism and self-responsibilization" to enact their best selves and lives (Ouellette and Hay 2008, 30; Weber 2009). Lifestyle television also addresses audiences as increasingly precarious in their housing and employment (Ryan forthcoming).

The 2008 global economic crisis complicated the dominance of neoliberal austerity somewhat, simultaneously producing both critiques of neoliberalism *and* the retrenchment of traditional and hegemonic gender roles as a response to the crisis. Both of these trends can be seen in contemporary media culture. For example, moments of failed neoliberal femininity, as discussed by Stephanie Patrick (2016) in relation to Snooki from the *Jersey Shore* and by Sean Fuller and Catherine Driscoll (2015) in relation to *Girls*, suggests popular interest in feminine figures who make visible what Lauren Berlant (2011) calls the "cruel optimism" perpetuated by neoliberalism. Indeed, the inability to ever attain "the good life" promised by neoliberal capitalism and the mediated visibility of these failures can eventually generate an awakening to the recognition that late capitalism is fundamentally crisis-prone (Piketty and Goldhammer 2014). More than that, it systematically produces gendered inequality. Feminist blogs such as *Jezebel* have recently worked to connect the recession to feminist issues such as pay equality, childbirth, and the work–life juggling act (see Baker 2013; Tolentino 2015;

Barry 2014; Ryan 2013), pointing to the ways in which neoliberal ideologies are being problematized within popular media culture.

Yet the recession and the lingering effects of the neoliberal turn have not produced an unequivocally feminist response. It has also led to varied attempts to reassert hegemonic power, as Negra and Tasker have shown, in the form of "recessionary images of female resourcefulness . . . that seek to retain traditionalist femininity under conditions of financial exigency," through images of thrifty housewives and cupcake-baking women (2014, 7). Indeed, popular media and dominant institutions have often clung to these "retreatist" (Negra 2009) postfeminist sensibilities following the financial crisis. Simultaneously, and perhaps in contradiction, women have been invited to "lean in" post-recession, assuming "a marketable self in relation to paid labor, so that wearing the most flattering hairstyle or cut of trousers is not only a way to snag a desirable man but also, and most importantly, a way to find and keep a desirable job" (Ouellette and Hay 2008, 119). In this sense, women are expected to reinvest themselves in the capitalist marketplace, performing a "new glamour-worker mode of feminine subjectivity" (Harris 2004, 19) constructed on the ideals of meritocracy and individual success (McRobbie 2009; Harris 2004).

This idea underpins what Catherine Rottenberg (2014) calls "neoliberal feminism," which incorporates core ideals of liberal feminism, such as "choice," "freedom," and "equality" within a framework that understands female success as an individual endeavor divorced from a critique of structural inequalities, power, and privilege. She writes, "In this emergent feminism, then, there is a liberal wrapping, while the content—namely, its mode of operation—is neoliberal through and through" (424–425). In this sense, neoliberal feminism dictates that the failure of women to succeed in the workplace is due to their own "ambition gap" rather than the structural inequalities that women face, including a lack of institutional or familial support for domestic and childcare duties and unequal pay. Facebook COO Sheryl Sandberg and her 2013 book *Lean In: Women, Work and to Will the Lead* popularized this neoliberal feminist discourse that may be understood as a hegemonic response to the 2008 recession (see Marchetti, this volume, for a discussion of Sandberg).

Rottenberg's discussion highlights the ambivalences of some of these emergent feminisms, calling attention to the ways in which emergent feminisms can remain affectively "stuck" (Ahmed 2004) to seemingly appealing postfeminist sensibilities. Indeed, Sandberg's neoliberal feminism espouses certain postfeminist sensibilities, including a focus on individualized social change and a lack of attention to class and racial privilege (see Gill 2016), yet is coupled with a feminist imperative to see more women in public life. Perhaps most importantly, the prominence of neoliberal feminism highlights the multiple iterations of feminisms that are currently visible, anchored in "political and ideological differences" (Gill 2016, 612). In this sense, emergent feminisms may not always offer us progressive politics or activist agendas, yet we contend that their materialization requires careful attention and analysis.

Finally, this conjunctural moment is marked by significant technological change, particularly with regard to media cultures. The development of digital cultures over the past decade, including the accessibility of high-speed broadband Internet, mobile technologies, and social networking sites, have led to new forms of engagement with media and the social world. Scholars have documented the ways in which people contribute to this "participatory culture" (Jenkins 2006) as producers and distributors of content rather than merely consumers. This is especially true for girls and women, many of whom are avid users of social networking sites and producers and curators of digital media content, including blogs, videos, websites, images, tweets, games, and graphics (Keller 2015b; White 2015; Dobson 2015; Kearney 2006). This widespread technological change has shaped media culture beyond the Internet, producing a convergent media landscape where content travels quickly across media, including television, film, magazines, and various digital platforms. What is produced in one medium will likely be shared on, and amplified across, a range of other media—and in this context, emergent feminisms (as well as anti-feminisms) can take hold with unexpected force. That is why in this collection we do not take a medium-specific approach. Instead we use terms like "media culture" and "postfeminist sensibility," which refuse to delimit the boundaries of the medium or text in question, instead acknowledging their permeability. Several authors in this collection explore how this convergent media landscape has been crucial to the circulation of emergent feminisms (for example, see Nygaard, this volume).

We reject a technologically deterministic perspective that would suggest digital technologies have in themselves produced a visible feminist politics. Yet we want to call attention to the ways in which digital culture has made feminism legible and accessible to many people unfamiliar with feminist politics (Keller 2015b). Girls and women may have more opportunities to not only produce media, but have it widely distributed as well, making it possible for unexpected audiences to flourish. Twenty-one-year-old Chicago native Tavi Gevinson is a prominent example of this. While Gevinson first attained visibility as a twelve-year-old fashion blogger, she eventually used her fame and industry connections to produce *Rookie* (rookiemag.com), an online feminist-inspired magazine for teenage girls. As a fifteen-year-old editor of the hugely successful website, Gevinson ensured that *Rookie* was "written with a feminist lens" (PBS 2012), including posts about sexual harassment, coming out as queer, and feminist icons such as Gloria Steinem, in between musings on fashion, beauty culture, and celebrity (see Keller 2015a, 2015b). Indeed, Gevinson exemplifies the ways in which the web has fostered the development of robust feminist dialogue, where the networking and distribution capacities of social media "cultivate new modes of feminist cultural critique and models of political agency for practicing feminism" (Rentschler and Thrift 2015, 1).

While some scholars have used a framework of postfeminism to examine girls' and women's digital practices (Dobson 2015), others have problematized the term's applicability to Internet cultures. For example, in her book *Producing Women*, Michele White (2015) argues that, "The usefulness of the term 'post-feminism' and its application to Internet settings is sometimes limited," noting that the concept of postfeminism "elid[es] promising aspects of women's use of Internet settings, including their articulation of creative cultures, collaborative production of identities and products, erotic engagements with other women while self-identifying as heterosexual and challenging whiteness" (8). As White's discussion suggests, girls' and women's digital engagements are complex, and require a nuanced examination that can account for their contradictory nature.

There is also a range of avowedly feminist media produced and circulated online, including blogs about feminist history (Keller 2015b), feminist political memes (Rentschler and Thrift 2015), personal testimonials of sexual assault and rape culture (Keller, Mendes, and Ringrose 2016), Twitter hashtags (Loza 2014; Thrift 2014; Horeck 2014; Khoja-Moolji 2015) and other forms of cultural commentary that discursively challenges patriarchal culture (Shaw 2012). Much of this media and its popularity amongst girls and women complicates some of the assumptions made in scholarship examining postfeminist sensibilities in media cultures. For example, while postfeminism as a cultural sensibility privileges a focus upon individualism, choice, and empowerment (Gill 2007), much of the digital feminist media reimagines collective solidarities in order to challenge sexism. To wit: Jessalynn Keller, Kaitlynn Mendes, and Jessica Ringrose (2016) discuss how hashtags such as #BeenRapedNeverReported generate an "affective solidarity" (Hemmings 2012) amongst hashtag users and audiences. Many feminist blogs, including the *Crunk Feminist Collective* and *Feministing*, operate as multi-blogger collectives, nodding to earlier forms of collective media production (Bains 2012). These blogs emphasize intersectionality and connect a range of issues to feminism, including the environment, racism, ability, and violence against queer and trans people (see for instance Britto Schwartz 2016; Germain 2016). And several blogs, such as *Black Girl Dangerous,* adopt a black feminist perspective that privileges the voices of women of color within the feminist blogosphere.

Of course, this does not mean that the web is unequivocally feminist, or that misogyny does not exist in media cultures. Power hierarchies are often reproduced online, which has led to important ongoing conversations about the reproduction of white feminism and privilege in online spaces (see Loza 2014; Daniels 2016). And as Sarah Banet-Weiser rightly points out, the circulation of popular feminisms on the web has been countervailed by the visibility of popular misogyny as well, in the form of misogyny and hate speech fostered on Twitter, 4chan, and *Return of Kings*. While misogynistic sentiment and behavior are not new, the web animates misogyny in new and more visible ways (see Jane 2014), and points to the ambivalence embedded within digital culture as offering opportunities for both progressive politics and the re-entrenchment of conservative values. With this, Banet-Weiser (2015) observes that, "We need to contend with how, and in what ways, misogyny has shifted its media tactics and tropes in response to popular feminism".

Banet-Weiser's assertion gives us pause and provides an important framework for this collection: How can we understand these emergent feminisms alongside a seemingly reinvigorated misogyny, embodied in popular figures such as Donald Trump and Milo Yiannopoulos? How do emergent feminisms problematize ongoing racism and anti-immigration discourses that are a part of media culture? How might we build on the feminist media practices and representations the authors of this anthology discuss in order to produce a more equitable future for all? These questions may have become more urgent as this collection goes to print in late 2017. While this book is meant to interrogate the feminisms that have emerged in the first half of the 2010s, we are now in a moment where renewed conversations about emergent feminisms may be more important than ever. In fact, this collection explores some of the feminist and anti-feminist politics that were afoot in the Obama era, despite what many people saw as an era of relatively progressive politics. The election of Donald Trump gave license to a widespread retrenchment of patriarchy, racism, and homophobia marked by an increase in racist hate crimes and white supremacist marches, the implementation of xenophobic and transphobic policies, and a rollback of women's rights. Yet—and this is the crucial point of our collection—feminists, queers, and people of color knew that these forces continued to shape societies across the globe. The terrain of struggle that we document in this book constitutes the lead-up to the full-blown resurgence of white patriarchal power.

And since 2016, we've also witnessed resistant feminist activism in the form of protest culture, such as the Women's March on Washington, its global sister marches, and the widespread protests against Islamophobia. This resistance to the Trump presidency is also often mediated within popular culture, and includes the politicization of commercial magazines like *Teen Vogue* (see Keller 2017), the use of social media platform to organize against Trump policies, and even the incorporation of anti-Trump sentiments into popular television programming (Beauchamp 2016). In this sense, this book sits at the uneasy crossroad between a retrenched rampant misogyny and what might be a re-energized feminist movement that builds upon some of the emergent feminisms we've analyzed here. Thus, we suggest approaching this collection not as an uncritical celebration of feminisms in the media but as an initial attempt to bring together some of the complex and contradictory ways in which feminisms are emerging within media cultures that remain shaped by patriarchy, racism, classism, heterosexism, and other forms of oppression.

Chapter Breakdown

The chapters in this collection are organized along thematic clusters, highlighting the broad themes we've laid out in this introduction. The first set of chapters is defined by **emergent identities**; how they are produced in the current conjuncture, and how they extend or complicate the identity politics of earlier moments.

Contemporary media culture is arguably producing more complicated, nuanced representations of feminine (and sometimes feminist) identities than perhaps were possible in earlier moments, partly as a result of some prominent female directors, screenwriters, and showrunners. Some of these nuanced feminine identities are articulated on popular quality dramas like *Girls*, *Transparent*, and *Orange is the New Black*, which deal with identity formation despite financial precarity (*Girls*), transgender politics and aging (*Transparent*), and an unjust prison system (*Orange is the New Black*). These texts have broadened the representational landscape of women's media and made new kinds of identities—ones that traverse the boundaries of race, class, and sexuality—increasingly visible and viable.

Thus, this section explores the ways in which mediated feminine and feminist identities are articulated, performed, and challenged across a number of popular media industries, texts, and genres. Amanda Rossie's chapter, "*Being Mary Jane* and Postfeminism's Problem with Race" begins this section with an analysis of black femininity in the popular BET television series. Rossie illustrates how, despite being embedded within postfeminist sensibilities, the show is highly critical of post-racial discourse and actively engages with a politics of blackness. Thus, her analysis asks important questions about the relationship between postfeminism, race, and feminist identities. Secondly, Bryce Renninger engages a political economy critique of celebrity journalism in order to map how celebrity feminism circulates within popular media cultures and the meanings it produces about contemporary gender politics. Renninger contextualizes this "trend" within a history of celebrity feminisms that have a lengthy history within popular culture. In chapter three, Taylor Nygaard examines what she calls Amy Schumer's "popular feminism" and theorizes the political potential inherent in the changing ways audiences use satirical television in an era of television connectivity. Her analysis also highlights the ways in which feminist identities and politics are mobilized to challenge postfeminist sensibilities, yet can simultaneously reinforce privilege around other identities including race and class. Finally, Alyxandra Vesey's chapter examines the creative practices of female musicians turned fashion designers, exploring how the fashion industry offers opportunities for feminine and feminist identity exploration within the constraints of neoliberal capitalism. Significant to Vesey's argument are the ways in which the musicians enact what she calls "citational feminism," which allows the artists the ability to rearticulate their own feminist identities and influences from the 1970s, 1980s, and 1990s, as part of their current fashion brands.

The current conjuncture has also produced new forms of **emergent solidarities** between and among girls and women, complicating Alison Winch's assertion that within postfeminist media culture, "solidarity among women is foreclosed" (2013, 2). Thus, the chapters in the second section explore how female friendships, solidarities, and collectivities remain not only viable, but increasingly recognized as necessary in the current conjuncture. First, Emilie Zaslow analyzes the #iammorethanadistraction online campaign, organized by middle school girls and their parents, to address school dress codes that unfairly discriminate against girls. Zaslow locates their political activism in the context of intergenerational feminist politics and the sexist body politics and beauty culture that saturates their adolescence. Also focusing her analysis on digital culture, Sujata Moorti examines how girls and women are using digital technologies to engage in feminist activism across both local and global contexts and produce solidarities across differences, drawing on Indian and Canadian case studies. Both Zaslow and Moorti's chapters speak to the ways in which many emergent feminisms privilege the building of solidarity and collective politics through digital media platforms. Next, Sarah Projansky analyzes how the discursive shift in relation to the 1972 Title IX educational amendment has been used to address the problem of rape culture on U.S. college campuses. Using the documentary film *The Hunting Ground* (2015) and media coverage of the Carry That Weight performance/campaign, Projansky articulates this discursive shift as indicative of emergent feminisms and collective activism that had made the issue of sexual violence visible within mainstream media. Verity Trott's chapter, "Black 'Ranting's: Indigenous Feminisms Online" interrogates the ways in which Australian Indigenous feminists have produced solidarities through online networks, challenging both postfeminist sensibilities and dominant Western feminist narratives of Indigeneity. Trott's discussion problematizes the mainstream media focus on digital feminisms that privilege whiteness and demonstrates the need to better understand the ways in which women of color are producing feminist media in creative and collaborative ways.

The third and final section of this collection recognizes the ongoing **emergent ambivalences** that shape contemporary feminisms. These chapters address the "sticky" (Ahmed 2004) relationship to postfeminist sensibilities, anti-feminist rhetoric, and neoliberalism manifested in diverse culture industries, including film, music video, and digital cultures. In this sense, the chapters in this section function to problematize an easy celebration of the visibility of feminisms by contextualizing them within the political economy of neoliberal capitalism and an increasingly visible mediated misogyny and anti-feminism. Cheryl Thompson addresses some of these concerns through an analysis of the "*new* Afro" in popular media culture, parsing out how the politicized hairstyle functions to problematize postfeminist notions of self-fashioning through styling (especially one's hair). Thompson compares the divergent reception of Beyoncé's "Formation" music video and Rachel Dolezal, both of whom engage in forms of racial "passing" through hairstyle appropriation, to show how the new Afro calls attention to the construction of race and destabilizes a universal white feminine subjectivity privileged within postfeminism. Next, Jonathan Cohn's essay demonstrates the ongoing ambivalence that feminist politics generate by drawing on Sara Ahmed's work on affect to discuss the #WomenAgainstFeminism posts on Tumblr and Twitter. His analysis points to the affective charge of both feminism and its failures, and the ways in which digital media is used by women to work through these feelings. In her contribution to this collection, Gina Marchetti explores the ambivalent nature of contemporary feminism in Hong Kong's geopolitical scene, focusing on filmmaker Barbara Wong and the ways in which her film *Wonder Women* (2007) embodies the contradictions of women's lives in post-Handover Hong Kong. Finally, in their chapter "@NoToFeminism, #FeministsAreUgly, and Misandry Memes: How Social Media Feminist Humor is Calling Out Anti-feminism" Emilie Lawrence and Jessica Ringrose explore how humor and irony are used as rhetorical and debating strategies to challenge problematic arguments against or about feminists by re-staging anti-feminist claims as absurd, ridiculous, and illogical. Focusing on three Twitter, hashtag, and meme case studies, the authors parse out the ways in which these digital media strategies function as feminist resistance and community-building, while also occasionally slipping into hegemonic discourses that ignore intersectional power structures.

Works Cited

Ahmed, Sara. 2004. *The Cultural Politics of Emotion*. Edinburgh: Edinburgh University Press.

Bains, Jess. 2012. "Experiments in Democratic Participation: Feminist Printshop Collectives." *Cultural Policy, Criticism and Management Research* 6: 29–51.

Baker, Katie J.M. 2013. "Women's Employment Numbers Are Up, But Don't Get Too Excited." *Jezebel.com*, June 10. Accessed July 14, 2016. http://jezebel.com/womens-employment-numbers-are-up-but-dont-get-too-ex-512349044.

Banet-Weiser, Sarah. 2015. "Popular Misogyny: A Zeitgeist." *Culture Digitally*, January 21. Accessed July 13, 2016. http://culturedigitally.org/2015/01/popular-misogyny-a-zeitgeist/.

Barry, Doug. 2014. "Women Filled ALL of the (Mostly Low-Wage) December Job Openings." *Jezebel.com*, January 11. Accessed July 14, 2016. http://jezebel.com/women-filled-all-of-the-mostly-low-wage-december-job-1499247601.

Beauchamp, Sarah. 2016. "'Broad City' will Treat Trump's Name as Profanity in Season 4." *NYLON.com*, June 14. Accessed September 12, 2017. https://www.nylon.com/articles/broad-city-season-four-trump-name-profanity?utm_source=facebook&utm_medium=social&utm_campaign=nylon.

Berlant, Lauren. 2011. *Cruel Optimism*. Durham: Duke University Press.

Bolotin, Susan. 1982. "Voices from the Postfeminist Generation," *New York Times Magazine*, October 17. pp 29–31+.

Britto Schwartz, Juliana. 2016. "Report: The Environment as the New Battleground for Human Rights." *Feministing*, June 22. Accessed July 13, 2016. http://feministing.com/2016/06/22/report-the-environment-as-the-new-battleground-for-human-rights/.

Brunsdon, Charlotte. 1997. *Screen Tastes: Soap Opera to Satellite Dishes*. New York: Routledge.

Butler, Jess. 2013. "For White Girls Only? Postfeminism and the Politics of Inclusion." *Feminist Formations* 25 (1): 35–58.

Chemaly, Soraya. 2011. "Violence Against Women Is a Global Pandemic." *Huffington Post*, December 1. Accessed July 13, 2016. http://www.huffingtonpost.com/soraya-chemaly/violence-against-women-is_1_b_1121001.html.

Daniels, Jessie. 2016. "The Trouble with White Feminism: Whiteness, Digital Feminism, and the Intersectional Internet." In *The Intersectional Internet: Race, Sex, Class and Culture Online*, edited by Safiya Umoja Noble and Brendesha M. Tynes, 41–60. New York: Peter Lang.

Dobson, Amy. 2015. *Postfeminist Digital Cultures: Femininity, Social Media, and Self-Representation*. New York: Palgrave.

Dosekun, Simidele. 2015. "For Western Girls Only? Post-Feminism as Transnational Culture." *Feminist Media Studies* 15 (6): 960–975.

Dow, Bonnie J. 1996. *Prime-Time Feminism: Television, Media Culture, and the Women's Movement Since 1970*. Philadelphia: University of Pennsylvania Press.

Duggan, Lisa. 2003. *The Twilight of Equality?* Boston: Beacon Press.

Farrell, Amy Erdman. 1998. *Yours in Sisterhood: Ms. Magazine and the Promise of Popular Feminism*. Chapel Hill: University of North Carolina Press.

Fraser, Nancy. 2013. *Fortunes of Feminism: From State-Managed Capitalism to Neoliberal Crisis*. New York: Verso.

Fuller, Sean and Catherine Driscoll. 2015. "HBO's Girls: Gender, Generation, and Quality Television." *Continuum: Journal of Media & Cultural Studies* 29 (5): 253–262.

Germain, Jacqui. 2016. "Defining Safety for All Queer People In the Wake of Orlando." *Feministing.com*, June 15. Accessed July 13, 2016. http://feministing.com/2016/06/15/defining-safety-for-all-queer-people-in-the-wake-of-orlando/.

Gill, Rosalind. 2007. "Postfeminist Media Culture: Elements of a Sensibility." *European Journal of Cultural Studies* 10 (2): 147–166.

Gill, Rosalind. 2009. "Mediated Intimacy and Postfeminism: A Discourse Analytic Examination of Sex and Relationship Advice in a Women's Magazine." *Discourse & Communication* 3 (4): 345–369.

Gill, Rosalind. 2016. "Post-Postfeminism?: New Feminist Visibilities in Postfeminist Times." *Feminist Media Studies* 16 (4): 610–630.

Grigoriadis, Vanessa. 2014. "How to Start a Revolution." *New York Magazine*, September 22. Accessed July 14, 2016. http://nymag.com/thecut/2014/09/emma-sulkowicz-campus-sexual-assault-activism.html.

Hall, Stuart. 1979. "The Great Moving Right Show." *Marxism Today* (January): 14–20.

Hamad, Hannah and Anthea Taylor. 2015. "Introduction: Feminism and Contemporary Celebrity Culture." *Feminist Media Studies* 6 (1): 124–127.

Harris, Anita. 2004. *Future Girl: Young Women in the Twenty-first Century*. New York: Routledge.

Harvey, David. 2005. *A Brief History of Neoliberalism*. Oxford: Oxford University Press.

Harzewski, Stephanie. 2011. *Chick Lit and Postfeminism*. Charlottesville: University of Virginia Press.

Hemmings, Clare. 2012. "Affective Solidarity: Feminist Reflexivity and Political Transformation." *Feminist Theory* 13 (2): 147–161.

Hewlett, Sylvia Ann. 1986. *A Lesser Life: The Myth of Women's Liberation in America*. New York: Harper Collins.

Horeck, Tanya. 2014. "#AskThicke: 'Blurred Lines,' Rape Culture, and the Feminist Hashtag Takeover." *Feminist Media Studies* 14 (6): 1105–1107.

Jane, Emma. 2014. "'Back to the Kitchen, Cunt': Speaking the Unspeakable about Online Misogyny." *Continuum Journal of Media and Cultural Studies* 28 (4): 558–570.

Jenkins, Henry. 2006. *Convergence Culture: Where Old and New Media Collide*. New York: NYU Press.

Joseph, Ralina. 2009. "'Tyra Banks is Fat': Reading (Post-)Racism and (Post-) Feminism in the New Millennium." *Critical Studies in Media Communication* 26 (3): 237–254.

Juzwiak, Rich. 2014. "Beyoncé is a Terrorist, According to bell hooks." *Gawker.com*, May 8. Accessed May 12, 2016. http://gawker.com/beyonce-is-a-terrorist-according-to-bell-hooks-1573771398.

Kearney, Mary Celeste. 2006. *Girls Make Media*. New York, Routledge.

Keller, Jessalynn. 2015a. "Girl Power's Last Chance? Tavi Gevinson, Feminism and Popular Media Culture." *Continuum: Journal of Media and Cultural Studies* 29 (2): 274–285.

Keller, Jessalynn. 2015b. *Girls' Feminist Blogging in a Postfeminist Age*. New York: Routledge.

Keller, Jessalynn. 2017. "Girl News, Woke Brands: Anti-Trump Resistance in *Teen Vogue*." Paper presented at Society for Cinema and Media Studies Annual Conference, March 24.

Keller, Jessalynn, Kaitlynn Mendes and Jessica Ringrose. 2016. "Speaking 'Unspeakable Things': Documenting Digital Feminist Responses to Rape Culture." *Journal of Gender Studies* 27 (1): 22–36.

Khoja-Moolji, Shenila. 2015. "Becoming an 'Intimate Publics': Exploring the Affective Intensities of Hashtag Feminism." *Feminist Media Studies* 15 (2): 347–350.

Lauzen, Martha. 2012. "The Funny Business of Being Tina Fey." *Feminist Media Studies* 14 (1): 106–117.

Leight, Elias. 2014. "Annie Lennox: 'Twerking is not Feminism'." *Billboard.com*, October 21. Accessed on May 8, 2016. http://www.billboard.com/articles/news/6289251/annie-lennox-twerking-not-feminism.

Lotz, Amanda. 2006. *Redesigning Women: Television After the Network Era*. Urbana: University of Illinois Press.

Loza, Susana. 2014. "Hashtag Feminism, #SolidarityIsForWhiteWomen, and the Other #FemFuture." *Ada: A Journal of Gender, New Media and Technology* 5. Accessed March 5, 2016. http://adanewmedia.org/2014/07/issue-5-loza.

McRobbie, Angela. 2004. "Post-Feminism and Popular Culture." *Feminist Media Studies* 4 (3): 255–264.

McRobbie, Angela. 2009. *The Aftermath of Feminism: Gender, Culture and Social Change*. London: Sage.

Mendes, Kaitlynn. 2015. *Slutwalk: Feminism, Activism and Media*. London: Palgrave Macmillan.

Merriam-Webster Dictionary. 2016. "Emergent." Accessed July 11, 2016. http://www.merriam-webster.com/dictionary/emergent.

Negra, Diane. 2009. *What a Girl Wants?: Fantasizing the Reclamation of Self in Postfeminism*. New York: Routledge.

Negra, Diane and Yvonne Tasker. 2014. *Gendering the Recession: Media and Culture in an Age of Austerity*. Durham: Duke University Press.

Ouellette, Laurie and James Hay. 2008. *Better Living through Reality TV*. Malden, Mass: Blackwell Publishing.

Oved, Marco Chown and Laura Kane. 2013. "Rape Culture: What do Steubenville, Rehtaeh Parsons and Frosh Chants have in common?" *Toronto Star*, October 19. Accessed July 11, 2016. https://www.thestar.com/news/insight/2013/10/19/rape_culture_what_do_steubenville_rehtaeh_parsons_and_frosh_chants_have_in_common.html.

Patrick, Stephanie. 2016. "I Want My Snooki: MTV's Failed Subjects and Postfeminist Ambivalence In and Around the Jersey Shore." *Feminist Media Studies*. doi: 10.1080/14680777.2016.1183139.

PBS. 2012. "*Makers* Profile: Tavi Gevinson." Accessed July 14, 2016. http://www.makers.com/tavi-gevinson.

Piketty, Thomas and Arthur Goldhammer. 2014. *Capital in the Twenty-First Century*. Cambridge, MA: The Belknap Press of Harvard University Press.

Press, Andrea, 2012. "'Feminism? That's So Seventies': Girls and Young Women Discuss Femininity and Feminism in America's Next Top Model." In *New Femininities: Post-feminism, Neoliberalism and Subjectivity*, edited by Rosalind Gill and Christina Scharff, 117–133. London: Palgrave Macmillan.

Projansky, Sarah. 2001. *Watching Rape: Film and Television in Postfeminist Culture*. New York: New York University Press.

Projansky, Sarah. 2014. *Spectacular Girls: Media Fascination and Celebrity Culture*. New York; London: New York University Press.

Rentschler, Carrie and Samantha Thrift. 2015. "Doing Feminism in the Network: Networked Laughter and the 'Binders Full of Women Meme." *Feminist Theory* 16 (3): 329–359.

Ringrose, Jessica and Emma Renold. 2012. "Slut-Shaming, Girl Power and 'Sexualization': Thinking Through the Politics of the International Slutwalks with Teen Girls." *Gender and Education* 24 (3): 333–343.

Rose, Nikolas, 1999. *Powers of Freedom: Reframing Political Thought*. Cambridge: Cambridge University Press.

Rottenberg, Catherine. 2014. "The Rise of Neoliberal Feminism." *Cultural Studies* 28 (3): 418–437.

Ryan, Erin Gloria. 2013. "Babies Not Even Worth It Anymore." *Jezebel.com*, July 9. Accessed July 14, 2016. http://jezebel.com/babies-not-even-worth-it-anymore-718813405.

Ryan, Maureen. Forthcoming. *Lifestyle Media in American Culture: Gender, Class, and the Politics of Ordinariness*. New York: Routledge.

Shaw, Frances. 2012. "Hottest 100 Women: Cross-platform Discursive Activism in Feminist Blogging Networks." *Australian Feminist Studies* 27 (74): 373–387.

Sills, Sophie, Chelsea Pickens, Kaishma Beach, Lloyd Jones, Octavia Calder-Dawe, Paulette Benton-Greig, and Nicola Gavey. 2016. "Rape Culture and Social Media: Young Critics and a Feminist Counterpublic." *Feminist Media Studies* 16 (6): 935–951.

Springer, Kimberly. 2007. "Divas, Evil Black Bitches, and Bitter Black Women: African American Women in Postfeminist and Post-Civil Rights Popular Culture." In *Interrogating Postfeminism: Gender and the Politics of Popular Culture*, edited by Yvonne Tasker and Diane Negra, 249–276. Durham: Duke University Press.

Stacey, Judith. 1987. "Sexism by a Subtler Name? Postindustrial Conditions and Postfeminist Consciousness in the Silicon Valley." *Socialist Review* 17 (6): 7–28.

Tasker, Yvonne, and Diane Negra, eds. 2007. *Interrogating Postfeminism: Gender and the Politics of Popular Culture*. Durham: Duke University Press.

Thrift, Samantha. 2014. "#YesAllWomen as Feminist Meme Event." *Feminist Media Studies* 14 (6): 1090–1092.

Tolentino, Jill. July 23, 2015. "Do Not Let the NYT Troll You About 'Young Women Planning Career Pauses'." *Jezebel.com*, July 23. Accessed July 14, 2016. http://jezebel.com/do-not-let-the-nyt-troll-you-about-young-women-planning-1719702857.

Towns, Armond R. 2016. "Geographies of Pain: #SayHerName and the Fear of Black Women's Mobility." *Women's Studies in Communication* 39 (2): 122–126.

Valenti, Jessica. 2014. "Beyoncé's 'Flawless' Feminist Act at the MVAs Leads the Way for other Women." *Guardian*, August 25. Accessed July 15, 2016. https://www.theguardian.com/commentisfree/2014/aug/25/beyonce-flawless-feminist-vmas.

Valenti, Jessica. 2015. "Anita Sarkeesian Interview: 'The Word "Troll" Feels too Childish. This is Abuse.'" *Guardian*, August 29. Accessed July 15, 2016. https://www.theguardian.com/technology/2015/aug/29/anita-sarkeesian-gamergate-interview-jessica-valenti.

Weber, Brenda. 2009. *Makeover TV: Selfhood, Citizenship and Celebrity*. Durham: Duke University Press.

West, Lindy. 2017. "Of Course Abortion Should Be a Litmus Test for Democrats." *The New York Times*, August 2. Accessed September 10, 2017. https://www.nytimes.com/2017/08/02/opinion/trump-democrats-abortion-litmus-test.html?_r=1.

White, Michele. 2015. *Producing Women: The Internet, Traditional Femininity, Queerness, and Creativity*. New York: Routledge.

Winch, Alison. 2013. *Girlfriends and Postfeminist Sisterhood*. Basingstoke: Palgrave.

Identities

1

BEING MARY JANE AND POSTFEMINISM'S PROBLEM WITH RACE

Amanda Rossie

In this chapter, I analyze BET's *Being Mary Jane* (2013–present) to more closely examine what happens when elements of a postfeminist sensibility are complicated by an intersectional analysis of race. BET is one of the few networks that targets black viewers, and its success is due, in part, to its emergence during a time defined by a dearth of representations of African Americans on TV, the rise of cable, and the widespread popularity of hip hop (Smith-Shomade 2007, xiv). Yet the success of BET has meant different things to different people. As Beretta Smith-Shomade writes in *Pimpin' Ain't Easy*, the black community has been divided on what BET's success means: some believed that the visual images of blackness proffered by the network (the "pimp," "bling," and hyper-sexualized women's bodies) made it a sellout that catered to white customers while others were left with feelings of accomplishment (Smith-Shomade 2007, xiv). Within BET's current slate of programming, *Being Mary Jane* targets black female viewers, and its success can be traced back to Mara Brock Akil, the series' showrunner, who is also known for shows like *Moesha* (UPN, 1996–2001) and *Girlfriends* (UPN, 2000–2008), which are some of the first and only shows to depict the realities of black female friendships. Hailed as BET's first hour-long scripted drama, *Being Mary Jane* is part of an emerging televisual genre of works that target black women, as evinced on networks like TV One, Centric, and OWN.

Being Mary Jane follows Mary Jane Paul (Gabrielle Union), a single woman who has worked hard to build a successful career as a news anchor in Atlanta. Along with local celebrity status, Mary Jane's job provides financial independence, cultural capital, and social power through consumption (i.e., high-end cars, designer fashion, and an upscale home). Although Mary Jane is empowered by having (heterosexual) sex for pleasure, she longs to find love and start a family—anxieties that drive much of the series' plot and situate Mary Jane at the center of a postfeminist panic around the timing of marriage and childbearing.

In these ways, *Being Mary Jane* is clearly situated within a postfeminist media landscape and set Mary Jane up to be a stereotypical postfeminist heroine. While viewing the series, I kept coming back to this nagging question: If postfeminism is about whiteness, then is *Being Mary Jane* postfeminist at all? However, I want to move away from this line of thinking. After all, one of the critiques of scholars using postfeminism as a framework is that we have become too satisfied in simply identifying common postfeminist tropes without mobilizing that analysis to push the field in new directions. A more productive line of thinking might be to explore what emergent identities this show offers viewers and what these identities say about the role of race within the current iteration of postfeminism.

Through a textual analysis of the show, I explore the ideological limits of postfeminism around questions of race, looking at specific elements that are often at the heart of postfeminist texts: the delicate balance between career, consumption, and time crises around marriage and motherhood. In the process, I argue that many of the aforementioned elements are inherently complicated by Mary Jane's blackness and her refusal to be deracialized in ways that challenge and disrupt postfeminism, therefore setting the show apart from similar texts featuring white protagonists. By highlighting situations where Mary Jane actively engages with and critiques post-racial discourse and refuses to be depoliticized, I demonstrate the nuanced ways the show is simultaneously embedded within postfeminist media culture *and also* invested in a racial critique. This racial critique is indicative of the ways in which feminist politics emerge in unexpected places, problematizing post-race fantasies that dominated many media texts in the mid-2000s.

Critiques of postfeminism have permeated the field of feminist media studies for the past two decades, and for good reason. Postfeminism is a "sensibility" (Gill 2007) that articulates how "feminism [has] achieved the status of common sense, while it [is] also reviled and almost hated" (McRobbie 2009, 6). Postfeminism naturalizes tenets of feminism, like women's "choice" and "empowerment," while simultaneously disregarding the need for a feminist politics or community because the work of feminism is perceived as finished—hence the *post* in postfeminism. However, there is plenty of evidence to show that the work of feminism is far from over. This particular historical moment is characterized by the revitalization of feminism in the public sphere alongside a resurgence of misogynistic, violent, and anti-feminist politics, thereby making feminism as urgent and politically relevant as it has ever been.

Feminist scholars have done well to identify hallmarks of postfeminism while also calling attention to new indicators that this sensibility is shape-shifting with the times. This work is important not only because it demonstrates the pervasiveness of postfeminism in contemporary popular culture but also because it reveals how postfeminism and its new iterations produce gendered and racialized scripts for contemporary femininity that affect the lives of women. But, if postfeminist critiques are to remain viable and relevant, we must ask how and where do women of color fit within the very paradigm that often renders them invisible? Perhaps women of color are not outside the bounds of postfeminism at all. Kimberly Springer writes, "[Race] is always present. Even when they are not on the screen, women of color are present as the counterpart against which white women's ways of being—from Bridget Jones to Ally McBeal to Carrie Bradshaw—are defined and refined" (2007, 249). The goal of this chapter is to locate one potential site in popular culture where women of color engage with postfeminism as protagonists (not counterparts), thereby changing the way we have come to understand postfeminism as *wholly* concerned with whiteness.

Tenets of Postfeminism

I use the term postfeminism throughout the chapter to represent ideological imperatives that shape contemporary femininity in the West. First, postfeminism frames women's empowerment through consumption and hypersexualization. These "fantasies of power" "insist that purchasing power and sexual power are more gratifying than political or economic power" (Douglas 2010, 5). The privileging of consumption over political efficacy or economic equality has detrimental effects on nearly all aspect of women's lives.

Second, there is a heightened focus on having a slender, sexy body sculpted through constant self-surveillance (Gill 2007, 149) that is only enhanced by new media technologies, social media apps, and camera phones that make women's bodies visible in new and more extreme ways (Rossie 2015). This heightened attention to the feminine body also explains the rise of a third aspect of postfeminist culture: the "makeover paradigm" (Gill 2007). Playing itself out in countless reality television shows like *What Not to Wear*, *Botched*, and *Extreme Makeover: Home Edition*,[1] the makeover paradigm

> requires people (predominately women) to believe, first, that they or their life is lacking or flawed in some way; second, that it is amenable to reinvention or transformation by following the advice of relationship, design or lifestyle experts and practicing appropriately modified consumption habits.
> *(Gill 2007, 156)*

These makeovers are not relegated to the body but also include one's wardrobe, home, and interpersonal relationships.

Fourth, postfeminism encourages women in their twenties to delay marriage and motherhood in lieu of higher education, careerism, and pursuing individual passions like travel. Yet, postfeminism does not remove these gendered imperatives from women's lives altogether, thereby creating time panics about romance and fertility later in life. As women agonize over whether they will ever achieve the identity markers of traditional femininity ("wife" and "mother") it becomes suddenly clear that what felt like postfeminism's promise to "cheat time" in their twenties materializes as an intense "calendarization" of women's lives once they reach their thirties (Negra 2009, 50).

A fifth element of postfeminism produces an apolitical feminine subject. As Yvonne Tasker and Diane Negra write, "the new female subject is, despite her freedom, called to be silent, to withhold critique in order to count as a modern, sophisticated girl. Indeed, this withholding of critique is the condition of her freedom" (2007, 34). This misrepresentation of feminist politics positions postfeminism as women's primary source of pleasure through shopping, sex, and—perhaps most importantly—an invitation to be apolitical. Through this logic, women's problems are personal and never structural. By emptying out the feminist rhetoric of "choice" and "empowerment" and filling it with "fantasies of power" that reify neoliberal discourses of individualism, postfeminism strives to create a generation of women who *feel* powerful but refuse to attach themselves to a concrete set of politics.[2]

A final hallmark of postfeminism is the idealization of a white, middle-class, heterosexual subject. Many scholars have written critically about the lack of racial diversity in postfeminist texts like *Sex and the City* (HBO, 1998–2004), *Ally McBeal* (FOX, 1997–2002), *Bridget Jones' Diary* (Dir. Sharon Maguire, 2001), and, more recently, *Girls* (HBO, 2012–2017). The consensus has been that many of postfeminism's "icons are white," but, as Springer duly notes, "the analysis seems to stop there" (2007, 249). Despite our best intentions, feminist scholars have failed to be fully intersectional in our critiques of postfeminism, therefore keeping whiteness front and center.

Tackling Postfeminism's Problem with Race

While there is much thoughtful feminist scholarship about how postfeminist media culture has reshaped the ways women's bodies and lives are sexualized, commodified, and policed (see McRobbie 2009, Gill 2007, Negra 2009, Banet-Weiser 2007), there is still work to be done when it comes to analyzing postfeminism's idealization of whiteness and, in turn, the devaluation and disregard of women of color within its ideological limits. Increasingly, scholars are beginning to diversify their objects of study and theorize postfeminism in intersectional terms to push forth a "critical lexicon for understanding contemporary culture" (Gill 2016, 620). Examining everything from pop culture icons like Beyoncé (Chatman 2015), Tyra Banks (Joseph 2009), and Snooki (Patrick 2016), to geisha stories (Hua 2009) and tourist films like *Eat Pray Love* and *Under the Tuscan Sun* (Marston 2016), feminist scholars have begun to interrogate the role of race beyond whiteness within the scope of postfeminist media culture.

Some of the earliest work about race and postfeminism by Kimberly Springer sought to highlight the ways "postfeminism takes demands for racial inclusion on the feminist agenda and makes race consumable," a process akin to bell hooks' notion of "eating the other," wherein racial difference is commodified and consumed to spice up the blandness of white culture (2007, 252). Springer argues that this "racialized postfeminism" updated historical racist stereotypes of black women (i.e., the welfare queen, mammy, jezebel, and black superwoman) for a new time. Tracing the diva, the black lady, and the angry black woman throughout popular films, reality television, and politics, Springer contends that, "for African American women, the postfeminist message is that black women need to know their place within the racial and gender hierarchy, even if they are permitted, in small numbers, to assume places in the middle class" (2007, 272).

Similarly, Sarah Banet-Weiser suggests that gender and race identities are "constructed in the present 'postfeminist' cultural economy as a 'flava'" or "a kind of product one can buy or try on" (2007, 202). While the current U.S. media landscape is rife with images of diversity, Banet-Weiser argues these images of empowerment are simply "lucrative commodities" in a "media marketplace" where only *certain* representations of race and gender are used to sell products to self-identified empowered consumers (2007, 216, 217). The result is an ambivalence around race because representations of racial diversity and stories about race relations have increased, thereby implying that "representational visibility no longer has the same urgency" (2007, 223). Under this logic, race simply becomes "an interesting way to feature the authentic, cool, or urban" (2007, 223).

Jess Butler's "For White Girls Only?" is another important contribution to the study of postfeminism and race. Butler highlights postfeminist literature's focus on texts featuring young, heterosexual, middle-class white women (2013, 47), yet she challenges the premise that women of color are inherently excluded from both media representations and the sensibility itself simply because postfeminism idealizes white women (2013, 48). Butler asks readers to forgo assumptions "that women of color are somehow unaffected by postfeminist discourses," citing reality television shows like *Bad Girls Club* (Oxygen, 2006–present), *Love & Hip Hop* (VH1, 2010–present), *The Real Housewives of Atlanta* (Bravo, 2008–present), and *The Real World* (MTV, 1992–present) as evidence of postfeminism "[making] space for women of color within its boundaries," even as it "strictly regulates and polices the forms their participation may take" (2013, 50). In other words, just because women of color are incorporated into postfeminism does not mean that the central tenets of postfeminism are disrupted (2013, 50). Butler argues that the women of color featured in these reality shows "clearly embody and enact postfeminism" by embracing femininity and consuming feminine goods; using empowerment language; and fashioning themselves as heterosexual subjects (2013, 48). However, it is with the language of "embody" and "enact" that I want to intervene. Butler's statement suggests that she views enacting and embodying to be synonymous actions; however, I want to propose that these two terms mean quite different things, especially when analyzing the ways white women and women of color engage with postfeminism.

According to *Merriam-Webster*, to embody means "to give body to; to make concrete and perceptible; to represent in human form." Enacting, by dictionary definition, means to "act out; enact a role." While it might seem like parsing hairs, I believe this semantic distinction matters when it comes to who can embody and who can enact postfeminism. Perhaps, it is even this division that signals "the versatility of postfeminism," which simultaneously "allows non-white women to participate in its deployment and enjoy its rewards, albeit in circumscribed ways," while "[working] to conceal the underlying power relations that reproduce hegemonic ideas about race, gender, sexuality, and class" (Butler 2013, 50).

Separating embodiment and enactment as two separate modes recognizes that the idealized postfeminist subject is white and whiteness will always be unachievable for women of color, even as they are able to tap into other parts of postfeminism and use it to their benefit in the same ways white women do. Feminists have made similar arguments about beauty standards, which idealize whiteness through long, straight hair, blue eyes, and a thin frame (Wolf 1991, Bordo 1993). Even though women of color approximate this white ideal through hair extensions, skin bleaching, contacts, and other bodily enhancements, they will never *be* white, thereby illustrating the difference between enacting beauty norms and embodying them. In much the same way, the difference between enacting and embodying—whether it be beauty norms or postfeminism—is a corporeal one. In what remains, I use this enact/embody framework to discuss how Mary Jane's relationship to postfeminism is shaped by her race.

Postfeminism with a Difference

When it comes to having a successful career, Mary Jane Paul is a vision of success. She hosts her own cable network news show, *Talk Back*, and her reporting is highly acclaimed. Mary Jane's father describes her as "a child who, from college to grad school to the newsroom, always went after what she wanted and got it" (S2:Ep5). Yet, nowhere does her career success make more of an impact than when contrasted with other members of her family. Both of her brothers, Patrick (Richard Brooks) and Paul Jr. (B.J. Britt), live off-and-on with their parents while struggling to graduate and/or find long-term employment. Patrick is a recovering addict and Paul Jr. has a lucrative side business selling marijuana, both of which reaffirm Mary Jane's image as the prodigal daughter. Mary Jane's niece, Niecy (Raven Goodwin), and her two children also live with her parents. Mary Jane frequently butts heads with family members around work and financial responsibility, situating her siblings and niece as foils that demonstrate the heights of her own career success.

Mary Jane's career paves the way for her consumption. With a closet full of designer clothes and shoes, Mary Jane's fashion is enviable. While shopping is never a considerable plot point in the series (unlike *Sex and the City*, which foregrounds shopping as form of therapy, female bonding, and empowerment), Mary Jane's consumption is always framed as a reward for working hard. Her Porsche and luxe, ultra-modern home also signal Mary Jane's wealth and status, and she fills each room with expensive accoutrements indicating financial security well beyond the middle class. Mary Jane's investment in material possessions is revealed when Niecy and her children stay with her for a brief time. A clueless Niecy burns Mary Jane's Le Creuset Dutch oven in an attempt to make breakfast, sending Mary Jane into a tailspin. Later, Mary Jane walks in on Niecy having sex with an ex-boyfriend on her bed. Niecy apologizes, hoping to quell her aunt's disappointment and anger by noting that they never got under the covers. Mary Jane retorts, "The duvet is the most expensive part!" (S2:Ep4). When Niecy and her children finally leave after a huge fight, Mary Jane meticulously puts her guest room back together, telling her father that she prefers it to look like a showroom. These examples not only point to the importance of having nice things but also demonstrate that these forms of consumption mean something to Mary Jane's sense of identity. These material goods and modern aesthetic personify her hard work and distinguish her from her struggling family members, thereby solidifying her position as a wealthy, self-made black woman.

While Mary Jane's home sends a message to viewers about her consumption habits, it is also where visions of herself as a domestic housewife and mother coexist alongside steamy sex scenes with various lovers throughout the series. The pilot episode opens with this very dichotomy, as viewers watch Mary Jane baking a cake in the kitchen in her pajamas. Suddenly, the doorbell rings and a drunken Andre Daniels (Omari Hardwick)—her latest lover—stands waiting at the door. "I need to see you," he says. "Can you let me in?" he begs, after apologizing for not calling. Mary Jane walks away calmly and then, once out of view, slides dramatically into her bedroom where she begins cleaning, ripping sticky notes with inspiring quotes from the walls and windows, and hiding her vibrator from view. Mary Jane removes the bandana, revealing long, flowing hair before frantically removing her bra and sweatpants, exposing a pair of cotton boy shorts—simple but sexy. Assessing herself in the mirror, she deems herself ready with a sigh of relief and coy smile. She lets Andre inside and they have sex in the entryway, transforming this quaint domestic scene into something quite sexier.

Suggesting that women find their empowerment through sex and sexuality is one of the markers of postfeminism, and Mary Jane has her fair share of sex and sexual pleasure over the course of the series.[3] But, as a woman well into her thirties, it is also clear that sex is a mechanism for more traditional relationships that provide a certain kind of cultural legibility for women—predominately the identities of "wife" and "mother." For example, as Mary Jane lies in bed with a sleeping Andre the following morning, she whispers, "Please God if he's mine, give me a sign" (S1:Ep1). As if on command, Andre wakes up and vomits. While cleaning up, he tells Mary Jane that he loves her, which seems to be the sign that she craves; however, as she walks through her living room to fetch a glass of water, she steps on the wedding band he removed before their sexual encounter. She kicks Andre out of her house, spraying him with the hose and calling him an "idiot." This moment when Mary Jane realizes Andre's infidelity is devastating. The sense of betrayal she feels is gut-wrenching and Mary Jane becomes enraged because she never wanted to be a mistress, a fact she states throughout the series. The relationship she has been investing in and banking on to be her "escape" from singlehood is a fraud. Sure, the sex was fun but only in the context of some kind of futurity. What Mary Jane craves is a traditional, heterosexual relationship not only because she finds fulfilment in companionship but also because being married and becoming a mother are both reflections of her desirability (to men) and her success as an ambitious woman who is used to achieving *all* of her goals. It is this opening scene that sets the stage for one of the most dominating and recurrent narrative arcs in the series: the ticking biological clock.

In her valuable work about the "postfeminist life cycle," Diane Negra argues that "ritualization of exemplary events of the female lifecycle"—everything from sweet-16 and bachelorette parties to baby showers—"serves to pin down time" and "essentialize femininity as a biological experience," thereby shoring up the "connections between femininity and domesticity, [rationalizing] event-related consumer spending on a grand scale, and [reinforcing] the connections to the nakedly hierarchical culture that postfeminism helps to produce" (2009, 51). Without these markers of femininity, "singlehood [is] encoded as a particularly temporal failure and a drifting off course from the normative stages of the feminine life cycle" (Negra 2009, 61). This "time crisis" is particularly relevant to *Being Mary Jane*, which features multiple examples of Mary Jane fretting about "running out of time" in her quest for a biological child.

In one instance, Mary Jane is baking a cake for Niecy's baby shower, and she turns her attention to the television where a baby product commercial is airing. Melancholia catches her off guard and she begins to cry. She walks over to her neighbor and network news colleague Mark Bradley's (Aaron Spears) house for solace and laments, "I'm so tired of all my misfires with guys. I don't want to be a cliché. You know, I want to be the exception to the rule. 'Cause you know I am the exception to the rule in every aspect of my life. Except *that* . . . Honestly, I just feel like I'm running out of time" (S1:Ep1). This moment signals the ways Mary Jane suffers in spite of her exceptionalism—or, perhaps *because* of it. Her identity is caught up in the perception that she has mismanaged her time, and she mourns the loss of what she could have had had she chosen differently. Later, Mary Jane's postfeminist time panic hits a crescendo when she realizes that her potential romantic future with longtime on-again–off-again beau David Paulk (Stephen Bishop) has come to an end because he has started dating another woman. In one of the series' more sensational plot points, Mary Jane asks her OB-GYN friend Lisa Hudson (Latarsha Rose) to inseminate her with semen she stole from the used condom and haphazardly froze after her last sexual encounter with David. Lisa tries to dissuade Mary Jane, reminding her, "[You] want to raise the baby with a man you love. Don't forget that important detail." But Mary Jane desperately insists, "I am running out of time. So please, inseminate me" (S1:Ep9). Scenes like these show Mary Jane's obsession with her biological clock and her desperate attempts to be culturally legible and marked in traditionally feminine ways. Without marriage and motherhood, Mary Jane's other exceptional qualities—career success, wealth, beauty, friendships, family—start to feel like bad decisions and misplaced priorities that keep her from achieving domestic bliss.

Mary Jane's push-and-pull between satisfaction with her career and dissatisfaction with her romantic life put the series in the company of other postfeminist media texts featuring a "miswanting" protagonist. Negra describes this narrative of "miswanting" as the point when "the heroine comes to realize that her professional aspirations are misplaced (2008, 53), leading her to "reprioritize romance and family" through some change, such as a retreat from the city to a hometown (Marston 2016, 8). While Mary Jane's job keeps her circumscribed to her hometown city of Atlanta through season three,[4] there is certainly a narrative of "miswanting" present in the series that is worth deconstructing. One of the first times Mary Jane articulates this "miswanting" is during Niecy's OB-GYN appointment with Lisa. Niecy leaves the room and Mary Jane admits her longing for children:

Lisa: Babysit sometimes!
Mary Jane: I do! That only leads to dreams of me kidnapping them. She and her sister have four kids between them. You know, I did everything right. What do I have to show for being a 'good girl'?
Lisa: A wonderful career. A beautiful house.

                                                                                    (S1:Ep1)

These types of material successes do not offer Mary Jane the same fulfilment that marriage and motherhood promise. The show establishes a clear tension between the sacrifices Mary Jane made to achieve career success, financial security, home ownership, and physical beauty and the lack of fulfilment she finds in the very things she fought so hard to achieve.

Later in season two, Mary Jane strikes up a relationship with renowned and mysterious attorney Sheldon DeWitt (Gary Dourdan). In preparation for an interview on her show, Mary Jane gives him a tour of the newsroom. When Sheldon asks why she chose her most recent segment about modern motherhood (in which Mary Jane goes through the process of cryopreservation, or egg freezing, for her viewers), she tells him "it just sort of felt like the right time" (S2:Ep4). She continues, "I've kind of had tunnel vision when it came to my career. This job has been my long-term relationship. One day I woke up and I wanted more. I wanted marriage and kids and the whole happy cliché" (S2:Ep4). Later, Mary Jane implodes her relationship with Sheldon after a series of hints help her discover that he does not "believe" in cohabitation, much less want a wife or children. For example, Sheldon's bathroom is stocked with disposable toothbrushes and he throws Mary Jane's away each morning, passive-aggressively signaling that she should not plan to stay too long. After Sheldon casually asks her when she will return to her own home, Mary Jane confronts him:

Mary Jane: You knew I was freezing my eggs. I tried to freeze my eggs on national television! The segment was called 'Modern Day Mother-hood.' Motherhood would imply that a child is what is hoped for.[5]

Sheldon: Look, I—I'm not in a rush here, okay? [. . .] I'm not going to give up my individuality for the promise of marriage and kids.

Mary Jane: And I don't want to waste my time. [. . .] I want a baby and you knew that when you barged into my life, when you came to my job—you knew I wanted a baby!

(S2:Ep12)

Mary Jane's refrain about wasting time is present again in this exchange, illustrating that any relationship that does not eventually lead to marriage and mother-hood is a waste of time.

When it comes to motherhood, there are two primary foils for Mary Jane's maternal desire: Niecy and Kara Lynch (Lisa Vidal), Mary Jane's ambitious executive producer at *Talk Back* and one of her closest friends. These relationships mirror back to Mary Jane the things she thinks she wants but in different packages. At face value, Kara is feminism's "women can have it all" writ large on screen. Kara has what Mary Jane wants: a husband, kids, and a successful career. However, Mary Jane witnesses firsthand Kara's constant struggle to balance work and family life. For example, Kara's son has a recital and her family comes to the newsroom so they can attend together. But, on the same day, a hurricane rips through Florida and their boss tells them *Talk Back* must broadcast the weather emergency indefinitely. Kara turns to Mary Jane and says, "Here I go breaking my little boy's heart again," before she breaks the bad news to her son amid a bustling newsroom (S1:Ep2). Later, Kara cites her demanding work schedule as the cause of her husband's affair, eventual dissolution of their marriage, and her decision to give primary custody to her ex-husband.

Niecy is another important character because she illustrates an alternative pathway to motherhood that might not measure up to Mary Jane's standards but, nonetheless, becomes a source of longing. Niecy has two children by two different fathers and no clear plan for her future. This perceived laziness and indecision frustrates Mary Jane. Mary Jane tries to mentor Niecy on the kinds of things she should want in her life, modeling a list of exceptional experiences that mirror her own. But Niecy finds the chink in Mary Jane's armor:

Mary Jane:	Kids your age are in college, they are studying abroad, they are having amazing life experiences. You have the rest of your life to have babies.
Niecy:	Like you? Because you did everything right, right? Where is your man? Where are your kids? Where's your happy ending?
Mary Jane:	[stunned] I'm fine. I am perfectly happy with my life.
Niecy:	Right. Maybe I'm not the only one here that's deluding herself.

(S1:Ep7)

This conversation highlights the tensions that shape their relationship: On one hand, Mary Jane wants motherhood but only if it is in addition to other kinds of achievements like higher education and travel; on the other hand, Niecy wants Mary Jane's economic success and beauty but not at the expense of her maternal identity. Marriage and motherhood become tokens of a different kind of success that seem unachievable to Mary Jane despite her achievements in nearly every other arena. This scene is crucial because it reifies Mary Jane's sense of failure and the resentment she feels about adopting a "good girl" persona that left her without a family of her own.

Enacting Postfeminism

The previous section exposes similarities between *Being Mary Jane* and other post-feminist media, showing how women of color *enact* postfeminism by using it to achieve contemporary definitions of feminine success while, at the same time, becoming susceptible to its gendered messaging. But the effects of this messaging on black women are different when paired with racialized historical, political, and economic conditions that intersect to create oppressions that white women do not face. To prove this, I first examine Mary Jane's quest for marriage with a critical attention to the politics of race to show how postfeminism's gendered requirements play out differently when applied to black women. Second, I high-light Mary Jane's refusal to be apolitical or deracialized, character traits that set her apart from postfeminist heroines and openly defy postfeminist imperatives for women to detach from social and political movements. These examples demon-strate how the series complicates a straightforward reading of Mary Jane as a post-feminist heroine through its explicit attempts to grapple with the intersections of race, gender, and class.

First, while marriage and motherhood are strong postfeminist narrative threads, achieving these things as a *black* woman are equally part of the show's discourse. The pilot opens with the following epigraph: "42% of black women have never been married" (S1:Ep1). From the beginning, viewers are presented with statistical evidence showing the difficulties black women face in achieving one of the greatest markers of traditional femininity. While both white and black women have anxieties about getting married (or "failing" to marry), the cultural contexts shaping those anxieties vary by race. A 2014 Pew Research Center study notes that whites (59%) are significantly less likely than blacks (77%) or Hispanics (74%) to place a high priority on finding a spouse or partner with a steady job. Additionally, whites are also much less likely than blacks or Hispanics to say that finding a spouse or partner with at least as much education as they have is very important to them (Wang & Parker 2014). Mary Jane's desires mirror this study's race-based emphases on career and education in romantic partnerships. These factors are important context for understanding why conversations about marriage are different for black and white women. While it can be argued that both groups want to find a "good" eligible bachelor who is educated and has a job, it is undeniable that education and career options are greatly shaped by economic resources, access, and networking, as well as inferential racism and discriminatory policies.

In the series, tensions around finding a "good black man" play out in a conversation between Sheldon and Mary Jane early in their dating history. When Sheldon argues that "the life of a black man today is significantly more difficult than any other single demographic," Mary Jane quickly retorts: "Well, except for that of black women" (S2:Ep6). "You want to talk hard?" Mary Jane asks. "Try finding an educated black man in America. Now that—that's difficult."

Sheldon: There's nearly 1.5 million black men in college, compared to 840,000 in the prison system.

Mary Jane: [Black] men are in college . . . *community* college, not the fiercely competitive ones that you and I attended. Those are the men I'm talking about. Where are they? . . . I mean, I'm not naive to understanding the systemic complexities of the journey but come on! At the end of the day, our men aren't there.

(S2:Ep6)

Mary Jane's point about the difficulties of finding "an educated black man in America" reflect growing conversations about the prison–industrial complex (Alexander 2010), poverty, and access to quality education that shape contemporary discussions about the black community and black men's place within it. These gendered disparities within the black community elucidate Mary Jane's concerns about finding a suitable romantic partner within her own race, which is defined by a unique set of political, economic, and historical oppressions.

Not only is marriage more difficult for black women to achieve but, according to the same Pew study, it is also more desired by blacks than whites: "While blacks are more likely than whites to have never been married . . . a much higher share of blacks (58%) than whites (44%) say that it's very important for a couple to marry if they plan to spend their lives together" (Wang & Parker 2014). *Being Mary Jane* reflects this data about race and marriage and sets

Mary Jane up as a black woman trying to beat the odds—odds that are not simply about "kissing too many frogs" to find her prince but, rather, a history of systemic inequalities that shape the lives, loves, and experiences of and within the black community.

In the example above, Mary Jane racializes an element of postfeminism using a clearly articulated sociopolitical history of the black community. In the next example, Mary Jane refuses to be an apolitical subject and uses her role as a journalist and her show *Talk Back* as vehicles for feminist and anti-racist critique. At the end of season one, Mary Jane expresses a personal conviction to tell the stories of people whose voices are not often heard, using *Talk Back* to report on a variety of cultural and political issues ranging from police brutality, racist beauty standards, immigration, to the widening gap between the rich and poor in America. Mary Jane also interviews real-world scholars, activists, and other public figures, thereby adding another layer of realism to the scripted series. For example, Mary Jane interviews Ava Duvernay (acclaimed director of the documentary *13th* and films *Selma, I Will Follow,* and *Middle of Nowhere*) about the prison–industrial complex. The segment ends with Mary Jane addressing dual audiences—those watching *Talk Back* and *Being Mary Jane*:

> The facts are indisputable. People of color make up 30% of the general population yet they make up 60% of the population behind bars. One in three black men in this country can expect to go to prison in their lifetime. I say enough is enough. We have to stop hiding behind rhetoric, legislation such as "three strikes," and sentences based almost entirely on the discretion of judges. If we remain indifferent to these injustices, we as individuals are no better than a system that has been problematic at best and morally bankrupt at worst.
>
> *(S1:Ep8)*

Mary Jane's job grants her a kind of authority that she strategically deploys to emphasize issues directly affecting the black community. What distinguishes this moment of direct address from, say, Carrie Bradshaw's disembodied voiceover narration in *Sex and the City*, is its political consciousness. Mary Jane is a black woman looking directly into the camera and critiquing institutionalized racism in a passionate and palatable way. Unlike Carrie Bradshaw, Mary Jane's blackness is embodied—it informs the stories she covers, her interviews and interactions with guests on her show, and signoff monologues like this one. Her politics are clearly attached to feminist and anti-racist political movements fighting for social justice in real time. This moment is one of many illustrating Mary Jane's refusal to erase race from the conversation or from her own body. She does not "choose" to be deracialized or disembodied, even when her refusal comes with consequences (like kickback from news executives or viewers who claim

Mary Jane's show no longer "speaks to them"). In moments like these viewers witness the limits of Mary Jane's potential to embody postfeminism and her refusal to enact it.

Another moment that tests Mary Jane's commitment to enacting postfeminism occurs in season two, when Cynthia Phillips (Kelly Rutherford), the white nightly news correspondent, calls in sick and Mary Jane is tapped to fill in. In her interview with Elizabeth Foy, a charter school advocate with a recently released book, Mary Jane goes off script and asks her tough questions about her ties with racists and religious fundamentalism. Foy says she feels "ambushed" by Mary Jane and her "liberal agenda," calling her a "race baiter" (S2:Ep10). Rather than shy away from the topic of race or return to the status quo script, Mary Jane pushes Foy to think intersectionally:

> [From] where I'm sitting, you're a woman. I'm a woman. But your mistake is that you seem to think that I only see things through the prism of race because I have black guests and I'm black. But just because you're Caucasian doesn't make you immune from discrimination or being ignored as a woman. If you were really paying attention to my show you would see that we're not all that different at all. I mean, granted, we may not agree on certain issues, but we're both fighting to be heard and fighting to be taken seriously and to be seen. So, when it comes down to it, when I look at you, I see an ugly black woman, too.
>
> *(S2:Ep10)*

This final line—"when I look at you, I see an ugly black woman, too"—goes viral and launches Mary Jane onto front page news, proving that being political in this way (a risky move in a postfeminist and post-racial workplace) does not necessarily inhibit career success. Yet, later, media executives make it clear that making *Talk Back* "too black" will hurt ratings and alienate white viewers. In a meeting with high-ranking network executive Shohreh Broomand (Kathleen Gati), Mary Jane is offered a spot on network news, which has been her ultimate career goal. But, this promotion comes with a condition. Shohreh asks, "When it comes to primetime, I will need you to tone down the all-black agenda and shift your focus over to doing some broader, more far-reaching stories. Can you do that for me?" (S2:Ep11). This rhetorical question inviting Mary Jane to deracialize and depoliticize herself and *Talk Back* creates a postfeminist double bind: either become the idealized apolitical subject and achieve great career success or forefront racial politics and suffer the consequences.

After the meeting, Mary Jane and Kara discuss the promotion behind closed doors and viewers watch as she struggles to keep her politicized identity *and* her job. While both agree that the promotion to primetime is a good thing because it is more visibility and prestige, Mary Jane hesitates to leave behind the work that has made her proud and popular:

Mary Jane: Right now, the possibilities are endless. I got people calling my agent offering me book deals, saying they want me to be a motivational speaker for fifteen grand a pop. I mean, even broadcast news is back on the table as a realistic option again.

Kara: Okay, I see where this is coming from. This isn't about making a difference. It's about making money.

Mary Jane: Why can't it be about both?

(S2:Ep11)

Mary Jane vacillates between racialized and postfeminist subject positions, weighing her desire for money and career success against her sense of pride in making media that matters for underrepresented communities. If, despite her freedom, the ideal postfeminist subject is "called . . . to withhold critique . . . [as] the condition of her freedom" (McRobbie 2007, 34), then Mary Jane sits at the crossroads of this turbulent intersection.

The examples above are just a sample of the challenges race poses to postfeminism in *Being Mary Jane*. Thinking intersectionally about postfeminism's gendered marriage imperatives does not account for the political, economic, and social histories of the black community that shape romantic and marital relationships in ways white women never have to contend with. Mary Jane reminds us of that. Thinking intersectionally about postfeminism's definition of career success (using empowerment phrases like Sheryl Sandberg's "lean in" that prioritize a privileged white, middle-class perspective on workplace dynamics) does not consider the ways black women's workplace experiences are shaped by the intersection of their gendered and raced identities.[6] Mary Jane reminds us of that, too.

These examples show two tensions at play that reinforce the space between enacting and embodying postfeminism: Mary Jane's inability to fully embody postfeminism because of its fascination and idealization of whiteness and Mary Jane's refusal to fully enact postfeminism if it means turning a blind eye to racial politics and the black community of her belonging. Mary Jane enacts postfeminism, but only to a point. Then, she claims her blackness in ways that transform her into someone quite different than traditional postfeminist heroines. The corporeal distance between Mary Jane and the idealized white postfeminist subject leaves room for her to inject identity politics into postfeminism. Mary Jane strategically enacts postfeminism and uses it to achieve career success, economic independence, sexual empowerment, and craft her personal brand. Nonetheless, her decision to enact postfeminism does not make her immune to the gendered pressures that white women feel—specifically the perceived "failure" of prolonged singlehood and fertility time panics—simply because she does not embody the white ideal. In most postfeminist media, the structural inequalities and histories of oppression shaping those pressures are erased—a fact that Mary Jane does not let viewers forget. Mary Jane's ability to foreground a concrete set of racial politics, histories, and material realities not only makes visible the ideological limits of postfeminism but also makes *Being Mary Jane* a radical departure from other postfeminist media.

Notes

1 For more about the gendered nature of makeover TV shows, see Weber 2009.
2 For a discussion of the links between postfeminism and neoliberalism, see Gill and Scharff 2011.
3 In one episode, Mary Jane masturbates at her office desk before going on a late-night date with David. This act of self-love destigmatizes masturbation and forefronts Mary Jane's connection to her own body and sexuality.
4 Season four of *Being Mary Jane* reveals that Mary Jane has relocated to New York City, the number one market in the country, where she attempts to start over at dating and find a husband.
5 One of the major storylines in season two revolves around Mary Jane's "Modern Day Motherhood" segment where she agrees to go through the process of freezing her eggs for her TV viewers. Although Kara is the one to propose the story, framing cryopreservation as "the modern day woman's insurance policy" (S2:Ep1), Mary Jane jumps on the opportunity out of personal fears that this might be her last chance to become a mother.
6 For a more in-depth discussion of Sheryl Sandberg's brand of "corporate feminism," see Gill 2016.

Works Cited

Alexander, Michelle. 2010. *The New Jim Crow: Mass Incarceration in the Age of Colorblindness*. New York: The New Press.
Banet-Weiser, Sarah. 2007. "What's Your Flava?: Race and Postfeminism in Media Culture." In Yvonne Tasker & Diane Negra (Eds.), *Interrogating Postfeminism: Gender and the Politics of Popular Culture* 201–226. Durham: Duke University Press.
Bordo, Susan. 1993. *Unbearable Weight: Feminism, Western Culture, and the Body*. Berkeley: University of California Press.
Butler, Jess. 2013. "For White Girls Only? Postfeminism and the Politics of Inclusion." *Feminist Formations* 25 (1): 35–58.
Chatman, Dayna. 2015. "Pregnancy, Then It's 'Back To Business.'" *Feminist Media Studies* 15 (6): 926–941.
Douglas, Susan J. 2010. *Enlightened Sexism: The Seductive Message that Feminism's Work is Done*. New York: Times Books.
Gill, Rosalind. 2007. "Postfeminist Media Culture: Elements of a Sensibility." *European Journal of Cultural Studies* 10 (2): 147–166.
Gill, Rosalind. 2016. "Post-postfeminism?: New Feminist Visibilities in Postfeminist Times." *Feminist Media Studies* 16 (4): 610–630.
Gill, Rosalind, and Christina Scharff. 2011. "Introduction." In Rosalind Gill & Christina Scharff (Eds.), *New Femininites: Postfeminism, Neoliberalism, and Subjectivity* 1–17. New York: Palgrave Macmillan.
Hua, Julietta. 2009. "'Gucci Geishas' and Post-feminism." *Women's Studies in Communication* 32 (1): 63–88.
Joseph, Ralina L. 2009. "'Tyra Banks is Fat': Reading (Post-)Racism and (Post-)Feminism in the New Millennium." *Critical Studies in Media Communication* 26 (3): 237–254.

Marston, Kendra. 2016. "The World is Her Oyster: Negotiating Contemporary White Womanhood in Hollywood's Tourist Spaces." *Cinema Journal* 55 (4) (Summer): 3–27.

McRobbie, Angela. 2007. "TOP GIRLS? Young women and the post-feminist sexual contract." *Cultural Studies* 21: 4–5, 718–737.

McRobbie, Angela. 2009. *The Aftermath of Feminism: Gender, Culture, and Social Change.* London: SAGE.

Merriam-Webster Dictionary Online. "Embody". Accessed January 28, 2017. https://www.merriam-webster.com/dictionary/embody.

Merriam-Webster Dictionary Online. "Enact". Accessed January 28, 2017. https://www.merriam-webster.com/dictionary/enact.

Negra, Diane. 2008. "Structural Integrity, Historical Reversion, and the Post-9/11 Chick Flick." *Feminist Media Studies* 8 (1): 51–68.

Negra, Diane. 2009. *What a Girl Wants?: Fantasizing the Reclamation of Self in Postfeminism.* London: Routledge.

Patrick, Stephanie. 2016. "I Want my Snooki: MTV's Failed Subjects and Postfeminist Ambivalence In and Around the Jersey Shore." *Feminist Media Studies* 17 (2): 181–197.

Rossie, Amanda. 2015. "Moving Beyond 'Am I Pretty or Ugly?': Disciplining Girls through YouTube Feedback." *Continuum: Journal of Media and Cultural Studies* 29 (2): 230–240.

Smith-Shomade, Beretta. 2007. *Pimpin' Ain't Easy: Selling Black Entertainment Television.* New York: Routledge.

Springer, Kimberly. 2007. "Divas, Evil Black Bitches, and Bitter Black Women: African American Women in Postfeminist and Post-Civil-Rights Popular Culture." In Yvonne Tasker & Diane Negra (Eds.), *Interrogating Postfeminism: Gender and the Politics of Popular Culture,* 249–276. Durham: Duke University Press.

Tasker, Yvonne, and Diane Negra. 2007. *Interrogating Postfeminism: Gender and the Politics of Popular Culture.* Durham: Duke University Press.

Time Warner Cable. 2017. *Being Mary Jane.* January 17. Retrieved from My On Demand: http://www.twcondemand.com/tv/bet/9219036/being-mary-jane.

Wang, Wendy, and Kim Parker. 2014. "Record Share of Americans Have Never Married: As Values, Economics and Gender Patterns Change." *Pew Research Center's Social & Demographic Trends project.* September 24. Washington, D.C. Retrieved from http://www.pewsocialtrends.org/2014/09/24/record-share-of-americans-have-never-married/.

Weber, Brenda. 2009. *Makeover TV: Selfhood, Citizenship, and Celebrity.* Durham: Duke University Press.

Wolf, Naomi. 1991. *The Beauty Myth: How Images of Beauty Are Used Against Women.* New York: Morrow.

2

"ARE YOU A *FEMINIST?*"

Celebrity, Publicity, and the Making of a PR-Friendly Feminism

Bryce Renninger

In November 2014, *TIME* magazine asked its online readers: "Which word should be banned in 2015?" The list of 15 nominated expressions included "kale," tech industry business terms "disrupt" and "influencer," slang exclamations "yaaasssss" and "obvi," and the word "feminism." Why is "feminism" on a list of words that need to go? On the page for the poll, *TIME* explains the reasoning behind the inclusion of the word: "You have nothing against feminism itself, but when did it become a thing that every celebrity had to state their position on whether this word applies to them, like some politician declaring a party? Let's stick to the issues and quit throwing this label around like ticker tape at a Susan B. Anthony parade" (Steinmetz 2014). Several online petitions and other instances of protest led the magazine's managing editor Nancy Gibbs to issue the following editor's note: "*TIME* apologizes for the execution of this poll; the word 'feminist' should not have been included in a list of words to ban. While we meant to invite debate about some ways the word was used this year, that nuance was lost, and we regret that its inclusion has become a distraction from the important debate over equality and justice" (Steinmetz 2014).

The *TIME* poll references a recent phenomenon in which the contemporary news ecosystem has inspired the development of two different kinds of celebrity identification with feminism: one in which celebrities are asked about their affiliation with feminism and one in which news outlets' critics contemplate whether or not a given celebrity's words and actions make them a feminist. These trends occur in a context in which postfeminist cultural politics have dominated popular media cultures. Postfeminism describes a "sensibility" (Gill 2007) based on the cultural belief that feminism is irrelevant because its goals have been achieved. According to Angela McRobbie (2004, 255), post-feminism works by suggesting:

> that by means of the tropes of freedom and choice which are now inextricably connected with the category of "young women," feminism is decisively aged and made to seem redundant. Feminism is cast into the shadows, where at best it can expect to have some afterlife, where it might be regarded ambivalently by those young women who must in more public venues stake a distance from it, for the sake of social and sexual recognition.

McRobbie's point, then, is that within a society that invests in postfeminist ideology, feminism is seen as outdated. This chapter seeks to intervene in this claim by examining the ways in which celebrity feminism has emerged as a response to postfeminism, suggesting that feminism deserves a place within contemporary cultural discourse.

This chapter argues that contemporary U.S. journalism's focus on celebrities' feminist status is indicative of a new trend in postfeminist media culture, one that makes feminism a topic of conversation in celebrity discourse. This renewed attention to feminism does sometimes change the course of popular cultural commentary to associate feminism with a positive valence, but it simultaneously encourages a simplistic understanding of what feminism is and can be. Individual journalists, online news outlets, and prevailing industry conventions have codified a new feminist moment, in which the "feminist" label is claimed by some celebrities . . . but often with hesitation and disclaimers. While much ink has been spilled on the decisions of specific celebrities to identify or not to identify as a feminist or on whether or not a certain celebrity (e.g. Beyoncé) qualifies as a feminist, the journalistic field has fostered and reinforced a limited view of feminism. I argue that far from "throwing this label around like ticker tape," journalists, with celebrities and their publicity teams, have co-created a stabilization of a popular definition of feminism as equality feminism that ignores many dimensions of privilege and obscures the systemic forces that create inequality.

To make these arguments, I start by comparing contemporary "celebrity feminism," in which celebrities are asked whether they identify as a feminist, with an earlier version of "celebrity feminism," in which feminist writers and critics became celebrities because their voices and ideas circulated in mainstream media outlets. I show how the recent version of celebrity feminism places the emphasis on the "feminist" identifier instead of feminist thought. I then use Edson Tandoc, Jr.'s (2014) analysis of the contemporary analytics-driven newsroom to show how and why journalistic outlets have decided to place so much attention on the "Are you a feminist?" interview question and the "X Is/Is Not a Feminist" headline. Following this, I argue that contemporary celebrity feminism seeks to give feminism a rebranding that eschews other potential meanings of the word to promote *equality* feminism.

How Celebrity Feminism is Negotiated

As Hannah Hamad and Anthea Taylor (2015) have noted, "discursive struggles over the meanings of feminism are now, perhaps more than ever, largely staged in and through media culture" (126). Thus, it is incredibly important to understand the "kinds of visibility" for feminism (Rosalind Gill 2016, 616) on offer from mainstream media outlets. As Gill points out, though feminism may be discussed more in mainstream outlets today, "many feminist media storms arrive *always-already trivialized*, be they about 'twerking,' footballers' private emails, inappropriate comments about a LinkedIn profile, or the latest feminist-baiting outburst from Donald Trump" (616). In this section, I compare contemporary celebrity feminism to the quite-different celebrity feminism of the mid- to late twentieth century to historicize the implications of having so many of these discursive struggles exist over whether or not a certain celebrity is or is not a feminist.

Jennifer Wicke (1994) writes about rifts in public feminisms in the late twentieth century. She notes the tensions over the meaning and priorities of feminism between academic feminists and grassroots movement feminism, but identifies one of the key factors of the postfeminist environment—that the U.S. in the late twentieth century has "no movement feminism" (752). To explain what does exist, she elaborates on the figure of the celebrity feminist, a "mixed blessing for materialist feminism" (754). She describes celebrity feminism as "the mediated nimbus around academic feminism . . . a new locus for feminist discourse, feminist politics, and feminist conflicts, both conflicts internal to feminism and feminism's many struggles with antifeminist forces" (753). Her examples of celebrity feminists from the 1990s operate in what she calls the celebrity zone, a place where public intellectuals and media commentators represented diverse, explicitly feminist viewpoints. These celebrity feminists include contrarian cultural critic Camille Paglia, anti-porn anti-sexual harassment legal scholar Catherine MacKinnon, *The Beauty Myth* author Naomi Wolf, and *The Nation*'s Katha Pollitt, who qualifies for using her gender column to participate in the celebrity zone by thematizing the gender politics of the Nancy Kerrigan/Tonya Harding rivalry and altercation.

Wicke argues that feminists will not—and in a way cannot—escape the celebrity zone as a viable way to circulate (media) messages. She describes the 1990s celebrity zone as being "fed by streams flowing from civil society: congressional hearings, Court TV, Hillary Clinton's health plan, the L.A. riots, controversial judicial or cabinet nominees, and so forth" (757). Wicke's 1990s celebrity feminism, therefore, is defined by the media environment of its time and sounds remarkably like an outline of the items on a contemporary cable TV news show popular during this period.

Though they focus on different historical moments, Wicke shares a general theoretical approach to the meaning of celebrity feminism with Anthea Taylor's (2014) analysis of "blockbuster" celebrity feminism. Taylor argues that in the second half of the twentieth century, authors of bestselling feminist books of non-fiction were the leading feminist celebrities. From Betty Friedan and her book *The Feminine Mystique* (1963), to Gloria Steinem and *Outrageous Acts and Everyday Rebellions* (1983) to Susan Faludi and *Backlash* (1991) to Naomi Wolf and *The Beauty Myth* (1990), "the key arguments of these books have been taken up within the mainstream mediasphere and become metonymic of feminism" (75). Taylor explains that these celebrities experience fame differently than other celebrities, but she also points out that in these cases, a unique feminist perspective or approach to understanding the world and the news causes the celebrity.

Richard Dyer's (1979) analysis of Jane Fonda's star figure shows how she and certain other stars have been able to be outwardly political, even feminist, while being respected actresses and sex symbols. The celebrity media infrastructure that existed while Fonda was becoming a full-fledged star, though, allowed celebrities to control their star-image much more closely. Dyer makes the case that Fonda was able to be a known feminist and political activist while retaining her fame by "reconciling the aims of the women's movement with 'acceptable,' 'normal' behavior" (94). He also reminds the reader of her all-American family upbringing and her non-threatening (i.e., non-lesbian) feminist star-image, aspects of her identity that allow her to maintain mass appeal while feminist.

Wicke and Taylor's celebrity feminism describe popular agenda-setters in feminist counterpublics, women who fostered Nancy Fraser's (1990) two functions for counterpublic communication: regrouping as a counterpublic, and agitating mainstream publics that do not take the counterpublic's concerns seriously. However, in contrast to these discourses, today's news media-facilitated celebrity feminism does not link these celebrity feminists to a feminist counterpublic. As Rhian Sasseen (2014) writes in *Salon*, "The rhetoric of personal choice has created a feminism that emphasizes sound bites over politics, draining the movement of any sentiment more complex than, 'Hooray, women.'" When journalists from mainstream news outlets ask celebrities whether or not they are a feminist, they attempt to pull a feminist identification out of an interview subject who did not offer it. This question, then, is more concerned with affiliation and individual labels rather than an active contribution to a feminist counterpublic, the communicative sphere where feminist priorities are discussed and debated, the place from which these concerns arise when they become popular discussions.

It is worth looking at specific examples of media commentary on celebrity feminism to illustrate the ways in which celebrity feminism does not spring out of a particular ideology. In the remainder of this section, I will explain how the focus on celebrity feminism today overemphasizes identification as a feminist instead of focusing on feminist thought or action.

Consider the way the "Are you a feminist?" question plays out in interviews. Eliana Dockterman (2014) starts her *TIME* interview with Shailene Woodley by noting that Woodley has previously discussed how it is important for her to think about "the kinds of messages that [she's] sending to young female fans when [she's] taking on roles." Dockterman ends her observation by asking, "do you consider yourself a feminist?" Woodley starts her answer,

> No, because I love men, and I think the idea of "raise women to power, take the men away from the power" is never going to work out because you need balance. With myself, I'm very in touch with my masculine side. And I'm 50 percent feminine and 50 percent masculine, same as I think a lot of us are. And I think that is important to note. And also I think that if men went down and women rose to power, that wouldn't work either. We have to have a fine balance.

Woodley's answer suggests feminism is synonymous with misandry, that being feminist is also synonymous with being feminine, and that feminism inherently argues for matriarchy. Her response assumes a meaning of feminism that is inconsistent and seems not to be based on any particular understanding of feminism. When *TIME* follows up on the story of Woodley's feminism (Alter 2015), the fact that they title their article "Shailene Woodley Still Adamant She's Not a Feminist" implies an expectation that she could have (and maybe should have) changed her tune.[1]

The story arc of celebrities' (non-)affiliation with feminism often extends beyond just one story. In her *Billboard* Woman of the Year acceptance speech, Katy Perry said that she was not a feminist. In a 2014 Australian morning show interview,[2] Perry explained "I used to not really understand what that word meant, and now that I do, it just means that I love myself as a female and I also love men." After refusing the term in 2012, Taylor Swift backtracked in a 2014 interview where she admitted that she did not know what the term "really" meant when she answered the question first. Her relationship with Lena Dunham, she said, helped her understand what feminism *really* was. She says, "Becoming friends with Lena—without her preaching to me, but just seeing why she believes what she believes, why she says what she says, why she stands for what she stands for—has made me realize that I've been taking a feminist stance without actually saying so" (Hoby 2014). The journeys of celebrities coming to feminism are sometimes not really journeys at all; the celebrities realize that they've been feminists all along. However, if being a part of a feminist conversation, discourse, counterpublic, or movement gives feminism meaning, what really is the use of these feminist announcements? The focus on the "Are you a feminist?" question in celebrity interviews gives extra "feminist" publicity to stars who do not actively participate in feminist movements.

The contemporary news system's obsession with celebrity feminism also takes shape in the pages of cultural commentary, op-eds, and think pieces, in which writers contemplate whether certain celebrities qualify as feminists. Perhaps the most popular celebrity to be subject to this debate about her feminist credentials is the pop star Beyoncé. Debate about Beyoncé's feminism hit a peak when three things occurred in 2013 and 2014. First, Beyoncé sampled Chimamanda Ngozi Adichie's TEDx talk "We Should All Be Feminists" on the song "Flawless" from her 2013 album. Second, she stood in front of a giant screen with the word "FEMINIST" emblazoned on it during a 2014 MTV Video Music Awards performance. Third, in a 2014 promotional short film, "Yours and Mine,"[3] she says "I've always considered myself a feminist, although I was always afraid of that word because people put so much on it." Various summaries and analyses of this video made it seem as if Beyoncé said that she considers herself, in the words of a CNN analysis of the video, a "'Humanist' rather than 'feminist'" (Hare 2014). In reality, the video voiceover includes Beyoncé saying that she has always considered herself a feminist and after an analysis of racialized gender politics says that she "considers herself a humanist," but in no way does that explicitly discount her earlier identification of her feminism as the CNN article supposes. Ironically, in an age that Graeme Turner (2010) describes as being oversaturated with celebrity content, Beyoncé, one of the world's biggest celebrities, has not subjected herself to a live, direct interview from 2013 through 2016. She has also not tweeted for the same period. She has only released new images into the world through Instagram and magazines like *Vogue*. Her only way of communicating with the public is in performances and in carefully edited videos like "Yours and Mine." Many cultural critics have questioned or defended her devotion to ostensibly feminist principles based on what she has put out into the world on her own terms (see Kendall 2013; Cooper 2013). In addition to Beyoncé's "feminist" commentary of 2013–2014 and well-worn arguments about sexualization and feminism, these critics often mention her empowerment anthems "Lemonade," "Independent Women," "Survivor," and "Who Run the World (Girls)." But they also have the servile Destiny's Child ballad "Cater 2 U" and "Drunk In Love" (which includes a line in Jay-Z's featured rap that casually alludes to Ike Turner's abuse of Tina Turner) to turn to for evidence of Beyoncé's lack of feminist awareness.

In the end, these essays that argue whether or not Beyoncé or anyone else is a feminist focus on whether or not someone's pre-existing thoughts and actions qualify them for the feminist label. Both these essays and the "Are you a feminist?" question presume that it is valid for feminism to be something that one can do without realizing, something one can be observed doing, and something which when offered should be questioned. These practices do not privilege feminism that is co-created with other feminists in conversations, counterpublics, and movements. They promote an individualistic form of feminism, a floating signifier label, not a feminist space for productive regroupment.

Contemporary Celebrity Feminism and Analytics-Driven Journalism

Graeme Turner (2010) justifies the importance of studying celebrity in the early twenty-first century by pointing to the growing influence of celebrity in contemporary news coverage, noting, "The growth of new media has generated new ways of representing, consuming and producing celebrity while online journalism – especially where it is developed as an additional platform for the mainstream print media – has also had an expansionary effect." (11). Even news outlets concerned with their reputation and a semblance of prestige have increased their coverage of celebrities, Turner argues. Edson Tandoc, Jr. (2014) argues that celebrity news, which often traffics in the ordinary actions of famous people, is incentivized in a news ecosystem that values measurements like clicks and social media shares. In this section, I explore the connections between the "Are you a feminist?" celebrity interview question and the contemporary online news political economy.

It seems suspect that the *TIME* editors actually thought that the inclusion of "feminism" on the banned words poll could have "invited debate" about the use of the word. A dark irony is present in *TIME*'s initial explanation of the inclusion of the word "feminism" on this list. While Steinmetz (2014) asked when it became "a thing that every celebrity had to state their position on whether the word applied to them," she should not have had to look further then the articles that were hyperlinked to her words on the article. *TIME* magazine, it turns out, has published several articles publicizing various celebrities' affiliation or disaffiliation with the "feminist" label. Many of these *TIME* articles are commentaries on interviews done by other outlets (Frizell 2014; Stampler 2014), but *TIME* also asked the question in at least one case. Eliana Dockterman's (2014) "Shailene Woodley on Why She's Not a Feminist" and the follow-up ten months later that pulled quotes from a *NYLON* magazine cover story interview with Woodley were both published in *TIME*. *TIME* magazine is, therefore, invested in perpetuating the "Are you a feminist?" celebrity interview question and the cultural politics therein. Again on the *TIME* website, a video interview with the "Miss Independent" singer Kelly Clarkson is titled "Kelly Clarkson: 'Not a Feminist'" and includes the singer saying the feminist identifier was "too strong" to define her.

In recent years, the work of journalists, especially those who publish online, has become dependent on analytics that indicate how many views an article has and how well an article is doing within various categories of referrals. As Tandoc's (2014) ethnography of the contemporary online newsroom has shown, editors for online outlets use analytics to both test and predict what headlines will be clicked on and shared. Referrals from social media sites have become especially important for the revenue generation of online news outlets, and it has become a part of news workers' jobs to title, illustrate, and position articles in particular ways on social media and to rearrange the display of articles on homepages to reflect what is learned about what makes people click from web analytics (Tandoc 2014). Web editors have been frank about how they use these tactics to gain more views (e.g., Mordecai 2014), but less frequent are explicit discussions about how web analytics crowds out valuable, quality content with articles that are less necessary and less worthwhile. Because web writers and editors can know whether and how many people read their articles, they are always attuned to ways in which they can earn clicks.

In a news media environment in which more people are getting their news from social media sites like Facebook and Twitter, headlines (and images) are especially important for convincing users to click on an article.[4] Because these new forms of news consumption do not rely on users visiting news outlets' homepages and because advertising revenue is based on the number of advertising impressions,[5] individual news stories must convince users to click and share. The popularity of celebrity coverage means that many outlets seek and gain access to the same public figures. The "Are you a feminist?" question is a popular way for journalists to distinguish their promotional or junket interviews from others. The headlines for the stories tied to many of these initial "X Is/Is Not a Feminist" interviews are instructive in developing an understanding of how journalists have begun to use the answer to the "Are you a feminist?" question to title and therefore sell the outlet's interviews with these celebrities. Consider the following headlines of interviews in which the journalist asked the celebrity the feminist question:

"Shailene Woodley on Why She's Not a Feminist," *TIME.* May 5, 2014.

"Miley Cyrus Opens Up to Tavi Gevinson About Heartbreak, Sex, and Feminism," *Elle.* April 8, 2014.

"Ellen Page: 'Why are People So Reluctant to Say They're Feminists?," *The Guardian.* July 3, 2013.

"Girls' Lena Dunham: Women Saying 'I'm Not a Feminist' Is My Greatest Pet Peeve." *Metro.* January 14, 2013.

"Katy Perry Is Still Confused By Feminism, Despite Her Best Efforts." *Huffington Post.* March 17, 2014.

All of these initial articles use the yes/no feminist declaration to entice readers to click and share, but not all articles that feature the question include notice of the answer in the headline. The original articles that tracked Taylor Swift's feminist development do not place her feminist identification in the title. The 2012 *Daily Beast* article in which Swift seemed unsure about the feminist label was titled "Taylor Swift Dishes on Her New Album 'Red,' Dating, Heartbreak, and 'Grey's

Anatomy',", and the 2014 *Guardian* interview in which Swift explains how Lena Dunham helped her realize the meaning of feminism has the title "Taylor Swift: 'Sexy? Not on My Radar." The questions about feminism were pointed, though, and several sites that reblogged or recontextualized the original interviews led with the feminist hook. The feminist blog *Jezebel* covered the *Daily Beast* interview with the article, "Don't Go Calling Taylor Swift a Feminist, Says Taylor Swift," and, *yes*, *TIME*'s coverage of the *Guardian* interview was titled, "Taylor Swift Finally Explains Why She's a Feminist and How Lena Dunham Helped." Though *The Daily Beast* and *The Guardian* both opted not to lead with feminism, their attention to the subject led to them being linked by several articles whose summary of the original interviews focused on the question of whether or not she identifies as a feminist. While it is hard to confirm whether or not these articles succeed in garnering clicks and shares because most sites keep their analytics private, these titles indicate what writers and editors think will entice viewers based on their experience of what typically works. These instincts are clearly at play in the promotion of the "Are you a feminist?" celebrity interview question.

The contemporary news ecosystem not only provides an incentive to ask celebrities whether or not they are feminists, but the articles that do so provoke other outlets to write their own commentary on the initial articles and gain their own cheap traffic. These commentary articles are inexpensive to produce, because they don't involve the process of setting up and waiting for the celebrity interview, and the interview that has already occurred has been transcribed and framed. These articles also benefit the original writers by linking back to the original story, sending a fraction of their readers to the original interview. This feedback loop of contemporary journalism is common, but in the context of celebrities' feminism, the contemporary news ecosystem has created an irresistible incentive structure for covering the topic.[6]

Celebrity Feminism Gives Feminism an Equality Rebranding

Earlier, I argued that contemporary celebrity feminism created by celebrity journalism promotes an individualistic view of feminism that legitimizes the act of assigning or simply picking up the feminist label. In this section, I argue that when the label is adopted by celebrity feminists in these contexts, equality feminism is privileged over other understandings of feminism. The dictionary definition of feminism—the online Oxford dictionary defines feminism as "The advocacy of women's rights on the grounds of political, social, and economic equality to men"—is often alluded to in these cases. The transformations of Katy Perry and Taylor Swift, for instance, into celebrity feminists are indicative of the way that celebrity feminisms are typically rebranded as equality feminism. Both Perry and Swift detailed to their respective interviewers that they changed their identification as feminists when they found out what "feminism really meant." Those celebrity interviewees who say they are not feminists often say they think the word is "too strong," and that it is associated with men-hating. Of course, there is no one definition of what feminism—like almost anything else—"really" means in all contexts.

One of the most popular instances of celebrity feminism in the past few years has been Emma Watson's speech at the launch of a United Nations #HeforShe campaign to bring men into the fight for women's equality worldwide. The speech by the white British actress was made in the context of the international organization in an era when the treatment of women in certain parts of the world has been used to justify destructive military policy (Stabile and Kumar 2005). It is difficult to know how this campaign or others like it will eventually be used to spur change and how it intends to navigate the complicated geopolitics of the early twenty-first century, but, of course, her decision to use the word "feminism," despite suggestions to avoid using it, in the speech became its own news (Dockterman 2015). The popularity of Watson's speech makes clear the widespread appeal of equality feminism, but the context of her speech as part of a United Nations program sponsored by the financial firm PricewaterhouseCoopers shows how equality feminism fits snugly with bureaucracy and global capitalism.

A similar dynamic is present in Sheryl Sandberg's (2013) blockbuster feminist book *Lean In* and its celebrity-friendly #BanBossy campaign, which focuses on predominantly, if not exclusively, women pursuing corporate success. The book features tips on how women can assert themselves in their relationships and in the workforce so that they can have a fulfilling work and home life. It also features a few sections in which Sandberg explains her reluctant acceptance of the "feminist" term to describe herself. But as bell hooks (2013) notes, Sandberg often sees the achievement of equality within the current (corporate) system as the be-all end-all. hooks writes, "From this perspective, the structures of imperialist white supremacist capitalist patriarchy need not be challenged. And she makes it seem that privileged white men will eagerly choose to extend the benefits of corporate capitalism to white women who have the courage to 'lean in.'" Sandberg's #BanBossy attempts to ban the use of the word "bossy" to describe young girls. Sandberg argues that "bossy" is used to hold young girls back from being too ambitious.[7] In fact, by pursuing a digital strategy for the campaign and enlisting celebrities to promote it, Sandberg sought to harness the same click-and-share incentives that celebrity journalists use to promote a "feminist" campaign that is both uncontroversial and completely invested in maintaining hierarchies.

Just as Anita Brady's (2016) observation that the contemporary debates over "good" and "bad" celebrity feminism and what constitutes "authentic" celebrity feminism actually redraws and reinforces our understanding of the feminist field itself, so too does the focus on equality feminism limit our perception of what constitutes feminism. As sites and platforms for feminist information and news proliferate on the Internet (e.g. *Feministing, Crunk Feminist Collective, Jezebel, Reductress*), Internet users have the opportunity to read or listen to a great many contemporary feminist perspectives on a number of today's news stories and issues. Users who are not professional media producers also have the opportunity to contribute to feminist conversations on social media sites and the comment sections of articles on mainstream and feminist news sites. I have been arguing that the phenomenon of contemporary celebrity feminism has been encouraged by particular attributes of the online news ecosystem. Likewise, a similar set of social technologies has fostered communication amongst feminists that is hostile (Loza 2014) and has also fostered a "popular misogyny" (Banet-Weiser 2015). In light of the complexity of contemporary feminism, one can understand why some might think that feminism might need a rebranding. But concentrating on the branding of the concept takes the focus off fostering substantive feminist conversations in counterpublic contexts.

My goal here is not to advocate an alternative to some celebrities' preferred version of feminism. I am only pointing out that "equality" feminism is being emphasized as a PR-friendly version of the word by the system that has created contemporary celebrity feminism. A phenomenon similar to feminism's "equality" rebranding has also occurred when LGBT struggles were organized around a "fight for equality" instead of "liberation" (see, for instance, Walters 2014). One can see how important defining the word feminism is to approaching feminist thought and action by comparing the difference between the dictionary definition of the word above and bell hooks' (1984) claim that "Feminism is a movement to end sexism, sexist exploitation, and oppression" (viii). The feminism created by contemporary celebrity feminism is a category broad enough to include "everyone" and narrow enough to limit the political possibilities of a feminist perspective. As the work of Jessalynn Keller and Jessica Ringrose (2015) has noted, even young celebrity news readers can feel patronized by celebrity feminism's limited scope. In almost all of the cases mentioned above, wealth, whiteness, and other signs of privilege are not challenged as cultural values. The question as commonly asked, "Are you a feminist?" or "Do you consider yourself a feminist?," frames the question as a personal identification and a belief in the value of equality. It does not frame the word as a systematic critique that extends beyond the individual. Identifying as a feminist often conforms to the consumerist self-empowerment ethos supported by various capitalist projects; it does not encourage the creation of feminist alternatives through counterpublic regrouping and political agitation (Banet-Weiser 2012).

Conclusions: Celebrity Feminisms in the Age of Trump

The contemporary conversations about celebrities' feminism discussed in this chapter occur in a particular journalistic ecosystem and a particular time in the history of feminism, where feminist politics must defend itself against postfeminist sensibilities. The very mundane, predictable paths that conversations around celebrity feminism carve out are the result of feminism's need to resist postfeminist irrelevance and popular misogyny via an assertion of relevance. Contemporary discussions of celebrity feminism are shaped by ad-supported journalistic projects and their analytics-trained writers and editors. These conversations, which occur within the social arenas of online publications—on social media, in the comment sections of news outlets, and in the social networks that connect various publications, focus on who is a feminist according to any given celebrity or writer, rather than what action feminist thought should be put to. For the most part, it has been journalists working for "mainstream" outlets that have pursued the line of questioning and reporting that in turn has created this particular celebrity feminism phenomenon. These stories are published in the pursuit of profit, but they often lead to news consumers following suit and policing the words and conduct of celebrities themselves. These stories have also spawned a genre of complementary commentary articles in feminist publications that take the "X Is/Not a Feminist" articles as jumping-off points.

Celebrities in the era defined in part by #BlackLivesMatter, the presidential candidacy of Hillary Clinton, and President Trump have leeway to be more openly political. The fact that Beyoncé followed her "feminist" VMA performance in 2014 with Super Bowl and VMA performances in 2016 that paid homage to the historical Black Power movement and contemporary #BlackLivesMatter movement shows this shift clearly. Celebrities now often do incorporate anti-racism or anti-capitalism and other intersectional political concerns into their public feminism. This shift indicates trends within at least the realm of celebrity—but also U.S. culture more broadly—that have made feminism politically relevant again. The obsession with asking celebrities whether they are feminists may be symptomatic of a weakening of the postfeminist sensibilities that Angela McRobbie and others have tracked. We are beginning to see what is "post-postfeminist." As this chapter and the recent work of Rosalind Gill (2016) have shown, interest in the concept of feminism can be exploited by media entities. But the insurgence of movement feminism has also led to the mobilization of millions of people all over the world to protest President Trump in the Women's Marches that occurred the day after his inauguration.

In light of discussions of the revolutionary potential of social media, the ways that celebrity feminism reporting has become a dominant genre of reporting about feminism is worth questioning. The popularity of social networking sites, the social algorithms that push articles to users on these sites, the labor practices of news workers, and the competing forces in contemporary feminism all combine to create the current popularity of celebrity feminism articles. It is necessary to interrogate and strategize around these phenomena. Feminist writers and editors in mainstream, alternative, and feminist publications who seek to activate and engage feminist counterpublics to pursue real change should be wary of the impact of too much focus on celebrity feminism. The standardized practices of celebrity journalism have propagated an unproductive, retrogressive focus on celebrities' feminism at the expense of fostering a productive discussion of feminist politics and a mechanism for feminist change.

Notes

1 In the follow-up interview, Woodley explains her dislike for the label by saying she doesn't like labels (*Nylon* 2015).
2 https://www.youtube.com/watch?v=H40rIbAc2ck
3 https://www.youtube.com/watch?v=x4pPNxUzGvc
4 According to a 2015 study, 41 percent of U.S. adults get news from Facebook, and 10 percent of U.S. adults get news on Twitter. Of U.S. adult users of these platforms, 63 percent of both Facebook and Twitter users use the platforms to get news (Barthel et al. 2015).
5 An impression is the loading of an individual advertisement on a web page.
6 For an explanation of how identity politics may be used to inspire clicks, see Adam Mordecai (2014).
7 A web video promoting #BanBossy produced by the cable network Lifetime includes Beyoncé, Jane Lynch, Jennifer Garner, Condoleeza Rice, and Girl Scouts CEO Anna Maria Chávez.

Works Cited

Alter, Charlotte. 2015. "Shailene Woodley Still Adamant She's Not a Feminist." *TIME*, March 20. Accessed February 2, 2017. http://time.com/3752855/shailene-woodley-insurgent-feminist/.

Banet-Weiser, Sarah. 2012. *Authentic™: The Politics of Ambivalence in Brand Culture*. New York: NYU Press.

Banet-Weiser, Sarah. 2015. "Popular Misogyny: A Zeitgeist." *Culture Digitally*, January 21. Accessed February 2, 2017. http://culturedigitally.org/2015/01/popular-misogyny-a-zeitgeist/.

Barthel, Michael, Elisa Shearer, Jeffrey Gottfried, and Amy Mitchell. 2015. "The Evolving Role of News on Twitter and Facebook." *Pew Research Center*, July 14. Accessed February 2, 2017. http://www.journalism.org/2015/07/14/the-evolving-role-of-news-on-twitter-and-facebook/.

Brady, Anita. 2016. "Taking Time between G-String Changes to Educate Ourselves: Sinead O'Connor, Miley Cyrus, and Celebrity Feminism." *Feminist Media Studies* 16 (3): 429–444.

Cooper, Brittney. 2013. "The Beyoncé Wars: Should She Get to Be a Feminist." *Salon*, December 17. Accessed March 6, 2016. http://www.salon.com/2013/12/17/a_deeply_personal_beyonce_debate_should_she_get_to_be_a_feminist/.

Dockterman, Eliana. 2014. "Shailene Woodley on Why She's Not a Feminist." *TIME*, May 5. Accessed March 6, 2016. http://time.com/87967/shailene-woodley-feminism-fault-in-our-stars/.

Dockterman, Eliana. 2015. "Emma Watson Says She Was Advised Not To Say the Word *Feminism* in U.N. Speech." *TIME*, December 1. Accessed February 2, 2017. http://time.com/4132059/emma-watson-feminism-heforshe-united-nations/.

Dyer, Richard. 1979. *Stars*. London: BFI.

Fraser, Nancy. 1990. "Rethinking the Public Sphere: A Contribution to the Critique of Actually Existing Democracy." *Social Text* (25/26): 56–80.

Frizell, Sam. 2014. "Taylor Swift Finally Explains Why She's a Feminist and How Lena Dunham Helped." *TIME*, August 23. Accessed February 2, 2017. http://time.com/3165825/taylor-swift-feminist-lena-dunham/.

Gill, Rosalind. 2007. "Postfeminist Media Culture: Elements of a Sensibility." *European Journal of Cultural Studies* 10 (2): 147–166.

Gill, Rosalind. 2016. "Post-postfeminism? New Feminist Visibilities in Postfeminist Times." *Feminist Media Studies* 16 (4): 610–630.

Hamad, Hannah and Anthea Taylor. 2015. "Introduction: Feminism and Contemporary Celebrity Culture." *Celebrity Studies* 6 (1): 124–127.

Hare, Breeanna. 2014. "Beyoncé Opens Up on Feminism, Fame, and Marriage." *CNN*, December 12. Accessed February 2, 2017. http://www.cnn.com/2014/12/12/showbiz/music/beyonce-feminism-yours-and-mine-video/.

Hoby, Hermione. 2014. "Taylor Swift: 'Sexy? Not on My Radar.'" *The Guardian*, August 23. Accessed February 2, 2017. http://www.theguardian.com/music/2014/aug/23/taylor-swift-shake-it-off.

hooks, bell. 1984. *Feminism Is for Everybody*. Cambridge, MA: South End Press.

hooks, bell. 2013. "Dig Deep: Beyond Lean In." *The Feminist Wire*, October 28. Accessed February 2, 2017. http://www.thefeministwire.com/2013/10/17973/.

Keller, Jessalyn and Jessica Ringrose. 2015. "'But Then Feminism Goes Out the Window!': Exploring Teenage Girls' Critical Response to Celebrity Feminism." *Celebrity Studies* 6 (1): 132–135.

Kendall, Mikki. 2013. "Beyoncé's New Album Should Silence Her Feminist Critics." *The Guardian* December 13. Accessed February 2, 2017. https://www.theguardian.com/commentisfree/2013/dec/13/beyonce-album-flawless-feminism.

Loza, Susana. 2014. "Hashtag Feminism, #SolidarityIsForWhiteWomen, and the Other #FemFuture." *Ada: A Journal of Gender, New Media & Technology* no. 5. Accessed February 2, 2017. http://adanewmedia.org/2014/07/issue5-loza/.

McRobbie, Angela. 2004. "Post-feminism and Popular Culture." *Feminist Media Studies* 4 (3): 255–264.

Mordecai, Adam. 2014. "What Tools Does Upworthy Employ to Test Its Headlines?" *Quora*, July 14. Accessed February 2, 2017. https://www.quora.com/What-tools-does-Upworthy-employ-to-test-its-headlines.

Nylon. 2015. "Shailene Woodley Is Our April Cover Star: Shailene Forever." *Nylon*, March 18. Accessed February 2, 2017. http://www.nylon.com/articles/shailene-woodley-april-cover.

Sandberg, Sheryl. 2013. *Lean In: Women, Work, and the Will to Lead*. New York: Knopf.

Sasseen, Rhian. 2014. "Feminism's Obsession with Celebrity: It's Time to Stop Making Our Pop Stars into Political Icons." *Salon*, May 14. Accessed February 2, 2017. http://www.salon.com/2014/05/14/feminisms_obsession_with_celebrity_its_time_to_stop_making_our_pop_stars_into_political_icons/.

Stabile, Carol A. and Deepa Kumar. 2005. "Unveiling Imperialism: Media, Gender and the War on Afghanistan." *Media, Culture & Society* 27 (5): 765–782.

Stampler, Laura. 2014. "Katy Perry: Maybe I Am a Feminist After All." *TIME*, March 18. Accessed February 2, 2017, http://time.com/28554/katy-perry-feminist-after-all-confused/.

Steinmetz, Katy. 2014. "Which Word Should Be Banned in 2015?" *TIME*, November 12. Accessed February 2, 2017. http://time.com/3576870/worst-words-poll-2014/.

Tandoc, Jr., Edson C. 2014. "Journalism is Twerking? How Web Analytics is Changing the Process of Gatekeeping." *New Media & Society* 16 (4) (June): 559–575.

Taylor, Anthea. 2014. "'Blockbuster' Celebrity Feminism." *Celebrity Studies* 5 (1–2): 75–78.

Turner, Graeme. 2010. "Approaching Celebrity Studies." *Celebrity Studies* 1, no. 1 (March): 11–20.

Walters, Suzana D. 2014. *The Tolerance Trap: How God, Genes, and Good Intentions Are Sabotaging Gay Equality*. New York: NYU Press.

Wicke, Jennifer. 1994. "Celebrity Material: Materialist Feminism and the Culture of Celebrity." *The South Atlantic Quarterly* 93 (4): 751–778.

3

"I'M COOL WITH IT"

The Popular Feminism of *Inside Amy Schumer*

Taylor Nygaard

Raucous comedian Amy Schumer has become an unlikely face of popular feminism. Indeed, 2015 was a banner year for the young comedian known for playing a self-lacerating version of herself as a ditzy and promiscuous blonde narcissist in both her stand-up routines and her Comedy Central sketch show *Inside Amy Schumer (IAS)*. In winter of 2014, Schumer won a Peabody award for *IAS*'s "smart, thoughtful humor, and an admirably feminist dedication to challenging and disrupting gendered expectations of women's behavior" (Peabody Awards 2014). The award set off a series of other nominations and launched her into the popular culture zeitgeist as a new feminist icon throughout 2015. That year she appeared on several magazine covers, hosted the MTV Movie Awards, and gave many highly publicized speeches about gender issues. Her mainstream exposure came about partly because of the extensive promotional campaign for the July romantic comedy she wrote and starred in, *Trainwreck* (a critical and box office success), in which she subverts some gendered aspects of the typical romantic comedy plot. Nevertheless, it was the visibility and success of her explicitly feminist third season of *IAS* that placed her in the center of conversations around popular feminism. The "spreadability" of her sketches, or the way online social networks shared her content as a new form of sociality (Jenkins, Ford and Green 2013), makes her particularly compelling when thinking about the role female comedians play in emerging feminisms.

The first episode of *IAS*'s third season generated two heavily shared sketches, one a *Friday Night Lights* parody that skewers the relationship between sports and rape culture when a football coach, played by Josh Charles, outrages his town with a "no raping" rule; the other a sketch about Hollywood double standards called "Last Fuckable Day," starring Tina Fey, Julia Louis-Dreyfus, and Patricia Arquette. While many of her sketches are viewed across online platforms, stats on just two possible online viewing platforms draw attention to the breakout success and spreadability of her third season. "Last Fuckable Day," for example, has been viewed 5.7 million times on YouTube and at least 215,000 times on the official Facebook video compared with an average of ~800,000 combined views on both platforms for her sketches from season one, and the 1 million views she gets from its airing on Comedy Central. And, this doesn't even include the number of views it gets from those watching it on numerous websites that embedded the cc.com video on their sites. Significantly, "Last Fuckable Day" seemed perfectly timed with the ACLU's announcement to investigate Hollywood's discriminatory hiring practices and the Sony Hack's revelation of the industry's gendered pay gap, which partially led to its increased views.[1]

These timely and sharable sketches (among others discussed in this chapter) reflect how *IAS* has become more overtly political and explicitly feminist over its run, which is a provocative and somewhat surprising move for a cable network that has historically targeted young men ages 18–34. As a result, this chapter contemplates the double address and layered appeal of Schumer's comic persona: her white, conventionally pretty, vain, and sex-crazed persona appeals to a young white male demographic while also offering a scathing feminist critique of the postfeminist culture that created her.

IAS offers a dynamic example of emerging feminisms at the intersections of comedy, television, and digital media. Schumer uses parody and satire not as a means to deflect or preempt feminist critique, like much humor in postfeminist media culture which typically offers images of female empowerment that fail to threaten patriarchal power hierarchies, but rather to inspire a sustained interrogation of postfeminist discourse as a dominant sensibility and to encourage a critique of lingering gender inequalities and double standards. Schumer's episodes with the most explicit feminist critiques get shared the most and have the most views on digital platforms, amplifying her popular feminism and allowing her critiques to reach a wide, diverse audience, beyond Comedy Central's target market of young men. Considering this context, this chapter explores the visibility of feminist humor on television and theorizes the political potential and limitations inherent in the complex ways comedians and audiences use satirical television to engage emerging feminisms.

The Complicated Politics of Satire TV

In *Satire TV: Politics and Comedy in the Post-Network Era*, Jonathan Gray, Jeffery P. Jones, and Ethan Thompson interrogate the rise of satire on television, its immense popularity with young people, and the increasingly important role it plays in political discourse. Highlighting everything from fake news like *The Daily Show* (1996–) to animated sitcoms like *South Park* (1997–) and sketch comedy like *Chappelle's Show* (2003–2006), they point out how TV satire has become an essential avenue for processing politics and has become its own thriving genre.

Significantly, they show how its rise in the early 2000s corresponded with a certain apathy and cynicism amongst viewers of mainstream news and political discourse: "Satire TV often says what the press is too timid to say, proving itself a more critical interrogator of politicians at times and a more effective mouthpiece of the people's displeasure with those in power, including the press itself" (4). Schumer's comedy builds on this critical legacy, and expands the male-dominated genre by talking about women's issues with blunter honesty than most mainstream media outlets. For example, on "Real Sext," Schumer's standup (that provides interludes to the various sketches on *IAS*) addresses rape with a candid humor: "We've all been a little bit raped," she says frankly. "Just a scooch?" she adds in a higher-pitched voice pinching her fingers together to highlight a small imaginary space on a spectrum between consensual sex and rape (S1E2). Her playful delivery of the slang "scooch," a combination of scoot and tush—as in "scoot your tush"—evokes a teasing innocence that incites a laugh by defamiliarizing rape from its context of a clear, purposeful, violent act.

The joke originally aired on Comedy Central two months after the rape conviction of Trent Mays and Ma'lik Richmond who publicly and repeatedly sexually assaulted an unconscious 16-year-old girl in Steubenville, Ohio—an act brazenly documented and flippantly discussed amongst her peers on social media. The highly publicized event threw into relief a variety of pressing social issues around sports, male privilege, and alcohol abuse, but it especially drew attention to social and cultural misconceptions about rape and consent, and particularly the seeming discursive limitations of the term "rape," which Schumer's joke touches on. In an interview with Terry Gross for NPR's *Fresh Air* (2013), Schumer explains her reasoning behind the joke:

> I—most women I know, that I'm close to, have had a sexual experience that they were really uncomfortable with and that if it wasn't completely rape, it was something very similar to rape. And so I say it's not all black and white. There's a gray area of rape, and I call it grape . . . there's just so many different things that can happen.

With this joke, Schumer articulates the blurriness or "gray area" around sexual assault that's a reality for many people. While the Steubenville event was clearly rape, Schumer's jokes about the word can resonate with the Steubenville teens involved in the rape who didn't understand or define it as such in their subsequent publicizing because of the albeit wrong yet common way that sexual assault, consent, and alcohol consumption are narrowly discussed and understood among teens. While Gross asks whether Schumer thinks her jokes "diminish the importance of talking about rape and of taking it seriously," Schumer says she hopes for the opposite, suggesting the joke can open up discussions of sexual assault in an arguably more approachable way than most of the patronizing, moralizing, and sensationalizing news media coverage of the Steubenville rape. Thus,

Schumer potentially makes serious feminist issues more resonant and more accessible to some younger audiences than the distancing extremity that coalesced in the Steubenville media event.

Schumer said in an interview in February 2012, "I like tackling the stuff nobody else talks about, like the darkest, most serious thing about yourself. I talk about life and sex and personal stories and stuff everybody can relate to, and some can't" (Dawson 2015). This personal focus manifests in sketches and standup bits with a raw, often self-deprecating honesty and sympathetic vulnerability. For example, much of this humorous honesty comes from a self-inflicted critique of the way she doesn't fit with Hollywood's unrealistic beauty norms. We see this self-deprecation when she nicknames herself "Agent butterface" in a parody of CIA action films (S1E3), and when she lands a plum animated movie role but learns she will be voicing a fat meerkat with exposed labia, who defecates onscreen (S2E5). She confronts this explicitly in the opening sketch of season two, asking an all-male focus group whether they liked the first season of IAS. The only comments they make are about whether she is hot enough for TV: "good tits, but not a great face."

Schumer takes this focus group concept even further in the Emmy-nominated, episode-long parody sketch of the classic jury film, "12 Angry Men, Inside Amy Schumer," where a jury of men played by (among others) Jeff Goldblum, Dennis Quaid, Paul Giamatti, Vincent Kartheiser, and Kumail Nanjiani provides a savage, brutally funny rumination on the question, "Is Amy Schumer hot enough to be on television?" Here, like in many of her sketches, the efficacy of the sketch is tied to the spot-on parody of the film's aesthetics—the black and white color palette, the cadence of the actors' performances, and the narrative pacing place the characters' misogynistic comments in the context of the 1950s. Yet, there's a disjunction between the contemporary language in the comments, the stars' recognizability, and their references to current stars like Blake Shelton on the one hand, and the dated aesthetics and performance styles on the other that render their insults towards Schumer similarly outdated. Her main point in the sketch is that very little has changed since the 1950s—that this is still how we judge women and therefore we still clearly need feminism.

New York Times critic Mike Hale (2015) praises the subtle tact with which Schumer performs this ironic self-deprecation: "It's a comfortable kind of self-deprecation, born of insecurity but delivered with a confidence that takes the sting out and gives the listener a snug feeling of complicity . . . no one has the audience so completely on her side." Schumer's ability to inculcate the audience with a sense of complicity in misogyny and gender inequality makes IAS's satirical critique particularly compelling given that Comedy Central's audience is made up of mostly young men. She levels intense feminist critiques at the very demographic that benefits from patriarchal privilege and is often accused of perpetuating gender inequality. Nevertheless, that very demographic is the reason that many critics are skeptical of Schumer's political value and the utility of her show in adding to the visibility and circulation of feminist politics within media culture today.

Falling on Comedy Central's Deaf Ears?

Schumer is in the place to use her Comedy Central platform to speak truth to power. But arguably, much of that potential depends on the audience watching and understanding the jokes and their feminist context. Many critics believe her feminist politics falls on deaf ears or think she is making jokes that perpetuate stereotypes about women rather than dismantle them (Thériault 2015). One can come to this conclusion because Comedy Central is a male-skewing network that explicitly targets young, straight, white men in its channel branding and core advertising arrangements, as well as one that for a long time arguably worked to alienate female audiences. Since Comedy Central's early days in the 1990s, the network has fostered a boy's club reputation. The ethos of *The Man Show* (1999–2014)—which simultaneously celebrated and lampooned the stereotypical loutish male perspective—still serves as the network's brand foundation, and the cable channel's audience remains roughly two-thirds men (Carter 2012).

Building on fellow Comedy Central comedian Sarah Silverman's disruption of gendered comedic norms, *IAS* participates in the network's ethos of foul language, political incorrectness, and gross-out humor in what was once a boys-only zone. For example, in the first-ever sketch of her series Schumer auditions for the illicit Internet video "Two Girls, One Cup,"[2] and talks herself into partaking in the absurd and demeaning scatological performance piece with another female porn star. Immediately following the sketch, she introduces herself via a standup set wearing a tight black dress and tall thigh-high leather boots with the line, "I'm sluttier than your average bear" (S1E1). On the surface she is the postfeminist fantasy of "the girl who can hang," partaking in masculine habits like drinking, swearing, potty humor, and casual sex, while retaining her feminine desirability. Yet, *The Guardian* critic Monica Heisey describes Schumer as a sort of Trojan horse for feminist politics: "Schumer's drunk party slut persona has proven a safe jumping-off point for increasingly politically minded satire on the show, all the while appealing to Comedy Central's largely male viewers with a classic trope: the hot girl with a potty mouth" (2015). Heisey points to how Schumer constructs an appealing but strategic comedic persona that frames *IAS*'s feminist critique and allows Schumer the performative space to make striking criticisms of gender inequalities and double standards.

Schumer is not the first comedian to confront controversy about the relationships between identity politics and target demographics on Comedy Central. The debates surrounding *IAS* in the press and amongst fans echo those from 2005 when Dave Chappelle left behind his incredibly popular Comedy Central series (and a $50 million paycheck). Bambi Haggins (2009) notes that Chappelle walked away from the network "in the wake of the Nigger Pixie," a sketch that made him "question whether his comedic discourse was becoming progressively more open to [mis]interpretation" (234). Beyond the easy comparisons between *IAS*'s and *Chappelle's Show*'s sketch comedy format, both shows confront the "possible dangers inherent in comedy that challenges cultural, social, and political sensibilities" (Haggins 2009, 234). Haggins argues Chappelle had "de facto crossover appeal" in his dual credibility—middle-class stoner and hip hop edginess—that allowed his show to speak for and to different demographics across racial lines. Similarly, Schumer has dual credibility—narcissistic millennial and foulmouthed cynic—that allows her to speak for and to different demographics, ultimately attracting 50–50 male–female demographics (Zinoman 2013). But, as Haggins points out, just as this dual credibility allowed the sketches on *Chappelle's Show* "to tell stories inflicted by multiple identities designed for multiple forms of identification," it also opens *IAS* up to the same discursive vulnerabilities. With broader appeal across different demographics, Schumer opens up the possibility that those in the audience may or may not be discerning the politics of representation embedded in the satire; they may not be able to determine if the series is exploding stereotypes or reinforcing them (Haggins 2009).

IAS is full of moments that are open for misinterpretation, particularly when Schumer pokes fun at structures of affluent white privilege or millennial narcissism, but the butt of the joke lands on individuals instead of the cultural context that shapes her. An illustrative example of this comes from "Herpes Scare," a sketch where Amy gets herpes and prays to God (Paul Giamatti) to get rid of it (S2E1). God asks her why he should help her over all the other people in the world. After she fails to see that her problems are relatively minor compared with the death and destruction wreaked by natural disasters across the world, God says, "I need to stop making so many white girls." Schumer's convincing, "straight" performance in the sketch runs the risk of reinforcing stereotypes of young women as vapid, narcissistic, and too irresponsible to handle their own reproductive health—a pressing social issue at the center of contemporary feminist politics. Yet, this ambiguity in her performance reflects what anthropologists Dominic Boyer and Alexei Yurchak (2010) deemed the American "stiob" prevalent on Comedy Central.

Drawing parallels between late-socialist political discourse in Europe and that of late-liberalism in the U.S., they define stiob as "a parodic genre based on over-identification that usually involves such precise mimicry of the object of one's irony that it is often impossible to tell whether this is a form of sincere support or subtle ridicule, or both" (185). Boyer and Yurchak suggest this performative mode has become prevalent because both late socialism and late liberalism share an increasing "hegemony of form" in the mediation of political culture and a hypernormalization of certain discourses—in this case, for Schumer, the gender norms of postfeminism. For many comics, like Schumer and Stephen Colbert (who is best known for his American stiob of conservativism), there is power in stiob's inherent ambivalence: the tension between the readability of the message and its radical uncanniness may result in a disenchantment of the dominant discourse. For Schumer it's disenchantment with postfeminist gender stereotypes as discussed below. But, it also risks looking so like what it critiques that it simply reinforces stereotypes, especially in Schumer's case because of the complex history surrounding the relationship between women, comedy, and feminism.

Feminists Aren't Funny?

In a Q&A for *Glamour* with her sister and co-writer on *IAS*, Kim Caramele, Schumer asserts, "I don't try to be feminist. I just am. It's innately inside me. I have no interest in trying to be the perfect feminist, but I do believe feminists are in good hands with me" (*Glamour* 2015). Schumer is just one of many explicitly feminist comedians to break out on American television recently; others include Whitney Cummings, Lena Dunham, Mindy Kaling, Chelsea Handler, Samantha Bee, and the creators of *Broad City*, Ilana Glazer and Abbi Jacobson. These women join an earlier generation of feminist comedians like Tina Fey, Amy Poehler, Julia Louis-Dreyfus, Wanda Sykes, Sarah Silverman, Ellen DeGeneres, Margaret Cho, and Kathy Griffin, who since the late 1990s have broken through the "boys' club" of entertainment comedy and laid the foundation for these young female comedians on American television. Although there is a long history of female comedians extending back to Mae West and beyond, these women make up a large part of the new "feminist zeitgeist" (Valenti 2014) on television and the mainstreaming of feminism in general over the past few years. By addressing feminist concerns in their humor around pay inequality, sex discrimination, sexual assault, unrealistic beauty standards, and other women's issues, they are demolishing the relentlessly persistent and libelous claims that women aren't funny and feminists are humorless.

As Linda Mizejewski points out in her contemporary genealogy of female comedians, *Pretty/Funny: Women Comedians and Body Politics* (2014), women's relationship to comedy is fraught with tensions and beset by unfair myths about their "suitability" to comedy or ability to make jokes. In particular, Mizejewski interrogates the comedy default that suggests women are either funny or they are pretty, but they can't be both (Hitchens 2007). Despite this seemingly gross generalization and limiting dichotomy, Mizejewski's book unpacks how the rich nuances of the pretty/funny dynamic actually inform many of the above-mentioned female comedians' humor, especially their critiques of contemporary gender norms. My arguments about Schumer in this chapter echo Mizejewski's subsidiary claim in *Pretty/Funny* that "women's comedy has become a primary site in mainstream pop culture where feminism speaks, talks back, and is contested" (6). Schumer, similar to the women Mizejewski writes about, complicates the pretty/funny dichotomy through her sustained satire of Hollywood's unrealistic beauty standards and her embodied parody of contemporary postfeminist femininity, thus defying the trope of the humorless feminist and offering new discourses of feminism on television.

As many feminist media scholars have noted, within a postfeminist media culture feminism is aged and represented as though it is no longer needed (McRobbie 2008, Negra 2008, Karlyn 2011). They note that from sitcoms to popular films and advertisements, feminists have been caricatured as old, aggressive, anti-sex, man-hating, ugly, and above all *humorless*. Part of this humorless legacy stems from the seriousness of feminist issues (rape, sexual assault, reproductive rights, domestic violence, sexual harassment, inequality, and misogyny) that often appeared antithetical to the lighthearted tone of most comedy entertainment. According to Sara Ahmed (2010), these issues coalesce in the figure of the "feminist killjoy" who disrupts our ability to enjoy the things that are meant to make us happy. As a result, feminists are rarely ever represented in the media as fun or funny, but this is arguably because they are so threatening to hegemonic media practices and representational norms that are built and sustained on the pleasures of patriarchal power structures.

As Angela McRobbie (2008) observes, rather than using humor for satirical critique, the prevailing use of irony in postfeminism was to allow the circulation of sexist images and discourse (particularly the sexual objectification of women's bodies) under the guise that they were not to be taken seriously. Rosalind Gill (2007) illustrates how irony framed overtly sexist imagery as silly, extreme, or just nostalgic (and therefore outdated) to preempt any criticism. Comedy Central's *Man Show* ethos is emblematic of this in the way it blatantly acknowledged the hosts' sexism and objectification of women (like when they bounced on trampolines in bikinis in the background). Humor, as it is predominantly utilized in the postfeminist sensibility, then, anticipated and forestalled "feminist thought critique," suggesting that to criticize postfeminist media culture was to not get the joke, to not be hip, and to be outdated. Yet, many contemporary female comedians like Schumer use irony, satire, and parody differently from these dominant comedic norms of postfeminist irony.

Much of Schumer's comedy on *IAS* draws attention to the disjunction between the way things are and the way they are represented in the joke, and especially the way a woman is represented or pressured to represent herself in contemporary postfeminist culture and the way she actually lives and feels. In a sketch from "Real Sext" (S1E2), for example, Amy sits eating plain pasta with her hands on the couch, wearing an oversized T-shirt with a cat emblazoned across the front—a drastic contrast with the obsessive preoccupation with idealized bodily femininity in most postfeminist media representations (Gill 2007, 149). Mid-bite she receives a flirtatious text from Bobby, a boy she is interested in, and she immediately calls a friend for advice on what to text back. The friend distractedly responds, "Just be yourself." Taking this advice seemingly too literally, as Amy attempts to text back she keeps writing and deleting replies that expose a raw and honest vulnerability meant to contrast with the typical self-assured flirt text-messaging communication encourages. From "I am so lonely all the ti—" and "I would love another shot at giving you a blo—" to "Tell me what all my remotes do," Schumer exposes a disjuncture between how many women actually feel and how they are pressured to present themselves to others. Rosalind Gill (2007) describes the pervasive sexualization of postfeminist culture, and particularly the newfound pressure women feel to present an eroticized version of themselves as sexually autonomous and "forever up for it," which this sketch is deliberately breaking down. The humor comes from Schumer's failure to live up to these self-sexualizing norms of postfeminism, but her endearing vulnerability, reflected in the honesty of her partially typed texts, encourages empathy rather than ridicule for her failure. This humorous empathy urges a critique of these postfeminist pressures and other aspects of postfeminism, which is a sustained project of *IAS* as a series.

Overall, *IAS* uses parody and satire not as a means to deflect or preempt feminist critique, but rather to inspire a sustained interrogation of postfeminist discourse as a dominant sensibility. McRobbie (2008) describes postfeminist media culture as perpetuating and even promoting a new sexual contract that represented a type of double bind where women were allowed certain freedoms—including limited economic independence, sexual independence, and behavioral independence. But, along with these new freedoms came "resurgent patriarchies and gender retrenchment" as well as an encouraged disengagement with any active form of political participation. For McRobbie and others, representations of "empowered girls" in postfeminist media culture actually conceal new modes of gender regulation. Yet, over the past few years there seems to be a new trend in women's media culture that Anne Helen Petersen (2015) has called "the postfeminist dystopia," a context where postfeminist discourse stops functioning as the map towards a fairy tale and instead "takes on the pointed corners of dystopia." Amy Schumer and other female comedians have arguably been crucial in producing a shift in conversation where the promises of postfeminism are not only problematized, but made visibly untenable.

Reviewing *Trainwreck*—Schumer's romantic comedy about a commitment-phobic career woman with unconventional feelings about monogamy and women's behavior—Petersen describes how the film reveals cracks in the postfeminist fantasy of single womanhood: "Sure, Amy screws, drinks, and writes like a man, but none of those things actually empowers her, or vaults her to a position of equality, or even makes her feel awesome, or competent, or in control . . . that 'fun' is still circumscribed by patriarchy" (2015). With her review, Petersen situates *Trainwreck* in series of films and television shows over the past five years, like *Young Adult* (2011), *Bachelorette* (2012), and *Girls* (HBO 2012–2017) that have highlighted the dystopic depths of attempting to adhere to the contradictory expectations of postfeminist empowerment. She argues that in these films, "what used to be the narrative backbone of the perfect rom-com looks increasingly gnarled, unseemly, undesirable." In many ways

Trainwreck is a culmination of several critiques of the postfeminist sensibility that Schumer works through on *IAS*.

Schumer's revelation of the postfeminist dystopia is particularly striking in the titular sketch from "Cool With It," where Amy goes to a strip club with her co-workers (S3E2). When her male co-workers assume she might not want to go, she assures them with phony nonchalance, "I'm cool with it." By constantly repeating this catchphrase, throughout the sketch Amy parodies an exaggerated form of what McRobbie deems the postfeminist masquerade—a performative compromise that women embody to make up for their place in the labor market without disrupting the gender hierarchies of patriarchal work structures. Clad in the stilettoes and tight pencil skirt that McRobbie says reinforce her performance of idealized heterosexual femininity and her desirability to men, Amy's assurance that she is "cool with" (or won't criticize as sexist) going to the strip club, drinking in excess, and paying for lap dances is supposed to assuage any threat to masculine hegemony she might provoke by gaining access to the labor market as a woman. Yet, throughout the sketch, Amy parodies the "phallic girl," a performative trope associated with the postfeminist masquerade that "gives the impression of having won equality with men by becoming like her male counterparts" (83). Like in her other sketches she fails to fully embody this postfeminist fantasy. We see this failure through her disingenuous delivery of the "cool with it" line, her crawling feebly onto the stage to dance with the stripper, her co-workers' increasing discomfort at her efforts, and her exaggerated overcompensation for her "otherness" by paying for everything. In her enthusiastic failure to participate in some of the habits of masculinity at the strip club—drinking, swearing, and enjoying the sexual objectification of other women—Amy mocks the performativity of the phallic girl who enjoys the freedoms of masculine sexual pleasures without critiquing masculine hegemony (83).

As the sketch escalates, Amy's forced complicity in the degradation of other women is rendered even more absurd as she eventually offers to bury a stripper killed by her co-worker. "I'm cool with it," she slurs as she sends her trepidatious co-workers home to finish the secret woodland burial herself: "I'll just be here doing 100% of the work, even though at work I only get paid 78 cents to the dollar," she says under her breath. The sketch then takes an abrupt turn when Schumer breaks character and talks directly into the camera. "Hi, I'm Amy Schumer," she says, "And, I'd like to talk to you about an important issue: the wage gap for women. Write to your congressperson today and tell them you are '*not* cool with it.' Or, just support raising the minimum wage, because two-thirds of minimum wage workers are women."

This somewhat pedantic and explicit political message is tied back to the original sketch when it is interrupted with a moment of slapstick comedy as Amy hits the suddenly awakened stripper on the head with the shovel. Significantly, rather than normalizing and celebrating the phallic girl or the broader postfeminist masquerade as real empowerment, Schumer ridicules and denaturalizes it in this sketch as she leads her audience to political actions that will work to remedy the unequal work culture that can lead women to such absurd places.[3] This sketch, along with others in the series, highlights the wage gap as part of the structuring compromise in postfeminism's new sexual contract that makes all the other inequalities around gender in the workplace possible. It is emblematic of the way Schumer and other comedians are using satire television to critique the dominance of postfeminism and offer new comedic discourses of feminist criticism.

Given Comedy Central's target market, however, like Dave Chappelle before her, Schumer risks audiences interpreting these sketches not as critiques but rather as simple stereotypes of incompetent young women to be laughed at as inferior to men. These sketches, therefore, illuminate tensions between *IAS*'s comedic discourse, its identity politics, and the multiple identity positions of its audience that have always been a part of the complicated politics of satire TV. Nevertheless, television distribution and exhibition have also changed dramatically since 2005 when Chappelle saw his racial satire being marketed for Comedy Central's relatively homogeneous audience of young, middle-class, white men. These changes ask us to think somewhat differently about the role of satire television in 2017, and particularly *IAS*'s emergent feminism potentially falling on deaf ears. As Nick Marx (2015) notes, networks like Comedy Central are beginning to seek more diverse audiences. He observes that by the early 2010s, Comedy Central had diversified its leadership and its programming lineup—for example bringing in network executive Brooke Posch who supervised program development and launched both feminist-leaning *Broad City* and *Inside Amy Schumer*. He observes, "the managerial moves, and the press discourses about them, highlight how above-the-line personnel at Comedy Central are involved in the construction of gendered identity politics seeking to differentiate the network from male-oriented competitors" (8). This new brand ethos would supposedly disrupt some of the tensions around interpretation discussed above.

Yet, Marx's central argument suggests that despite the network's seemingly progressive representational impulses, the promotional discourses of the network still work to reinforce hegemonic gender and racial hierarchies that re-value the network's target demographic as predominately young white men. He discusses how ads for shows like *IAS* focus on catch-phrases and pared-down images that he argues "circumscribe the potential of the programs' cultural critiques" and how the ads tend to rely on "gendered caricatures designed for fleeting consumption by a presumed male audience in a distracted, multi-screen viewing environment" (12). Marx doesn't acknowledge, however, the changing dynamics of how television is consumed and how television spreads beyond the branded spaces of network control, thus enabling *IAS* to avoid some of the pitfalls that Chappelle encountered. As Henry Jenkins, Sam Ford, and Joshua Green note, with rising media consumption on a variety of social media platforms, television content now moves from consumer to consumer, marketer to consumer, and consumer to marketer with the logics of spreadability—dispersing content through both formal and informal networks (2013). While the network may work to frame its content, like *IAS*, in restricted ways—because as Posch notes "Comedy Central's ad buys are for men, so we can't lose them"—many of the show's viewers won't, in fact, watch *IAS* in the context of this network branding, nor will they be part of its desired target market (Zinoman 2013).

The Spreadability of Satirical Feminism(s)

One of the reasons for the widespread development and popularity of satire TV since the early 2000s can be attributed to its "viral qualities and cult appeal," which developed "along with the technological apparatus that now allows such satire to travel far beyond the television set almost simultaneously" (Gray, Jones, and Thompson 2009, 4). In this era of media convergence, segments of satire television programs are actually viewed across digital platforms. Millennials, in particular, have different entertainment consumption practices from previous generations and they are increasingly distancing themselves from traditional television programming and TV sets (Steel and Marsh 2015). This shift is especially significant for basic cable networks like Comedy Central that target the millennial demographic and increasingly seem to be losing audiences to online platforms.

IAS's viewership exemplifies these changing viewing habits. For example, despite the critical buzz surrounding *IAS*'s third season, the series returned to its smallest opening audience to date, averaging 1.006 million on traditional television sets. Yet, when calculating season three's views across social media and digital platforms, the first seven episodes garnered over 37 million views [27,007,746 on YouTube; 4,531,357 on Facebook; 1,222,943 on Hulu; 4,249,479 on Snapchat; 1,400,000 linear] (Weiner 2015). These fragmented numbers are the new reality for Comedy Central in a post-TV era, where the television industry is facing upheaval as it learns to track and monetize these multiplatform viewing habits. These changing viewing habits are also leading to content like *IAS* reaching different demographics beyond those targeted by Comedy Central as well as bringing new audiences to the network's other satirical content. In particular, the diverse ways *IAS*'s sketches circulate online attests to the show's popularity and resonance with a wider, more diverse audience. Most *IAS* sketches range from two to six minutes, which render them easily digestible in online platforms like Facebook when users scroll quickly through their newsfeeds.

IAS's sketch comedy format is also ideal for spreadability because of its layered intertextual appeal. Audiences are given multiple entry points for appreciation and understanding a sketch. For example, "Football Town Nights," which skewers the symbiotic logic between football and rape culture, might attract fans of *Friday Night Lights*, the television show it parodies aesthetically, or viewers interested in high school football, or fans of Josh Charles who developed a large following of older women from his role in *The Good Wife*, or fans of Connie Britton who Schumer parodies and who played a fan-favorite role on *FNL*. After Schumer's Peabody award and subsequent publicity, entertainment news outlets, feminist blogs, and online comedy channels were sharing her sketches across media platforms, demographics, and the typical silos of feminist discourse, reflecting a certain detachment from its Comedy Central brand and broader reach than most television comedy.

While her sketches still hold the potential for misinterpretation, particularly as they are stripped from their context and can reach any number of unwitting audiences, their spreadability nevertheless encourages a newfound visibility for her mode of humorous feminist politics. Her parodies of postfeminism can be seen as a way to reconnect a variety of viewers to feminist thought and politics through entertaining, accessible, and sometimes all-too-familiar representations that are rendered with uncanny or dystopic edges. And, spreadable media has arguably made her show appear even more feminist-centric, since the sketches that tend to get picked up are those that are more directly and intelligently feminist; those that are less overt tend to be forgotten.

The tensions and contradictions of her sketches provide especially productive fodder for debate and discussion across media convergences; they have the potential to spark debate that disrupts easy questions or assumptions about contemporary womanhood and what feminism should or should not look like, which is incredibly important in this age of popular feminism. In her interrogation of what the rise of popular feminism means for feminist politics, Sarah Banet-Weiser (2015) laments the discursive dominance of the "Are you a Feminist?" question. She suggests that it is increasingly easy for women, particularly celebrities, to say "yes" to this question, but points out that their quick and resolute answers preclude a more sustained understanding of what that actually means as well as any other sustained engagement with feminist politics (see Renninger, this volume). Schumer's show, with her parody of postfeminist femininity, her complicated performances of stiob and their tensions between the familiar and the uncanny, as well as the way her comedy spreads across media platforms offer a productive example of how satire TV can provide a sustained engagement with emerging feminist discourses that weave in and out of mainstream media.

Yet, it's important to reiterate that Schumer's satirical mode of feminist discourse is not "perfect" and highlights the need to interrogate who is able to participate in these increasingly visible emergent feminisms and who remains marginalized. For example, many continue to see Schumer's elevated platform as a straight, white, cis-gender, able-bodied, conventionally pretty woman as evidence of the limited version of feminism that attains mainstream mediated visibility. Schumer has been rightly called out for her "shockingly large blind spot around race" (Heisey 2015) and for perpetuating racism in several jokes where she described Latina women as "crazy," Mexican men as rapists, and participated publicly in a presumptive and prejudiced conversation about athlete

Odell Beckham Jr. with Lena Dunham. This criticism of her lack of attention to intersectional feminism came to a head in the fall of 2016, when she released a parody lip-synch version of Beyoncé's powerful and highly political music video for "Formation." Although Schumer has tried to defend the video as a "tribute," most read it as insensitive and thought it was making fun of Beyoncé's celebration of African American womanhood—to the point where the hashtag #amyschumergottagoparty trended on Twitter, reflecting a majority of viewers' frustration with Schumer's persistent failure to acknowledge her privilege, her complicity in perpetuating racism, and her continued centrality to discussions of popular feminism despite these major failings.

While these criticisms of Schumer are vital to the productive development of feminist politics and the way feminists engage with mainstream media as a form of activism, her show and the responses it elicits from diverse audiences exemplifies the "affective labor of ambivalence" Banet-Weiser claims is increasingly needed in this age of popular feminism. Many viewers, scholars, and media critics are ambivalent about what the mainstreaming of feminism in the media means for on-the-ground intersectional feminist politics and making changes to structural and institutional inequalities. Nonetheless, I believe Schumer's show, its humor, and audience's varied reactions gets into the messy, sometimes contradictory trenches of feminist political discourse in a postfeminist age so that, hopefully, we can come out on the other side.

Notes

1 In November 2014, a hacker group leaked confidential data from the film studio Sony Pictures, allegedly as a demand that Sony pull *The Interview*, for its critical depiction of North Korean leader Kim Jong-un. The data included controversial revelations including that high-profile actresses, like Jennifer Lawrence, were compensated much less than their male co-stars, giving proof of Hollywood's sexism and pay gap.

2 "Two Girls, One Cup" is the nickname for the trailer of *Hungry Bitches*, a 2007 Brazilian scat-fetish pornographic film featuring two women conducting themselves in fetishistic intimate relations, including defecating into a cup, taking turns consuming the excrement, and vomiting into each other's mouths. The trailer became one of the best-known shock videos to circulate in the mainstream.

3 As Schumer breaks character in direct address, notcoolwithit.com pops up in text on the bottom of the screen. Typing the URL into a web browser directs you to the Pay Equity and Discrimination page for the Institute for Women's Policy Research Website: http://www.iwpr.org/initiatives/pay-equity-and-discrimination.

Works Cited

Ahmed, Sara. 2010. "Feminist Killjoys." *The Promise of Happiness*. Durham, NC: Duke University Press.

Banet-Weiser, Sarah. 2015. "Whom Are We Empowering? Popular Feminism and the Work of Empowerment." Paper presented at Console-ing Passions International

Conference on Television, Video, Audio, New Media and Feminism. Dublin, Ireland. June 18–20, 2015.

Boyer, Dominic, and Alexei Yurchak. 2010. "American Stiob: Or, What Late-Socialist Aesthetics of Parody Reveal about Contemporary Political Culture in the West." *Cultural Anthropology* 25 (2): 179–221.

Carter, Bill. 2012. "In the Tastes of Young Men, Humor Is Most Prized, a Survey Finds." *New York Times*. February 19.

Dawson, Mackenzie. 2015. "Why Every Woman (and Man) needs to be Watching Amy Schumer." *NY Post*. April 16.

Gill, Rosalind. 2007. "Postfeminist Media Culture: Elements of a Sensibility." *European Journal of Cultural Studies* 10: 147–166.

Glamour. 2015. "Amy Schumer's Life Goals: 'I Want to Make Women Laugh. I Want Them to Use Their Voice. And I Want a Jet.'" *Glamour*. July 7.

Gray, Jonathan, Jeffery P. Jones, and Ethan Thompson. 2009. "The State of Satire, the Satire of State." Introduction to *Satire TV: Politics and Comedy and the Post-Network Era* 3–36. New York: NYU Press.

Gross, Terri. 2013. "*Inside Amy Schumer*: It's Not Just Sex Stuff." *Fresh Air*. Philadelphia: NPR. Accessed May 1, 2015. https://www.npr.org/2013/06/25/188698578/inside-amy-schumer-its-not-just-sex-stuff

Haggins, Bambi. 2009. "In the Wake of 'The Nigger Pixie': Dave Chappelle and the Politics of Crossover Comedy." In *Satire TV: Politics and Comedy and the Post-Network Era* 233–251. New York: NYU Press.

Hale, Mike. 2015. "In 'Amy Schumer: Live at the Apollo,' Tart Words on Men, Women, Sex and Herself." *New York Times*. October 15.

Heisey, Monica. 2015. "Amy Schumer: Comedy's Viral Queen." *Guardian*. June 28.

Hitchens, Christopher. 2007. "Why Women Aren't Funny." *Vanity Fair*. January.

Jenkins, Henry, Sam Ford, and Joshua Green. 2013. *Spreadable Media: Creating Value and Meaning in a Networked Culture*. New York: NYU Press.

Karlyn, Kathleen Rowe. 2011. *Unruly Girls, Unrepentant Mothers: Redefining Feminism on Screen*. Austin: University of Texas Press.

Marx, Nick. 2015. "Expanding the Brand: Race, Gender, and the Post-politics of Representation on Comedy Central." *Television & New Media* 17 (3): 1–16.

McRobbie, Angela. 2008. *The Aftermath of Feminism: Gender, Culture and Social Change*. Los Angeles: Sage.

Mizejewski, Linda. 2014. *Pretty/Funny: Women Comedians and Body Politics*. Austin: University of Texas Press.

Negra, Diane. 2008. *What a Girl Wants?: Fantasizing the Reclamation of Self in Postfeminism*. New York: Routledge.

Peabody Awards. 2014. "Inside Amy Schumer (Comedy Central)." Peabodyawards. com. Accessed May 1, 2015. http://www.peabodyawards.com/award-profile/inside-amy-schumer

Petersen, Anne Helen. 2015. "In *Trainwreck*, Amy Schumer Calls Bullshit On Postfeminism." *Buzzfeed*. July 18. Accessed August 1, 2015. http://www.buzzfeed.com/annehelenpetersen/postfeminist-bullshit#.xmxl3XdNM8

Steel, Emily, and Bill Marsh. 2015. "Millennials and Cutting the Cord." *New York Times*. October 3.

Thériault, Anne. 2015. "Amy Schumer isn't as Feminist as the Internet Thinks." *Daily Dot*. June 10. Accessed June 12, 2015. http://www.dailydot.com/opinion/amy-schumer-feminist-comedy-women/

Valenti, Jessica. 2014. "When Everyone is a Feminist, Is Anyone?" *Guardian*. November 24.
Weiner, Jonah. 2015. "Comedy Central in the Post-TV Era: The Network is in the Middle of a Creative Renaissance—and a Business-model Crisis." *New York Times Magazine*. June 18.
Zinoman, Jason. 2013. "Funny Girl." *New York Times*. April 21.

4

PLAYING IN THE CLOSET

Female Rock Musicians, Fashion, and Citational Feminism

Alyxandra Vesey

While unwinding from her band's 2007 European tour, Gossip frontwoman Beth Ditto talked with *BUST* about whether the fashion industry's embrace of the "fat, lesbian, and blatantly feminist" singer as a style icon signaled an expansion of fashion's narrow parameters (Rems 2008, 52). At the time, Chanel's creative director Karl Lagerfeld invited the singer to perform at various label events. Ditto also became a London nightlife fixture by stepping out with model Kate Moss (Hattersley 2009), an activity that seemed at odds with Ditto's humbler beginnings.

As a queer woman of size who grew up poor in rural Arkansas, Ditto got involved with music through riot grrrl, a feminist rock movement that originated in the Pacific Northwest and developed without commercial support during the early 1990s. Many journalists fixated on participants' appearance by evacuating their girlish play with barrettes and Mary Jane shoes of its critique against female infantilization and sexual violence, prompting a media blackout from the movement's participants (Marcus 2010). But riot grrrl also helped Ditto express subcultural and intergenerational belonging through clothing independent of financial status. As she said in her *Guardian* advice column, "fashion is something that is prepackaged, bought, and sold, but style, like art, is a primal instinct. My number-one theory in life is that style is proportional to your lack of resources—the less you have, the more stylish you're likely to be" (Ditto 2007, 17).

Ditto's distinction between fashion and style clarified her hesitation in returning the fashion industry's embrace, as she claimed that its representatives "make you feel as uncomfortable as possible so you'll appreciate what they have. But fashion is a world that I'm starting to dabble in now, and it's like dancing with the devil a little bit" (Rems 2008, 52). Over the next few years, Ditto "dabbled" as a runway model and minor celebrity (Phelps 2010; Trebay 2009, A21). She also partnered with British retailer Topshop to create two capsule collections for its plus-size Evans line, which debuted in February 2009 (Pool 2009, 2).

Drawing upon industry discourse, this chapter investigates female rock musicians' work as capsule collection designers. Capsule collections are self-contained, often mass-produced seasonal wardrobes of affordable basics that can be easily integrated into consumers' closets and worn with more upscale pieces. In recent years, retail chains have increasingly pursued celebrity tie-ins to compete with online retail (Sherman 2016). Capsule collections have been an opportunity for big-name designers to partner with discount retailers, as Prabal Gurung and Lilly Pulitzer did with Target (Lutz 2013; Schneier 2015). Capsule collections have also attracted celebrities like Rihanna and Gwyneth Paltrow to team with luxury brands like Armani and Valentino (Phelan 2011; Reed 2015). Many of these collaborations promise to grant access to a celebrity or label's aura for young women who cannot afford to cycle through seasons of high-end couture for their school, leisure, and work wardrobes. Due to their emphases on celebrities' particular glamour and consumerism's promise of personal transformation, these collections often adhere to Rosalind Gill's claim that postfeminism is a sensibility that prioritizes women's individual achievement, empowerment, and productivity removed from sociohistoric contexts around collective action on broader social and political issues, both past and present (2007).

However, this chapter claims that rock subcultures' sartorial impact have influenced female rock musicians' involvement in capsule collection design and extended women's intergenerational participation in music through fashion. While individuality informs the production and marketing of these collections, certain female rock musicians' work in capsule collection design cannot be neatly codified as postfeminist because of how they use fashion to interface with their fans and favorite female artists across generations. By drawing inspiration from women associated with French pop, classic rock, and new wave, this chapter shows how Sonic Youth bassist Kim Gordon, Best Coast frontwoman Bethany Cosentino, and Beth Ditto used their capsule collections for Urban Outfitters and Topshop to enact "citational feminism," a term I use to describe the act of explicitly referencing feminine and female emblems of popular culture as an intergenerational expression of women's solidarity through creative inspiration. These musicians, who all self-identify as feminists, champion feminized popular culture's transformative potential in a manner similar to recording artists' synthesis of their favorite records to create new sounds.

Yet knowledge about fashion is often discredited by male rock professionals— even though rock has always been preoccupied with self-presentation—in order to deny women recognition as musicians. These capsule collections intervene by insisting that female musicians' style is integral to their influence and by extending their legacies to shoppers. Such creative practices function as a form of emergent feminism in two respects. First, it demonstrates important historical continuities between female musicians, the women who influenced their sound and self-presentation, and the fans who may express their support of these artists by wearing their designs. Second, it operates within a contemporary context of celebrity branding and the ways in which such work is often distanced from global retail's decentralized labor practices and immaterial consumption patterns, and therefore espousing a kind of feminism that is often compliant with, if not ambivalent about, neoliberal capitalism.

Thus, borrowing from Stuart Hall, such citations are conjunctural (1979). These collections are historically specific as recent commercial utterances that reference the music and fashion of French mod culture in the mid- to late 1960s, California soft rock in the early to mid-1970s, and New York's downtown club scene at the turn of the 1980s. Yet at the same time these collections represent feminism's ongoing difficulties responding to the needs of multiple groups—particularly on the basis of race and size—through the designers' uneven attention to the needs of different consumer groups and fashion's environmental and labor costs. Thus, in a manner similar to punk's incorporation, these collections illustrate how female recording artists espouse a negotiated feminism by paying tribute to their musical foremothers and calling upon their fans to join the celebration while reckoning with the limits of citation by complying with the structures of capitalism in order to commemorate their heroines' style.

Gathering Materials

Sara Ahmed (2013) defines "citation" as "a way of reproducing the world around certain bodies." She builds upon Judith Butler's claim that "performativity must be understood not as a singular or deliberate 'act,' but, rather, as the reiterative and citational practice by which discourse produces the effects that it names" (1993, 2). The women in this case study accomplished this by using their favorite musical artists to create products to be worn instead of heard, an important yet under-observed aspect of how rock uses influence to elicit commerce. The labor around the design and manufacture of these garments requires consideration for how capsule collections reproduce the world around certain bodies by attempting to address various consumer demands and through partnerships between rock musicians and multinational corporations. As a result, citational feminism traverses geographical borders. For one, e-commerce facilitates their distribution. Such consumption patterns reflect the pervasiveness of online shopping, as well as Urban Outfitters' and Topshop's status as transnational entities with stores in North America and Western Europe and a burgeoning presence in Central America and parts of Asia. Both companies also outsource the manufacture of their goods to workers in South and Southeast Asia and Latin America, which often distances executives and celebrity designers from the realities of how these garments are produced. Thus, capsule collection design exists within and adheres to the biopolitical regimes that organize mass production, making citational feminism an expression of what Radha S. Hegde refers to as "the gendered subject of globalization," a transient figure who "has to be situated within shifting formations of power" and in relation to "the flow of capital, with its complex global infrastructure of commodities, resources, and bodies" (2011, 1).

Thus, this chapter draws upon scholarship on gender's ideological circulation to understand female rock musicians' subcultural practices and entrepreneurship. In particular, this chapter posits that as designers, Kim Gordon, Bethany Cosentino, and Beth Ditto negotiate with what Angela McRobbie refers to as the postfeminist masquerade in their mobilization of female musicians as creative inspiration for their own ventures into fashion design. Embodied by the figure of the fashionista, a style-conscious woman represented by popular female characters like *Sex and the City* protagonist Carrie Bradshaw and hipster icons like filmmaker Sofia Coppola and singer-actress Zooey Deschanel (Lewis 2011; Tortorici 2010), McRobbie defines the postfeminist masquerade as "a knowing strategy which emphasizes its non-coercive status" and as "a highly-styled disguise of womanliness which is now adopted as a matter of choice" (2008, 67). According to McRobbie, the masquerade relies upon the illusion of volunteerism to "conceal that patriarchy is still in place, while the requirements of the fashion and beauty system ensure that women are in fact still fearful subjects" that must obey the dictates of conventional femininity (2008, 69). It also helps reinstate "whiteness as a cultural dominant within the field of the fashion-beauty complex" through the fashion industry's reductive and exclusionary celebration of iconography associated with feminine glamour and decontextualized images of retro nostalgia that deny or erase historically grounded images of women of color (McRobbie 2008, 69). Finally, the masquerade positions its subjects as luminosities. Drawing upon this Deleuzian concept of visibility, McRobbie uses luminosities to describe how the postfeminist masquerade creates "clouds of light which give young women a shimmering presence" in public life in order to "mark out the terrain of the consummately and re-assuringly feminine" (2008, 60). To McRobbie, luminosities represent ephemeral forms of female power. Young women can only capture the light for the brief duration of their youth and can only bend it as individuals, thus disallowing for more sustainable and transformative collective action between coalitions of women, across generational bonds, and within particular historic contexts.

In some ways, these capsule collections similarly function as a shimmering presence in the marketplace that reinforce conventional femininity through fashion's compressed temporality. Yet Kim Gordon and Bethany Cosentino's Urban Outfitters collections and Beth Ditto's Topshop line are unsatisfied with limiting the cultural legibility of women's agency to a few tiny flickers in darkness, and thus use fashion design as a tactic to initiate a cross-generational exchange between their rock heroines and their fans. They also use these collections to strengthen their personal affiliations with other women. Gordon and Cosentino reflect on the familial bonds between mothers and daughters in their designs.

However, Gordon and Cosentino's emphasis on biological heritage suggests an implicit heteronormativity that Ditto cannot fulfill as easily as a queer woman. Thus, Ditto approaches design as a way to connect with other fat women whose needs are often ignored by the fashion industry, and to interrogate how clothing manufacture impacts the global workforce, a critique that Gordon and Cosentino do not make.

These musicians use attribution as a form of feminist cultural production because, so often, women and girls' contributions to rock history are often ignored, discredited, or erased. Angela McRobbie's and Jenny Garber's taxonomy of female archetypes like the mod and the hippie doubles as a corrective against the masculinist assumptions embedded in previous research on the signification practices and incorporative strategies that organized teddy boy and punk style (2000). Riot grrrl also negotiated incorporation. For example, Gayle Wald claims that Gwen Stefani and Courtney Love benefitted from the mainstreaming of riot grrrl by positioning girlishness "as a mode of culturally voiced resistance to patriarchal femininity, as a token of a sort of 'gestural feminism' that is complicit with the trivialization, marginalization, and eroticization of women within rock music cultures; and as an expression of postmodern 'gender trouble' that potentially recuperates girlhood in universalizing, ethnocentric terms" (2002, 193).

Yet feminine influence may also invite the possibility of ventures like capsule collection design to do more than gesture to feminism by explicitly placing generations of female rock musicians in a dialogue with each other through designers' explicit references to their predecessors as artistic influences on their work. Scholars have identified the importance of practicing feminism through citation in other contexts. Mary Celeste Kearney argues that riot grrrl not only appropriated punk's gleeful amateurism, but fused it with British post-punk's theoretical approach to modern gender relations and women's music's confessional and proudly queer songwriting (1997). She thus places riot grrrl on a continuum with women's musical contributions across generations and scenes while avoiding reductive comparisons between female artists.

Furthermore, women and girls may also risk feminism's dilution to assure their place in music history. Catherine Strong observes that female grunge musicians were often confused with riot grrrl participants or vilified, demonstrating the implicit sexism that often enables women's erasure from subcultural memory (2011). Strong builds upon Helen Davies' work on women's limited visibility in British music journalism (Davies 2001). Davies argues that credibility is the yardstick against which women are measured because their claims to authenticity are "automatically denied" if they are perceived "as being in any way manipulated or not in control of their own material," due to the discrediting of their intelligence and the hostility with which their subcultural participation is frequently met (Davies 2001, 306). This definition of credibility could dismiss female musicians' forays into capsule collection design. But such work allows them to elaborate upon their musical influences for creative purposes as feminist entrepreneurs, which warrants further consideration.

Contemporary recording artists also increasingly position themselves as entrepreneurs, as Eric Harvey (2011), Tim Anderson (2013), and Jeremy Morris (2014) observe. Such industrial pressure informs the rise of "360 deals," a recording industry strategy that Matt Stahl and Leslie M. Meier argue encircles "the contracted artist so that non-record-related activities and revenues formerly beyond the reach of the recording contract become subject to 'participation' by the contracting company" (2012). Pop stars tend to be associated with these arrangements, as Kearney (2010) and Morgan Genevieve Blue (2013) imply in their analyses of Miley Cyrus' endorsement work with Daisy Rock Guitars and D-Signed, Disney's tween fashion line, respectively.

However, David Hesmondhalgh's investigation of British independent bands' international distribution deals with American-based major labels clarifies that indie rock always relied upon entrepreneurial hustle (1999). Kim Gordon's and Beth Ditto's bands benefitted from similar support. Geffen Records subsidary DGC represented Sonic Youth from 1991 to 2007 (Browne 2008). In the mid-2000s, Columbia subsidiary Music With a Twist acquired Gossip from Kill Rock Stars, an Olympia-based independent label that nurtured riot grrrl associates like Bikini Kill (Sheppard 2007). Morris applies Michael Scott's definition of "cultural entrepreneurship" as "the process of trying to convert a lack of financial resources into economic success through cultural capital and artistic influence" to electronic artist Imogen Heap (Morris 2014, 276). This term pertains to artists' musical and non-musical ventures. For example, Dirk Gindt observes that Icelandic singer Björk worked with designer Alexander McQueen and photographer Nick Knight on the cover art and music videos for 1997's *Homogenic* to supplement her album's mediations on nationality (2011). Gindt extends Noel McLaughlin's notion of "the performative power of clothes" in music, wherein "the *meaning* of dress will be inflected, altered, amplified, or contradicted by the musical and performing conventions and associations within which they are placed" (2000, 271). Such power is embedded in musicians' style and informs its translation into fashion. This process is further complicated by Gordon's, Ditto's, and Cosentino's use of capsule collections to honor female musicians' influence on women's and girls' intergenerational self-fashioning.

Getting Dressed

In her memoir, Kim Gordon recalls a photo shoot for Sonic Youth's *Daydream Nation*:

> "Do you want to look cool, or do you want to look attractive?" [photographer] Michael [Lavine] asked me, as if the two were mutually exclusive. The silver paint; glitter-dabbed, faded cutout jeans; and crop

top with the sheer jeweled panel marked a turning point for me and my look. . . . I didn't want to just look cool, or just look rock and roll: I wanted to look more *girl*.

(2015, 161)

This quote contextualizes Gordon's status as a riot grrrl interlocutor. Gordon influenced the movement with her deadpan vocalizations and her thematic interests in desire, sexual violence, body dysmorphia, mother–daughter dysfunction, and women's commodification as a songwriter. However, Gordon's commitment to "look more girl" also informed riot grrrl's visualization of feminine leisure, subcultural practice, and labor in musicians' self-presentation.

Such preoccupations inform the music video for Sonic Youth's 1994 single "Bull in the Heather," which depicts a pregnant Gordon writhing in a children's bed and playing with her band in a baby-doll dress and a hot-pink miniskirt as Bikini Kill's Kathleen Hanna dances around them. Gordon's clothes gesture to riot grrrls' appropriation of kidswear to confront the recording industry's infantilization of female talent and observe how women straddle motherhood's cultural and biological imperatives at work. Hanna supports this critique by dancing alongside Gordon in a ringer t-shirt, star-print underpants, tights, dirty topsiders, and pigtails—a collision of punk and childhood signifiers that was emblematic of riot grrrl style.

"Bull in the Heather" also doubles as an advertisement for Gordon's X-Girl clothing line, since both women wear its merchandise in the video. Gordon started X-Girl in 1993 with former X-Large clerk Daisy Von Furth, the daughter of a prominent D.C.-area real estate developer and the younger sister of guitarist Julia Cafritz. X-Large specialized in men's skate wear. With co-owner Eric Bonerz' encouragement, Gordon and Von Furth used their network and encyclopedic knowledge of thrift-store fashion to launch X-Girl as X-Large's sister brand with a store front on Lafayette Street in New York City (Thompson and Swerdloff 2012). They enlisted graphic designer Mike Mills to create the logo and guitar strap designer Wendy Mullin as their pattern maker.

X-Girl's house style—a riff on the prep school uniforms Gordon hated wearing during adolescence and revised with mod's graphic impact and punk's lean androgyny—enjoyed commercial interest upon arrival (Gordon 2015). It received placement in teen fashion magazines and MTV's *House of Style* filmed a segment on its first show, days before Gordon gave birth to her daughter, Coco (Seymour 1994). However, X-Girl was a short-lived venture. By 1998, Gordon and Von Furth sold it to Japanese company B's International, and Gordon used her stake to put toward a down payment on her Northampton home once her daughter was old enough for kindergarten (Gordon 2015, 224). Nonetheless, Gordon claimed that X-Girl gave her "far more notoriety than Sonic Youth ever did" (2015, 199). Such notoriety allowed her to model in print campaigns for Marc Jacobs and Calvin Klein during the late 1990s and introduce her band to new audiences through appearances on ironic teen dramedies like *Gilmore Girls* and *Gossip Girl* and Indiewood features like *Last Days* and *I'm Not There*. The accumulation of these experiences eventually resulted in Mirror/Dash, her 2009 Urban Outfitters collection.

Inspired by French yé-yé singer Françoise Hardy, who favored the sleek designs associated with the transition from mod and hippie fashion during her mid-1960s heyday, Gordon used the collection to fill "a need for clothes for cool moms" that the youth-oriented company often overlooked (Chang 2013; "50 Ways to Rock the P.T.A." 2008). But she considered herself "a stylist wannabe" instead of a designer, and collaborated with Jeffrey Montiero and Melinda Wansbrough on its look and marketing (Lau and Friday 2010; Chang 2013). And despite Gordon's admiration for Hardy's personal style, she assumed Urban Outfitters shoppers would not "buy a pantsuit, no matter how cool it looks" and offered a demure set of blazers and dresses in black, off-white, and grey for cool moms and their college-aged daughters (Lau and Friday 2010). It was tasteful and affordable, but lacked X-Girl's assertiveness. However, another female rock musician soon followed Gordon's lead with her own Urban Outfitters capsule collection.

Bethany Cosentino was approached to design for the company's Urban Renewal line in late 2011. Her band Best Coast already established a relationship with the chain when their record label licenced exclusive streaming rights for their debut album, *Crazy for You*, to the company's website (Dombal 2010). To extend the commercial life of their follow-up *The Only Place*, Cosentino partnered with Urban Outfitters on a summer capsule collection (Mathieson 2012). As a long-time Sonic Youth fan who shopped at X-Girl's Los Angeles boutique during her teen years, Cosentino was also inspired by Gordon's success with the retailer (Pelly 2012). But despite her previous experience as a fashion intern at *Fader*, Cosentino had little prior design experience and worked extensively with the design and branding teams via email to establish the collection's aesthetic and necessary materials ("Best Coast on her Fashion Line" 2012).

Cosentino received criticism for partnering with the company, which received considerable derision for its sweatshop labor conditions and pervasive cultural appropriation, after it was revealed that CEO Richard Hayne donated to conservative Republican Senator Rick Santorum (Miles 2012; Haruch 2014; Weiner 2012). Cosentino rationalized that "[i]f my landlord supported an anti-gay company, I wouldn't stop living at my house. . . . Not to mention, when you get asked to do a clothing line, you say yes" (Weiner 2012, 55). Instead, Cosentino saw the collection as an opportunity to honor the "girls that come to Best Coast shows" and the "different references in pop culture, like *Clueless*, *The Craft*, Stevie Nicks, all these things that shaped my personal style," thus connecting her own adolescent longing to her young fans' 1990s-era nostalgia, upon which Urban Outfitters hoped to profit ("Best Coast on her Fashion Line" 2012). As she told *SPIN*, the collection was "an extension of Best Coast" and that "[t]he first time I see someone wearing Bethany Cosentino for Urban Outfitters at one of my shows [i]t'll be like when I heard Best Coast on the radio for the first time" (Reilly 2012, 48).

Bridging her California roots with her interest in vintage fashion, Cosentino described the collection as "Stevie Nicks and Cher from *Clueless* had a baby and they took her to a séance" (Mau 2012). Its citational politics were embedded in its marketing, and thus better allowed Cosentino to challenge postfeminism's ahistoricism by making the collection's feminist cultural influences legible and demonstrating young women's and girls' ability to identify with previous generations of feminist figures. In contrast to Gordon's comparatively obscure approach to inspiration for Mirror/Dash, almost every item in Cosentino's collection was named for a female celebrity or character she idolized, including a lace mini-dress inspired by an outfit worn by *Clueless* protagonist Cher Horowitz in Amy Heckerling's 1995 hit film ("Best Coast on her Fashion Line" 2012). Cher (Alicia Silverstone) is also named for the chameleonic pop diva, thus tying her to the memory of her mother's youth and her best friend, Dionne (Stacey Dash), who is also named for a famous singer who does infomercials.

This intertextual relationship between pop stardom and endorsement is relevant to Cosentino's design work. Not only was *Clueless* a touchstone, but its female-driven alternative soundtrack influenced Best Coast's anthemic sound (Shirway 2015). She used the collection to pay tribute to her favorite recording artists, naming a high-waisted plum-colored jumper after singer-songwriter Jenny Lewis and a black cape for Stevie Nicks (Pelly 2012). Cosentino also traced this influence back to her mother's identification with Laurel Canyon's 1970s soft-rock scene as a young designer who wore "long, witchy dresses and boots and lots of jewelry" (Pelly 2012). This intergenerational exchange was best illustrated in the collection's "Joni jacket," a cropped letterman jacket inspired by merchandise Cosentino's mother acquired from singer Joni Mitchell's 1976 U.S. tour. It also allowed Cosentino and the design team to render hegemonically masculine garments in more feminine silhouettes, thus recontextualizing signifiers of youth culture from normative masculinity in a manner evocative of riot grrrl's sartorial play. Finally, Cosentino was inspired by her own experiences as a performer. She included a pair of ruffle shorts because "I don't really wear a lot of pants. . . . And I named them the 'tour' shorts, because I'll be wearing them every day [on the road]" (Pelly 2012). In doing so, Cosentino also broke with the collection's branding strategy by naming a garment after an integral professional activity that requires mobility and comfort instead of after a female icon.

Such professional concerns inform Gossip vocalist Beth Ditto's partnership with Evans in the late 2000s as an extension of her music fandom and associations with the riot grrrl movement. However, Gordon and Cosentino ultimately reinforced normative conventions of female beauty with Urban Outfitters by designing clothes that flattered slender bodies and were not rescaled to accommodate plus-sized customers. Much like riot grrrl reorganized cultural space by bringing girls to the front at shows, Ditto used her 2009 and 2010 Topshop capsule collections to rearrange the fashion industry's priorities by centralizing underserved consumers eager to wear youthful clothes made for their bodies. The singer identified with their needs, stating that what excited her most about working with Topshop was to "make something special, just for us, something never seen before" in mass-produced apparel (Manning 2009).

Ditto also sought to reimagine pop music history by inserting unruly bodies into a cultural memory that used absence as a regulatory tool. Her sequined, jewel-toned collections paid homage to Deborah Harry and Grace Jones, women whose associations with New York City punk and disco in the late 1970s and early 1980s made them famous—but they were not fat women. Jones modeled prior to signing with Island Records, while the petite Harry was a Playboy Club waitress before starting Blondie (Kershaw 1997; Simon 2010). But Ditto's collections expanded their decadent glamour's potential by adapting Harry's and Jones' love for short hemlines, broad shoulders, bold patterns, and glittery embellishments for large bodies. They also offered a rare example of how citational feminism honored difference through capsule collection design. While Gordon's and Cosentino's muted palettes favored the pale coloring of their white muses, Ditto's penchant for deep teals, blues, and purples nodded to 1980s excess and the spectrum as a symbol of queer liberation. Such a vivid palette also recognized that Jones gravitated toward those colors because they accentuated her features as a dark-skinned woman.

But Ditto's Topshop partnership also revealed her ambivalence in commodifying women's style, particularly when it compromised her political convictions. In 2004, she declared boldly in *Rockrgrl* that "[t]o be a fat person wearing tight clothes is activism in itself" (Case 2004, 35). She spoke from experience as a survivor of disordered eating and child molestation in her early life who suffered a nervous breakdown in late teen adolescence before coming out as a lesbian and relocating to the riot grrrl hub of Olympia, Washington with Gossip drummer Kathy Mendonça (Rems 2008; Anderson-Minshall 2012). Ditto was committed to using music as a platform for fat activism and often confronted audiences with her physicality by stripping and wearing homemade t-shirts with body-positive slogans like "Punk Rock Will Never Diet" on stage (Case 2004, 35). However, Ditto's fat pride conflicted with Topshop's corporate image. While it was willing to create plus-size collections with Ditto, Topshop was unwilling to use "fat" in its marketing and also declined her request to use Miss Piggy for a t-shirt because, according to Ditto, "it would send the wrong message" (Mapes 2016). This may have influenced Ditto's presence as a model for both collections' print campaigns. Gordon and Cosentino did not appear in the advertising for their collections, perhaps because Urban Outfitters had a roster of willowy models to employ. While Topshop's marketing centralized Ditto, it also suggested that the company could not find or chose not to look for plus-sized models. It may have also implied that Topshop required a celebrity spokesmodel rather than an unrecognizable model that fit into preordained beauty parameters in order to sell plus-size clothes to its consumers.

Finally, Ditto was displeased with Topshop's reliance upon sweatshop labor. Both collections were "made in India, which caused a lot of conflict for me," Ditto stated in 2012 after her spokesperson contract with Topshop had expired (Mapes 2012). She believed that such manufacturing decisions were symptomatic of Topshop's superficial interest in the plus-size market, which was indicative in the company's lack of "real thought about [pattern and design] . . . I don't think there are a lot of plus-sized people behind it, and I don't think that's fair" (Anderson 2016). This resulted in both collections' overreliance upon sack-like mini-dresses that were easy to duplicate but did not recognize fat women's diverse bodies and tastes. In the aftermath, Ditto resolved to create a brand that embodied her dreams for the fashion industry.

Pulling Threads

In late 2015, Beth Ditto announced her first U.S. clothing line, which was available for purchase through her website the following February. Having left Gossip to pursue a solo career Ditto was free to devote her energies to clothing design. She also returned to an industry with greater interest in the plus-size market and celebrity fashion than when she had left it. However, her previous struggles with Topshop prompted her to work with "no investors, no bank, no umbrella company" in order to apply "punk rock feminism and DIY culture" to her disco-inspired self-titled label (Mapes 2016). Ditto claimed that the business decision assured better quality control, and made sure her line was produced in Manhattan under fair labor conditions (Mapes 2016). In this regard, Ditto more explicitly positioned herself as a feminist entrepreneur by making manufacturing decisions that safeguarded against labor exploitation rather than trumpeting postfeminist appeals to individual achievement and empowerment while letting exploitative manufacturing practices within the fashion industry go unchallenged.

But Ditto's arrangement sacrificed price point for fit, at least in the short term, as individual pieces ranged between $65 and $395. This discrepancy between cost and tailoring was also evident in plus-size actresses Melissa McCarthy's mid-range independent venture Seven7 and Rebel Wilson's inexpensive capsule collection for Torrid, a U.S. chain formerly owned by mall-goth purveyor Hot Topic (Lodi 2015; Friedman 2015). Ditto also drew upon musical influence to publicize her forthcoming collection by collaborating with designer Jean-Paul Gaultier on a limited edition t-shirt for plus-size clientele that featured lithograph prints of the corsets Gaultier created for Madonna's Blonde Ambition tour (Figure 4.1). This citation let Ditto acknowledge the Material Girl's significance as a symbol of agentic female sexuality while reimagining the corset as a playful design element on a loose-fitting t-shirt. It also allowed Ditto to realign with the riot grrrl movement by donating a portion of t-shirt sales to the Girls Rock

FIGURE 4.1 Beth Ditto wears her limited edition t–shirt designed in collaboration with Jean-Paul Gaultier. Author screenshot from *Klonblog.com*

Camp Foundation (Vivinetto 2015). However, the t–shirt's $165 price tag limited its reach among consumers, casting the singer's distinctions between style and fashion into relief.

Kim Gordon's subsequent work, a fall 2011 Sportmax collection and twelve-piece collection with French boutique Surface to Air, faced similar challenges. While working with Surface to Air's company designer Dorothée Loermann, Gordon transferred the bright oranges, earth tones, and wild prints associated with late-1960s psychedelia into utilitarian tank dresses, blouses, and leather jackets by using French pop singer Catherine Ribeiro to symbolize glamorous sophistication for adult women expected to deftly master the work–life balance. "I'm a mom too," Gordon said, "but I don't always want to look just like that. It's the idea of finding things that work and are comfortable, but in which you can still feel like you have an identity" (Frank 2012). The collection's early 2012 release also followed the dissolution of Gordon's twenty-seven-year marriage to Thurston Moore, and subsequently their band. Thus Gordon, a divorcée with a daughter in college and a thirty-year music career, began to consider her legacy and what ambitions she wanted to pursue in her middle age (Halberstadt 2013).

After collaborating with Sportmax and Surface to Air, Gordon formed experimental music project Body/Head with guitarist Bill Nace and wrote her memoir. She and Coco also appeared in print campaigns for Marc Jacobs and Daryl Kerrigan's Madewell collection, decisions that stitched her maternity to her status as a fashion icon and nodded to X-Girl's legacy as a contemporary of Kerrigan's mid-1990s East Village boutique, Daryl K (Mau 2016). They also reinforced the intergenerational exchange between the adult women who imagined and orbited riot grrrl and the girls eager to try it on and revise it. Such nostalgic zeal manifest in various ways during the first half of the 2010s, from *Rookie* editor Tavi Gevinson professing riot grrrl's influence on her to clothing company Nasty Gal commissioning slip dresses designed by Courtney Love (Cadenas 2010; McKenzie 2016). However, Gordon did not reteam with Urban Outfitters, a decision that suggested Gordon wanted to look "more woman" than girl by appealing to a more mature and moneyed clientele (Halberstadt 2013).

Recently, Cosentino focused on recording and touring instead of fashion. However, in early 2016 she wrote candidly about her personal experiences in the recording industry. This complemented Ditto's and Gordon's forays into autobiography, a professional move that many female rock musicians pursue in the later stages of their lives and careers, including punk poet Patti Smith, Slits' guitarist Viv Albertine, singers Pauline Black and Grace Jones, and Sleater-Kinney's Carrie Brownstein. It also drew upon Cosentino's experience as a fashion blogger, a medium that expects writers to supplement trend forecasts and product reviews with personal narratives. In solidarity with Dirty Projectors' Amber Coffman, who used Twitter to upbraid music publicist Heathcliff Berru for his pattern of abusive behavior against women in the recording industry, Cosentino wrote a missive for Lena Dunham's e-letter *Lenny* about the sexual harassment she endured from Berru, male concert-goers, and journalists and readers who scrutinize her appearance online (2016). Such admissions are powerful, particularly in light of recent events like Runaways bassist Jackie Fuchs' allegation that she was raped by manager Kim Fowley and Speedy Ortiz leader Sadie DuPuis' decision to install a phone hotline for female fans to assure their safety at her band's concerts (Cherkis 2015; White 2015).

Conclusions: The Possibilities and Limitations of Citational Feminism

Cosentino's, Gordon's, and Ditto's examples demonstrate the systemic inequality that female musicians experience due to sexist and misogynistic misperceptions about gendered self-presentation. This is not only evident in their work in capsule collection design, but it is bound up in their work as musicians and the sexism they have confronted on stage and in public life by harnessing the feminist potential of feminized performance and self-presentation. It is evident in Cosentino's claim that a critic's assessment of her stage appearance "revealed how he thought a woman who he saw as 'sexy' should behave" and in Ditto's declaration that her plus-size fans "deserve to be draped in seven yards of fucking silk" (Cosentino 2016; Mapes 2016). Though Ditto's commitment to provide this for them on her own is admirable, Cosentino's admission brings to mind how confession became a powerful tool for feminist consciousness-raising and coalition building during the 1970s. Gordon, Cosentino, and Ditto use citational feminism to engage in a cross-generational dialogue between musicians and fans through fashion. Though their capsule collections still comply with a model of individual achievement inherent in postfeminist sensibilities, they also use design as an opportunity for feminist coalition-building by elevating earlier generations of female artists into style icons; acknowledging their indebtedness to them as musicians; and using capsule collection design as an opportunity to reflect on how women develop style not only as a form of self-expression, but in relation to their layered identities as mothers, daughters, sisters, and fans. Yet these endeavors also reveal absences within citational feminism through capitalism's ability to create distance between celebrity designers, the global work force responsible for the execution of their designs, and the complex needs of customers, as well as the necessary work ahead for feminists to harness style as a tool for systemic change within the fashion industry. Thus, female recording artists' maneuvering between style and fashion reinforces how citation reproduces the world around certain bodies, and necessitates a critical eye toward the potential and limits of their assembly.

Works Cited

"50 Ways to Rock the P.T.A." 2008. *New York Times*, September 5. http://www.nytimes.com/slideshow/2008/09/05/fashion/20080907-PULSE_3.html.

Ahmed, Sara. 2013. "Making Feminist Points." *Feminist Killjoys*, September 11. http://feminist killjoys.com/2013/09/11/making-feminist-points/.

Anderson, Kristin. 2016. "Beth Ditto's Clothing Line Is Finally Here! Get Your First Look Now." *Vogue*, February 12. http://www.vogue.com/13398654/beth-ditto-style-clothing-brand-plus-size-fashion/.

Anderson, Timothy J. 2013. *Popular Music in a Digital Music Economy: Problems and Practices for an Emerging Service Industry*. New York: Routledge.

Anderson-Minshall, Diane. 2012. "Beth Ditto Interview: Diamonds are Forever." *Advocate*, December 3. http://www.advocate.com/print-issue/cover-stories/2012/12/03/cover-story-interview-gossip-front-woman-beth-ditto.

"Best Coast on her Fashion Line—Noisey Meets Bethany Cosentino (#10)." 2012. *Noisey*, April 18. https://www.youtube.com/watch?v=UjrLE-FrmpA.

Blue, Morgan Genevieve. 2013. "*D-Signed* for Girls: Disney Channel and Tween Fashion." *Film, Fashion & Consumption* 2 (1): 55–75.

Browne, David. 2008. *Goodbye 20th Century: A Biography*. Boston: Da Capo Press.

Butler, Judith. 1993. *Bodies That Matter: On the Discursive Limits of "Sex"*. New York: Routledge.

Cadenas, Kerensa. 2010. "Tavi Gevinson is Fashionable, Feminist and Just 14." *Ms.*, October 8. http://msmagazine.com/blog/2010/10/08/tavi-gevinson-is-fashionable-feminist-and-just-14/.

Case, Mairead. 2004. "Ditto to Ditto." *Rockrgrl* 50: 35–36.

Chang, Bee-Shyuan. 2013. "Indie Frock: Kim Gordon's New Line." *T*, February 4. http://tmagazine.blogs.nytimes.com/2009/02/04/indie-frock-kim-gordons-new-line/?_r=0.

Cherkis, Jason. 2015. "The Lost Girls." *Huffington Post*, July 8. http://highline.huffingtonpost.com/articles/en/the-lost-girls/?ncid=tweetlnkushpmg00000067.

Cosentino, Bethany. 2016. "Burgers, Bitches, and Bullshit." *Lenny*, February 2. http://www.lennyletter.com/life/a248/burgers-bitches-and-bullshit-bethany-consentino/.

Davies, Helen. 2001. "All Rock and Roll is Homosocial: The Representation of Women in the British Rock Music Press." *Popular Music* 20 (3): 301–319.

Ditto, Beth. 2007. "What Would Beth Do?: Today's Dilemma for Beth: I Can't Sew and I'm Not Skinny. How Can I Look Great on a Budget?" *Guardian*, May 25: 17.

Dombal, Ryan. 2010. "Hear Best Coast's Album in Full." *Pitchfork*, July 12. http://pitchfork.com/news/39425-hear-best-coasts-album-in-full/.

Frank, Alex. 2012. "Now Collaborating: Kim Gordon + Surface to Air." *T*, February 7. http://tmagazine.blogs.nytimes.com/2012/02/07/now-collaborating-kim-gordon-surface-to-air/?_r=0.

Friedman, Megan. 2015. "Rebel Wilson's New Plus-Size Fashion Line Is Here—And It's Badass." *Marie Claire*, November 2. http://www.marieclaire.com/fashion/news/a16720/rebel-wilson-new-plus-size-fashion-line-torrid/.

Gill, Rosalind. 2007. "Postfeminist Media Culture: Elements of a Sensibility." *European Journal of Cultural Studies* 10 (2): 147–166.

Gindt, Dirk. 2011. "Performative Processes: Björk's Creative Collaborations with the World of Fashion." *Fashion Theory* 15 (4): 425–450.

Gordon, Kim. 2015. *A Girl in a Band: A Memoir*. New York: Dey Street Books.

Halberstadt, Alex. 2013. "Next Stage." *The New Yorker*, June 3. http://www.newyorker.com/magazine/2013/06/03/next-stage.

Hall, Stuart. 1979. "The Great Moving Right Show." *Marxism Today* (January): 14–20.

Haruch, Steve. 2014. "Is Courting Controversy an Urban Outfitters Strategy?" *NPR*, December 16. http://www.npr.org/sections/codeswitch/2014/12/16/370329870/is-courting-controversy-an-urban-outfitters-strategy.

Harvey, Eric. 2011. "Same as the Old Boss? Changes, Continuities, and Careers in the Digital Music Era." In *Managing Media Work*, edited by Mark Deuze, 237–248. London: Sage.

Hattersley, Giles. 2009. "The Brilliance of Beth," *The Sunday Times*, June 14: 8–13.

Hegde, Radha S. 2011. "Introduction." In *Circuits of Visibility: Gender and Transnational Media Cultures*, edited by Radha S. Hegde, 1–20: New York: NYU Press.

Hesmondhalgh, David. 1999. "Indie: The Institutional Politics and Aesthetics of a Popular Music Genre." *Cultural Studies* 13 (1): 34–61.

Kearney, Mary Celeste. 1997. "The Missing Links: Riot Grrrl—Feminism—Lesbian Culture." In *Sexing the Groove: Popular Music and Gender*, edited by Sheila Whiteley, 207–229. New York: Routledge.

Kearney, Mary Celeste. 2010. "Pink Technology: Mediamaking Gear for Girls." *Camera Obscura* 25 (2.74): 1–39.

Kershaw, Miriam. 1997. "Performance Art." *Art Journal* 56: 19–25.

Lau, Venessa and Kim Friday. 2010. "Kim Gordon: Making Noise." *Women's Wear Daily*, May 3. http://wwd.com/eye/fashion/kim-gordon-making-noise-3056975/.

Lewis, Caitlin. 2011. "Cool Postfeminism: The Stardom of Sofia Coppola." In *In the Limelight and Under the Microscope: Forms and Functions of Female Celebrity*, edited by Su Holmes and Diane Negra, 174–198. New York: Continuum.

Lodi, Marie. 2015. "Melissa McCarthy Launches Website for Clothing Line." *Jezebel*, December 20. http://jezebel.com/melissa-mccarthy-launches-website-for-clothing-line-1749015826.

Lutz, Ashley. 2013. "Prabul Gurung's Line is the Smash Hit That Target Needed." *Business Insider*, February 11. http://www.businessinsider.com/prabal-gurung-for-target-sold-out-2013-2?0=retail.

Manning, Sara. 2009. "Think Big." *Guardian*, July 7. http://www.theguardian.com/lifeandstyle/2009/jul/07/beth-ditto-evans.

Mapes, Jillian. 2012. "Beth Ditto Talks the Gossip's New Album, Starting 'the Ikea' of Plus-Size Lines, and Her Beef With Karl Lagerfeld." *Vulture*, May 24. http://www.vulture.com/2012/05/beth-ditto-has-beef-with-karl-lagerfeld.html.

Mapes, Jillian. 2016. "Beth Ditto Stays Radically Fat With New Clothing Line and Solo Career." *Pitchfork*, February 19. http://pitchfork.com/thepitch/1026-beth-ditto-stays-radically-fat-with-new-clothing-line-and-solo-career/.

Marcus, Sara. 2010. *Girls to the Front: The True Story of the Riot Grrrl Revolution*. New York: Harper Perennial.

Mathieson, Craig. 2012. "Surf Pop's New Wave." *Sydney Morning Herald*, December 14. http://www.smh.com.au/entertainment/surf-pops-new-wave-20121213-2bagq.html.

Mau, Dhani. 2012. "Best Coast's Bethany Cosentino on Her New Urban Outfitters Line and '90s Style Influences." *Fashionista*, May 10. http://fashionista.com/2012/05/best-coasts-bethany-cosentino-on-her-new-urban-outfitters-line-and-90s-style-influences.

Mau, Dhani. 2016. "Why Madewell Teamed up with '90s Cult Brand Daryl K." *Fashionista*, February 8. http://fashionista.com/2016/02/madewell-daryl-k.

McKenzie, Lesley. 2016. "Courtney Love, Sophia Amoruso Fete Their Nasty Gal Collab." *Pret-a-Porter*, January 14. http://www.hollywoodreporter.com/news/courtney-love-sophia-amoruso-love-856098.

McLaughlin, Noel. 2000. "Rock, Fashion, and Performativity." In *Fashion Cultures: Theories, Explorations and Analysis*, edited by Stella Bruzzi and Pamela Church Gibson, 264–285. New York: Routledge.

McRobbie, Angela. 2008. *The Aftermath of Feminism: Gender, Culture, and Social Change*. Thousand Oaks, CA: SAGE.

McRobbie, Angela and Jenny Garber. 2000. *Feminism and Youth Culture*. New York: Routledge.

Miles, Kathleen. 2012. "'Sweatshop' Conditions Found in LA Fashion District at Contractors for Urban Outfitters, Aldo, Forever 21." *Huffington Post*, December 14. http://www.huffingtonpost.com/2012/12/14/sweatshop-la-fashion-urban-outfitters-aldo-forever-21_n_2302493.html.

Morris, Jeremy. 2014. "Artists as Entrepreneurs, Fans as Workers." *Popular Music and Society* 37 (3): 273–290.

Pelly, Jenn. 2012. "Best Coast Talks Urban Outfitters Collaboration." *Pitchfork*, March 2. http://pitchfork.com/news/45619-best-coast-talks-urban-outfitters-collaboration/.

Phelan, Hayley. 2011. "Rihanna Breaks Into Design With a Capsule Collection for Emporio Armani Underwear and Armani Jeans." *Fashionista*, November 22. http://fashionista.com/2011/11/rihanna-breaks-into-design-with-a-capsule-collection-for-emporio-armani-underwear-and-armani-jeans.

Phelps, Nicole. 2010. "Spring 2011: Jean-Paul Gaultier." *Vogue*, October 1. http://www.vogue.com/fashion-shows/spring-2011-ready-to-wear/jean-paul-gaultier.

Pool, Hannah. 2009. "Does Fashion's New Love for Curves Go Beyond Beth Ditto?" *Guardian*, February 19: 2.

Reed, Sam. 2015. "Gwyneth Paltrow Launches Valentino Collab, Goop Pop-Up Store," *Hollywood Reporter*, November 19. http://www.hollywoodreporter.com/news/gwyneth-paltrows-goop-x-valentino-842238.

Reilly, Phoebe. 2012. "Feel Good, Inc." *SPIN* 28 (4): 46–51.

Rems, Emily. 2008. "Beth Threat." *BUST* (December/January): 52–56.

Schneier, Matthew. 2015. "Lilly Pulitzer for Target: They Came, They Waited, They Went Home Mad." *New York Times*, April 22. https://www.nytimes.com/2015/04/23/fashion/is-target-in-the-consumers-bulls-eye-after-the-lilly-pulitzer-dustup.html.

Seymour, Corey. 1994. "Are You Xperienced?" *Rolling Stone* 692: 60–63.

Sheppard, Justin. 2007. "The Gossip Sign with Columbia." *Prefix*, March 8. http://www.prefixmag.com/news/columbia-signs-the-gossip/9637/.

Sherman, Lauren. 2016. "What's Next for the American Department Store." *Business of Fashion*, January 3. http://www.businessoffashion.com/articles/intelligence/whats-next-for-the-american-department-store.

Shirway, Richard K. 2015. "Episode 48: Best Coast, 'Feeling Okay.'" *Song Exploder*, August 27. http://songexploder.net/best-coast.

Simon, Scott. 2010. "How Times Have Changed, Ex-Playboy Bunnies Say." *NPR*, June 10. http://www.wbur.org/npr/127495661.

Stahl, Matt and Leslie M. Meier. 2012. "The Firm Foundation of Organizational Flexibility: The 360 Contract in the Digitalizing Music Industry." *Canadian Journal of Communication* 37: 441–458.

Strong, Catherine. 2011. "Grunge, Riot Grrrl and the Forgetting of Women in Popular Culture." *Journal of Popular Culture* 44 (2): 398–416.

Thompson, Elizabeth and Alexis Swerdloff. 2012. "An Oral History of X-Girl." *Paper*, August 20. http://www.papermag.com/an-oral-history-of-x-girl-1426244090.html.

Tortorici, Dayna. 2010. "You Know It When You See It." In *What Was the Hipster?: A Sociological Investigation*, edited by Mark Greif, 122–135. New York: Sheridan Press.

Trebay, Guy. 2009. "When a Punk Artist Finds Herself in the Throes of Fashion." *New York Times*, March 10: A21.

Vivinetto, Gina. 2015. "Beth Ditto Creates Plus-Size Clothing Line." *Advocate*, December 15. http://www.advocate.com/music/2015/12/15/beth-ditto-designs-plus-sized-clothing-line.

Wald, Gayle. 2002. "Just a Girl: Rock Music, Feminism, and the Cultural Construction of Female Youth." In *Rock Over the Edge: Transformation in Popular Music Culture*, edited by Roger Beebe, Denise Fulbrook, and Ben Saunders, 191–215. Durham: Duke University Press.

Weiner, Jonah. 2012. "Sunshine and Dread." *Rolling Stone* 1163: 52–55.

White, Caitlin. 2015. "Speedy Ortiz Launch Help Hotline to Ensure Fans Feel Safe at Their Shows." *Stereogum*, September 7. http://www.stereogum.com/1829067/speedy-ortiz-launch-help-hotline-to-ensure-fans-feel-safe-at-their-shows/news/.

Solidarities

5

#IAMMORETHANADISTRACTION

Connecting Local Body Politics to a Digital Feminist Movement

Emilie Zaslow

In the late spring of 2014, thirteen-year-old Gabriella woke up to discover that the temperature in her New Jersey suburb would reach 88 degrees by midday.[1] As she always did, she got dressed with comfort and style in mind. Not all of the classrooms in Forest Park Middle School had air conditioning, so Gabriella wore shorts and a T-shirt. As Gabriella waited for her first class of the day to begin, the school principal made his morning announcement and, as he did daily, included a reminder to the girls that the "fingertip rule" would be enforced. In math class, Gabriella's teacher asked the girls to stand up with their hands down at their sides to make sure that they met the conditions of the school dress code. Her fingertips were just above the tip of her shorts but the rule in the school handbook was that "to be appropriate shorts or skirts must reach to the fingertips of the extended arm." The female students had been told repeatedly that they had to follow the dress code so as not to distract the boys and disrupt the learning environment. As she stood there, with her arms at her sides, Gabriella felt angry, afraid, and shameful. Pushing her emotions aside, Gabriella joined with four other girls and their parents to launch a local feminist campaign that became a digital feminist movement to fight school dress codes that unfairly discriminate against girls. These intergenerational feminists created the #iammorethanadistraction social media campaign and ultimately worked with the local school district to revise its dress code.

Based on an ethnographic study of the girls and their parents, including focus groups with both, this chapter locates their political acts within the feminist, postfeminist, and body/beauty cultures that defines the particular historical moment of emergent feminisms. In the panic surrounding postfeminism and girl power, teen girls are often positioned as ideal subjects of postfeminist sensibility, easily manipulated by a powerful neoliberal celebrity feminist culture that simultaneously sexualizes them, encourages them to see themselves as the empowered architects of their own sexual display, and disciplines their sexuality to conform to normative tropes of beauty. Yet, the group of young activists discussed in this chapter actively negotiates the contradictory discourses in which emergent feminisms reside and challenges the forces of disarticulation by building an intergenerational solidarity. Embracing collective feminist politics, the teen girls in this study create a feminist messaging, using both digital technology as well as traditional grassroots political action, that attempts to embrace their bodies while refusing to be sexualized by their academic institution.

This empowered statement by young feminists and their parents complicates our understanding of a "postfeminist sensibility" (Gill 2007). Bound within colliding messages of power, the girls and parents who coordinated the #iammorethanadistraction campaign are aware that their bodies serve purposes other than sexual arousal and that they should not be held responsible for disrupting the learning environment should they choose to expose their shoulders or thighs at school. Yet, while these activists are operating within a capitalist girl power culture that promotes sexually explicit styles and uncritically markets these as feminist empowerment, they reject the positioning of their bodies as "always already unruly and requiring constant monitoring, surveillance, discipline and remodeling" (Gill 2007, 149). In addition, this campaign defies the logic of generational feminism. Generational categorization, best known through the wave metaphor, has long been the predominant approach to studying shifts in feminist notions of power and strategies for social change, suggesting that feminists of different generations may not share a political affiliation with one another. Yet, as young feminists born into third-wave feminism, raised in a girl power media culture by parents who had benefitted from the gains of the women's liberation movement, and coming of age in an era of body positivity and digital technology, this movement incorporated theories of the body and strategies for social change that span multiple waves of feminism.

Postfeminism and Girl Power Discourses

That same March of 2014, *Seventeen* magazine published its "Girl Power Issue" with articles on how to "make your own style," "get your dream job," "be a beauty rock star," and learn "what makes you powerful." In each of these articles girls were instructed that the way to power was personal, individual, and self-directed; girl power was not the power *of* girls but "your power" *as* a girl. Just as Sheryl Sandberg's (2013, 137) *Lean In* suggests that individual will and "making the best choices we can" is the key to gender equity, *Seventeen*'s girl power lessons propose that if you work hard, stay strong, and give as much as you can to your personal project, you can "get everything you want." In the following month, *Seventeen* advanced its theme from girl power to feminism. Explaining that some readers don't identify as feminists due to old, worn-out definitions of the term, the magazine declared that feminism is "not some giant movement—it's personal. . . . It's about . . . being confident, embracing your femininity however you choose to, and just being *you*" (Moscatello 2014, 122). Directing the onus for change on the individual and her choice-making, *Seventeen*'s girl power feminism obfuscates well-established institutions and practices that sustain gender oppression.

As in *Seventeen,* the implication in the popular culture in which these activists are growing up is that individual responsibility and choice are at the root of feminist identity. A girl power feminist makes choices in her own interest, without thinking about the political implications of those choices or about the social structures within which those choices are made. Because the world is depicted as already ripe for self-determination, social movements such as feminism need not be intersectional, collectivist, or committed to structural or systemic change (Zaslow 2009). In this paradigm, what must change is not society but the individual girl. The self then becomes the site upon which one must enact regulation, discipline and improvement (Gill 2007). If power is waiting to be claimed, it is the unsuccessful girl who has failed to claim her prize.

Sexuality, Power, and Body Positivity

The movement against gender biased dress codes, which attracted public attention in the late 20th century (Pomerantz 2007) and gained momentum with the #iammorethanadistraction hashtag, must also be read against the backdrop of the conflicting and contradictory discourses about sexuality, bodies, and power that dominate this generation's media culture. Unlike their foresisters and foremothers, the girls in this study were not growing up in a culture in which objectification of the female body as available for men's gaze was a given. While schools were telling them to cover up and hide their bodies, popular media was telling girls that they should celebrate their bodies with a feminist pride. Their parents may have been raised within a second-wave feminist political culture that equated the personal with the political in ways that sometimes celebrated an anti-beauty culture, but the girls in this study are coming of age within a third wave that embraces style, femininity, and female sexuality.

Third-wave feminism critiqued the anti-fashion, anti-beauty, and anti-sex discourses they felt were emblematic of second-wave feminism. Not only did these discourses feel alienating and restrictive, some young feminists felt that it also reeked of a victim mentality with which they did not want to associate (Budgeon 2015). Moreover, third wavers claimed that their adoption of a style that sometimes included traditionally feminine sexiness should be understood as flexible and not evidence of their exploitation by a commodity market (Baumgardner and Richards 2000). At the center of third-wave feminism was the notion of choice; with the fortification of gender studies in the academy, increasing numbers of women in positions of power in the culture industries, and the proliferation of user-generated media on the Internet, third-wave feminists claimed that choice within feminism was their birthright.

As the new millennium was ushered in, critics began to document the capitalist incorporation of the pro-sexuality, choice discourse of the third-wave feminist movement—what scholars like Rosalind Gill (2007) discuss as a "post-feminist sensibility." Across media, third-wave discourse was co-opted and repurposed as girl power; the same neoliberal market-friendly discourse that marked individual success as the pinnacle of gender equality also identified sexuality as the foundation of female power (Zaslow 2009). Ariel Levy (2006) argued that young women were being encouraged to participate in a raunch culture in which they enthusiastically embraced the hypersexualization of other women and themselves under the guise of empowerment and feminist liberation. In fashion, too, girls' clothing began to incorporate girl power's sexual empowerment motif. Gill (2003) contends that in popular culture, not only has sexual subjectification replaced objectification but that, because it is ever-present and continues to perpetuate white thin women as desiring and desirable sexual subjects, it has become a new regulatory mandate. In the name of self-determination and empowerment, women must choose to be sexy, adopt the normative codes of sexiness, and work hard to maintain their sexy appearance within social norms (Gill 2003).

More recently, however, alongside the pornification of culture is an upsurge in body positive discourse. Body positivity is the belief that we should embrace all body sizes, shapes, colors, types and abilities rather than praising only those that meet normative standards of beauty. The recent swell in body positive blogs and websites and an organized movement spearheaded by teen girls against the perpetuation of teen magazines' thin ideal has led to the mainstreaming of this language (Sastre 2014; Tolman 2012). Body positivity also became the trend *du jour* of teen girl culture through more traditional media forms. Studies have long found contemporary teen magazines to address girls with contradictory messages about their bodies. On the one hand, they construct a girls' desirable body as "smooth, trim, toned, long, lean, strong, young, sexy, clean and free of odor and [certain body] hair," attainable through the purchase of consumer products (Ballentine and Ogle 2005, 290). At the same time, girls and young women are increasingly encouraged to accept and love their natural bodies and to challenge dominant beauty ideals. After 2012, in response to pressure from teen girl activists, *Seventeen* magazine released a "Body Peace Treaty" pledging to "celebrate every kind of beauty" and to "never to change girls' body or face shapes." The magazine has since included body positive rhetoric and narratives (Haughney 2012).

Female pop singers also embraced a duplicitous version of body positivity in the years leading up to the #iammorethanadistraction movement through their embrace of feminism. These performers challenge their listeners to love their bodies and their cosmetic-free faces while simultaneously working as paid spokeswomen for the biggest cosmetics brands. In 2010, Pink sang that she was "done looking for critics" who "don't like my jeans . . . [and] don't get my hair" and begged her listeners, "pretty, pretty please . . . don't you feel like you are less than . . . perfect." In 2012, Lady Gaga asked fans to join in her body revolution to celebrate all body types and on 2014's "Flawless," Beyoncé celebrated natural beauty singing "I woke up like this." All three have signed spokesperson deals with cosmetics companies (Cover Girl, MAC, and L'Oréal, respectively), and Beyoncé has admitted to wearing Spanx shapewear, the modern-day version of a girdle, leaving girls to make sense of the contradictions between body positive star texts and the support of a multi-million-dollar beauty industry that literally thrives on creating, sustaining, and offering to fix the dissatisfaction women and girls feel about their appearances.

These celebrities' beauty campaigns were not the only reason that body positive messages were front and center in 2014 as the Forest Park girls began their fight against the school district. In addition, body positive discourse had begun to focus not just on loving one's body, but on loving one's sexual body. The previous winter, the world had been abuzz with news that Kim Kardashian had "broken the Internet" when her husband posted a *Paper* magazine photo shoot image featuring Kardashian's nude behind covered in a shiny substance. Once the summer began, a focus on the female derriere began in earnest. In early June, Meghan Trainor released the video for her single, "All About that Bass" in which Trainor told women that even if they weren't "a size two," they should know that "every inch of you is perfect from the bottom to the top" because "Boys like a little more booty to hold at night." A few days later Jennifer Lopez released her single "Booty," reminding women, "What you got a big booty/ My baby, you're gorgeous/I mean you're fine, you're sexy." Later that summer Nicki Minaj released "Anaconda," in which she sang the praises of the "fat ass" and claimed that men "don't want none unless you got buns, hon." Although many girls, including some of those in the study, did not like these songs because Trainor and Minaj called thin women "skinny bitches" and thus engaged in "skinny shamming," or because they called out that it was men's desire that made having a larger butt appealing, both were largely deemed emblematic of a kind of new body positivity seeping into popular culture.

While the girls in this study embrace the concept of body positivity, critics challenge the authenticity of body positivity as well as its limitations. Beyond becoming common parlance, body positivity has been incorporated into the marketplace as a technique for selling products to women. Rosalind Gill and Ana Sofia Elias (2014) have documented the problematic nature of this commodification demonstrating that the use of "love your body discourses" in advertisements is false in that most companies continue to use cosmetics and computer software to modify the bodies of the "real women" in advertisements. This discourse also creates a new regulation in which it is no longer "enough to work on and discipline the body . . . [now] the beautiful body must be accompanied by a beautiful mind, with suitably upgraded and modernized postfeminist attitudes to the self" (2014, 185). Alexandra Sastre (2014) found that body positive blogs also focused on a kind of self-disciplining that was fulfilled by following a prescribed therapeutic process reminiscent of those on makeover shows. In her analysis, feeling positive about one's body becomes a new mandate to which women must conform. Furthermore, as Gabriella's mother laments, body positivity seems to have become equated with positivity about the sexy body. She says, "You never see 15 ways to look more classy or how to look more intelligent. It's always how to look more sexy."

Conflicting rhetorical displays by celebrity feminists make sense in a marketplace feminism that alludes to a movement but emphasizes personal transformation (Zeisler 2016). Girls may be left feeling a sense of discordance when their mediascape does not align with their social and political realities (Zaslow 2009). At the same time, the young activists who launched #iammorethanadistraction are actively negotiating the discursive contradictions of contemporary culture. Stella explains, "From a very young age girls are shown the messages that women are inherently sexual objects but also that we should not explore our femininity or sexuality. It offers this weird duality and it's like which one is it?" They called upon body positivity discourse as a means to challenge the postfeminist sensibilities that don't resonate with them. Elizabeth cited body positive blogs, hashtags and online magazines such as *Rookie* as antidotal to mainstream media's normalization of the white, thin, hairless female body. Calling these blogs "safe spaces," she says that they have helped her to think of herself, and not of others, as she chooses her clothing and finds things that make her feel confident.

Invested in body positivity, these girls want to love their bodies, and believe that women should embrace their sexuality, but they reject a consistent and institutionalized sexualizing and disciplining of their bodies. While schools often use gender-neutral language, and focus on promoting safety and limiting distractions, dress codes that focus on the length of shorts and the thickness of tank top straps put girls in the position of being responsible for maintaining the school's morality. Like the participants in Kate Gleeson and Hannah Frith's (2004) study, the girls in this study see the act of styling themselves to be one in which they maintain power and control over their own bodies within these confusing systemic relations of power. For the Forest Park girls, power means reclaiming the right to define themselves by dressing against the school code and to find meaning in the conflicting discourses. Demonstrating the dualism in the message and the taking back of power, Alexa asks, "You want me to wear a bra, but you don't want to see it?! It's like, I'm a teenage girl. I have a bra on. Sorry. It's not breaking news." Elizabeth extends the argument to choice and confidence, suggesting that girls lose power to define themselves and find what feels right for their bodies when "at some point you are telling me to wear this and I don't feel confident in it or I feel more confident when I was wearing what I wore before."

The #iammorethanadistraction campaign resists the way that dress codes mark certain modes of dress, and thus certain forms of girlhood, as good/acceptable and others as bad/amoral (Raby 2010). As Stella said during our focus group, the various pressures on girls to dress in certain ways—including school dress codes—create a feeling that

> You are always trying to see yourself through the lens of other people. You are dressing to make guys like you or dressing to make the school happy and especially in such an impressionable time, our age group, it is such an important time to be able to understand what you want to do and what you are most comfortable with. If you are getting all these external messages it can be very hard not to internalize them and that kind of stunts your growth in a way and [you are] constantly thinking that you are there just for someone else to look at you. It doesn't really build a culture of confidence. It builds a culture of insecurity.

Stella is arguing against the policing of her body and the way that the dress code asks her to imagine her body as an object and constantly be responsible for regulating the extent to which it publically communicates sexuality. Further, the girls identified that the dress code was not equally enforced; some bodies were more likely to be targeted for discipline than others. The girls noticed that both race and size were factors in who was called out for violating the dress code. Girls whose bodies did not represent a normative feminine beauty were more likely to be the objects of surveillance than those who were white and thin. This uneven application of the dress code was a concern for them because in their embrace of body positivity, they rebuff the postfeminist sensibility that their bodies are problems that require constant surveillance (Gill 2007).

Feminism at the Dinner Table

If media was telling them that feminism was a movement for individual power, their local culture was communicating something different. To contextualize the relationship of the girls who launched this campaign to feminism, it is important to understand how their local community and families are participating in the framing of their feminist politics. Forest Park, where the girls all live, is a racially diverse, socially, and politically progressive, wealthy commuter suburb. Located outside of a major city, the town attracts many artistic and intellectual people who work in fields such as media, performing arts, healthcare, and academia. Further, all of the girls' parents—both father and mothers—are highly educated working professionals. For the girls, this local political climate translates into both an educational and community environment that welcomes resistive and critical voices. Teachers, parents, and students alike have been discussing gender issues throughout their lives. As Gabriella summed up, her family "talks about feminism at the dinner table all the time."

While their parents' level of involvement with feminism and other political causes varied, all consider themselves progressive and all of the parents and the girls in this study identified as feminists even before they became involved with the #iammorethanadistraction movement. The parents' own political activism in the 1970s and 1980s was inspired by their parents before them; their lessons in activism occurred before neoliberal individualism pervaded social movements. One girl's grandparents met at a labor rally and her family has together attended protests in support of universal healthcare and reproductive freedom. Another girl's father had identified as an activist since the late 1970s when he first started fighting for gay rights. Others, who did not have a strong activist history, had taken their children down to Wall Street when the Occupy movement had taken over Zuccotti Park in 2011.

These girls may be coming of age in a postfeminist, girl power culture, but they are also being educated about their parents' beliefs in collective struggles, rather than individual achievement, and in structural systems, rather than free choice, as the focus of change. For these girls, social movements included not only tweets and Beyoncé performances, but also people uniting for policy and systematic change. Likewise, as Jessalynn Keller (2015) found with the young women she studied, the concept of body politics for these teens extended beyond the right to sexually objectify themselves to the right to healthcare, a living wage, and reproductive rights. Angela McRobbie (2009) has posited that the neoliberal disarticulation of feminism, in which a politics of feminism is cast as outdated while simultaneously the rhetoric and symbolism of feminism has been reappropriated as a commodity with exchange value in the popular culture market, operates to reduce the likelihood of solidarity across generations. The #iammorethanadistraction movement in which parents and youth worked together both online and offline may suggest, however, that the force of disarticulation may not always be effective in containing feminist identification and politics. Further, the overlapping, varied discourses, in and through which these girls are defining their feminist politics, supports the recent challenges made to the historicizing of feminism as occurring within distinct waves (Laughlin et al. 2010).

#iammorethanadistraction: Dress Codes and Protest

Most schools in the United States have some stated code of conduct that includes how students should dress for school. Dress codes may be used to enforce a conservative moral code and/or in an effort to protect girls from a toxic capitalist pornification of culture. School administrators often argue that dress codes are written in order to minimize distractions, promote positive self-esteem, and create a respectable image for the school (Pomerantz 2007). As the porn-chic trend grew, concerns about sexualized clothing were fueled by fear and early research that suggests girls who wear sexualized clothing may be more likely to hold sexualized beliefs about themselves (McKenney and Bigler 2014). Further, studies have suggested that the negative consequences of girls' internalization of these sexual images include increased body dissatisfaction, feelings of shame about their bodies, monitoring of the body, and disciplining the body (American Psychological Association 2007). With the support of some parents, many school districts have sought to protect girls from a culture that they believe could be detrimental to their physical and mental health as well as their sexuality. More often, dress codes are founded in a heterosexist and sexist fear that boys (and male teachers) will not be able to concentrate or control themselves around girls with exposed legs or shoulders.

Protest movements against school dress codes have been at the forefront of millennial feminist sartorial politics. At the core of these movements is the understanding that clothing choice is "situated body practice" which is used to craft one's identity for herself and the world (Entwistle 2000, 11). Despite the personal nature of clothing, the act of selecting clothing and getting dressed is performed within the cultural constraints of dominant ideologies and social norms including the patriarchal-bound sexualization of the female body. Enacting a style at this age, according to Gabriella's mother, is a process of weeding through the messages about gender and sex to come to a place of power and understanding. She says that she tells her daughters that "Clothing is an expression of you as an individual but it doesn't always have to be you as a sexual being." Though parents wanted their daughters to think critically about their dress, they supported their daughters' fight against the dress code.

Thinking through the relationship between dress codes and feminism is difficult for the most seasoned feminist. Peggy Orenstein (2014) mused that she did not want her daughter to "feel shame in her soon-to-be-emerging woman's body" but that, "even as I object to the policing of girls' sexuality, I'm concerned about the incessant drumbeat of self-objectification: the pressure young women face to view their bodies as the objects of others' desires. . . ." Orenstein questions whose legislation it is more dangerous to resist: the governmental legislation of the school or the capitalist legislation of the fashion and media industries. For the girls and parents in this study there is a somewhat clearer divide; media should be held accountable, but schools should not take on a paternalistic role that polices girls' bodies and insinuates a moral code. Moreover, schools should not be marking girls' bodies as sexual nor should they hold girls responsible for maintaining attentiveness and civility and for dressing to protect their bodies from unwanted attention.

The day that Gabriella was asked to prove her adherence to the fingertip rule, she rode home from school with four other friends, Alexa, Becca, Elizabeth, and Stella. The girls talked about the daily reminders specifically addressed to girls and about the new pool party dress code which prohibited girls from wearing two-piece bathing suits but made no requirements on boys' attire. Behind the steering wheel, Ronin, one of Alexa's fathers, listened to the girls; he heard them argue that it wasn't fair, it was gender biased and it made them feel responsible for boys' distraction. His own experiences as a political activist in the gay rights movement told him never to sit back and let inequitable policies be left unchallenged. He told the girls that they could do something.

The girls of Forest Park created a hashtag that united a number of nationwide dress code protests online. Their hashtag, #iammorethanadistraction, was not used simply for their own small town efforts to change the local dress codes but was adopted as a rallying cry by girls across the country and at the time of this writing, is still being used widely. As social media has blossomed, girls across the U.S. and Canada have used the hashtag to support and broadcast online petitions, organize sartorial protests, and post images of the outfits in which they have been coded (Figure 5.1). As school began again in the autumn of 2015, evidence that the hashtag gained national momentum could be found in mentions of the movement in *The Atlantic, The Huffington Post*, and a *Buzzfeed* story entitled, "Young Women Are Protesting Against Dress Codes With #IAmMoreThanaDistraction."

To start, the girls met with Ronin and decided that they wanted to speak to the principal. Ronin says that while he gave them guidance, it was important to him that they took ownership of the resistance. They researched the issue and prepared note cards with their talking points. The girls had always believed in the promise of egalitarianism, which is what motivated them to discuss and act

Props to whoever did this!
#iammorethanadistraction

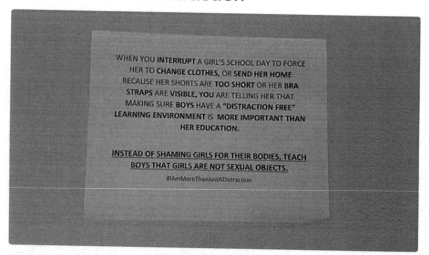

WHEN YOU INTERRUPT A GIRL'S SCHOOL DAY TO FORCE HER TO CHANGE CLOTHES, OR SEND HER HOME BECAUSE HER SHORTS ARE TOO SHORT OR HER BRA STRAPS ARE VISIBLE, YOU ARE TELLING HER THAT MAKING SURE BOYS HAVE A "DISTRACTION FREE" LEARNING ENVIRONMENT IS MORE IMPORTANT THAN HER EDUCATION.

INSTEAD OF SHAMING GIRLS FOR THEIR BODIES, TEACH BOYS THAT GIRLS ARE NOT SEXUAL OBJECTS.

#IAmMoreThanJustADistraction

3:21 PM - 2 Jun 2015

FIGURE 5.1 A tweet using the #iammorethanadistraction hashtag shares activism from a high school hallway. Author screenshot from *Buzzfeed*

on this issue, but it was during this research process, he says, that "They were becoming political . . . and saw what was going on. It was eye opening to them." The girls decided to focus on three points: teaching boys respect rather than blaming girls, giving parents and students the authority to determine appropriate clothing guidelines, and changing society's attitudes toward women. He recommended that they make sure to present the facts and a resolution and also "that you write everything down because it shows you mean business." When the girls met with the principal their organizational skills impressed him, he told Ronin, because they came with their notecards and a designated note taker. Perhaps because of their presentation, the principal was receptive to their concerns and agreed to explore the issue.

The girls and their parents decided that their campaign would be more effective if they had a digital presence. Ronin came up with several hashtags for the girls to choose from and after discussion, the girls had a formal vote and selected #iammorethanadistraction because, as Stella explained, "We were just seen as a distraction and so it's like we are not *just* distractions; there is a whole other side to us. You can't see it this way anymore. We are people. We are girls. We are not just the sum of our body parts." They also liked that the hashtag made the movement more expansive than just a dress code. As Elizabeth explains, it is also saying, "The underlying ideas are more than the clothes" and can link to issues such as rape culture and slut shaming. Finally, they felt that the hashtag included a built-in response to their critics; Alexa says, "If you say you are not a distraction, people can argue that you are." The word "more" is key to their stance; the girls reject the premature sexualization of their bodies by others and fight to live in their bodies without institutional discipline but they also have an affiliation with the sex-as-power discourse represented in both celebrity and body-positivity cultures.

Unbeknownst to the girls at Forest Park, parents at another school in their district were also struggling against the ways in which the biased enforcement of the dress code stigmatized their daughters. One of these parents wrote an article about the issue on a popular daily web magazine which linked to the #iammorethanadistraction Facebook page and then orchestrated a BBC News story about the girls at both schools. Once the BBC News story aired, the hashtag gained traction; the mainstream press began to report on it, and the district began to respond. Not only did the school principals agree to reconsider their building dress codes, but the Board of Education also began the process of examining its own more broadly written district dress code. The parents from both schools met with the district's lawyer who supported their concern; "There is no argument," he told them, as Becca's mother remembered, "This is a civil rights issue. You can't take out the girls or the girls with big boobs [from class] all the time because it is not equal education."

While the school district was exploring new language for the dress code policy, the hashtag began to blossom. Because the girls were still in middle school, they had restrictions on screen time and much of the initial posting was done by parents. They tweeted about their daughters being highlighted in the media as well as articles related to unjust dress codes. Then, young people around the country began to tweet details of their own experiences being coded for "indiscretions" such as wearing shorts, leggings, and tank tops. Tweets like "so I missed 6th and 7th bell today bc I'm showing 'too much leg' & can't do that in an environment w/ adult males," "today I was asked to tape together the sides of my shirt because of the one inch of skin showing" and "when you are not allowed to wear thigh length shorts and it is 120 degrees" were commonplace. Others posted pictures of groups of girls wearing T-shirts with the hashtag in protest of their own schools' policies.

Finally, both the school and the district eliminated the gender-biased language in their policies and pledged to eliminate it in their enforcement as well.[2] The new district policy, the revision of which was overseen by the student representative to the board, included the statement: "Enforcement of the dress code will be done without regard to race, color, religion, ancestry, gender, sexual orientation, gender identity and expression, physical characteristics, or disability."

A Developing Feminist Perspective

The Forest Park girls' involvement in this campaign has been monumental in how they are developing their comprehension of sexuality, gender, fashion, and power. Though they initially thought of their movement as limited to dress code, seeing the tweets and articles about their campaign, says Stella, "helped us [in] understanding rape culture and double standards and become more aware of it." The impact of the hashtag campaign also shaped the girls' understanding and appreciation of participatory activism. Critics have questioned the efficacy of hashtag activism deeming it slacktivism for a generation that wants a quick-fix, feel-good participation in social movements (Morozov 2009). For these girls, the hashtag and local movement together worked to cement their beliefs in the power of political engagement suggesting that there is a link between digital and traditional activism rather than the former taking the place of the latter (Christensen 2011).

For Alexa, the online dialogue that she and her father had with naysayers was impactful in that it allowed them to help others understand their position. Stella and Elizabeth were moved by the way that the campaign helped other girls around the country to become more aware of dress codes in their schools and to take action. Elizabeth felt that it was inspiring to see how "people would tweet with the hashtag and they would make petitions for their own schools and that could affect other people on a national level."

Though at the time of the interviews (which was prior to the 2016 presidential election) none of the girls was actively involved in any feminist campaigns, they felt, as Becca expressed, "I am more aware socially and my values are more broad" than they were before launching #iammorethanadistraction. Rather than focusing on activism, the girls are involved in feminist education. Stella completed a blog-based project that asked girls to consider "how modern society affects self-image." Through this project she has learned to explore body image "in a racial and feminist sense and how these ideas that we were trying to combat in #iammorethanadistraction affect a girl's daily life and how she sees herself and how she acts and how she dresses." Four of the five girls were also involved in a feminist consciousness-raising group in the high school where they were discussing intersectional feminism. The group discussions are helpful in seeking out social media and traditional media that is positive and feminist and in thinking through how to live a feminist life. According to Elizabeth's mom, "You can see that the light bulbs are really going on, now."

Not only are these girls establishing a public space for themselves where their voices can be heard, but they are beginning to understand the institutional relations of power that organize that space (Harris 2008; Keller 2012). As Eszter Szücs found of the girls she studied in a girl-focused website, the girls of Forest Park, "inhabit a different form of political agency that is based on a reinterpreted connection among individualism, community and politics" so that "political engagement becomes an essential . . . signifier of their distinct individuality" (2015, 677). As they begin to frame individual concerns within local institutions and, more broadly, within global systems and structures, they identify as feminist learners and teachers, sharing their knowledge with peers in a way that may alleviate the fears of those who, like me, have raised concerns about the individualizing, depoliticizing force of a girl power feminism steeped in neoliberal ideologies (Zaslow 2009).

Conclusions: The Power of Intergenerational Feminisms

When dress is considered in a feminist context, the purpose of the female body is always a consideration: Is the body an object of desire awaiting a male gaze or a desirous subject holding command over the gaze? Is the body an instrument of labor requiring flexibility and mobility? Is the body a political billboard staking its subjective position as agent? If so, what is the agent declaring its right to express? Moreover, how does a young teen understand her body and the ways in which others view it? These girls are coming of age in both a feminist and media culture that hails female sexuality and body positivity as empowerment. As feminist critiques of normative beauty culture and sexual objectification have been neutralized and incorporated into feminist iconography and mainstream media, female bodies are at once coded as powerful, sexual, political, distracting, agential, and in need of control.

The girls in this study live within the contradictory and conflicting spaces of a school culture that enforces a paternalistic, moralistic dress code, a feminism that celebrates female sexuality as empowerment, a capitalist beauty culture that commodifies female sexuality, and a body-positive discourse that seeks to embrace all bodies and forms of beauty. Significantly, the girls who participated in this action also live in homes with parents who were involved in second-wave feminism and other political movements, in which being a feminist is a part of the familial identity. This intergenerationally shared value system served as a navigational tool for the girls as they worked together with their parents and school administrators to create a dress code that meshed with what they had learned about being a girl. This case study challenges the logical assignment of postfeminist sensibilities to contemporary girls. The work of these girls and their parents suggests that while feminism may be wisely defined as occurring in waves for the purposes of classification, we must remain cognizant of the water metaphor which implies movements that have fluid ingresses and egresses through which feminist logics flow (Buszek 2006, 21). This movement spawned a nationally embraced social media activist movement as well as fomenting the emergence of five thoughtful feminists.

Notes

1 Forest Park is a pseudonym as are all the names used, but the movement is real and widely reported on in the digital press. Therefore, although the location of the action is traceable, I have made every effort to protect the identity of the girls.
2 The girls say that non-gender-biased enforcement has improved but remains inconsistent.

Works Cited

American Psychological Association, 2007. Report of the APA Task Force on the Sexualization of Girls.
Ballentine, Leslie Winfield and Jennifer Paff Ogle. 2005. "The Making and Unmaking of Body Problems." *Family and Consumer Science Research Journal* 33 (4): 281–307.
Baumgardner, Jennifer and Richards, Amy. 2000. *Manifesta: Young Women, Feminism, and the Future.* New York, NY: Farrar, Straus and Giroux.
Budgeon, Shelley. 2015. "Individualized Femininity and Feminist Politics of Choice." *European Journal of Women's Studies* 22 (3): 303–318.
Buszek, Maria Elena. 2006. *Pin-up grrrls: Feminism, Sexuality, Popular Culture.* Durham: Duke University Press.
Christensen, Henrik Serup. 2011. "Political Activities on the Internet: Slacktivism or Political Participation by Other Means?" *First Monday* 16 (2). Accessed on January 25, 2018. doi:http://dx.doi.org/10.5210/fm.v16i2.3336.
Entwistle, Joanne. 2000. *The Fashioned Body: Fashion, Dress & Modern Social Theory.* New York: Polity.
Gill, Rosalind. 2003. "From Sexual Objectification to Sexual Subjectification: The Resexualization of Women's Bodies in the Media." *Feminist Media Studies* 3 (1): 100–106.
Gill, Rosalind. 2007. "Postfeminist Media Culture: Elements of a Sensibility." *European Journal of Cultural Studies* 10 (2): 147–166.
Gill, Rosalind and Ana Sofia Elias. 2014. "'Awaken Your Incredible': Love Your Body Discourses and Postfeminist Contradictions." *International Journal of Media & Cultural Politics* 10 (2): 179–188.

Gleeson, Kate and Hannah Frith. 2004. "Pretty in Pink: Young Women Presenting Mature Sexual Identities." In *All About the Girl*, edited by Anita Harris, 103–144. London: Routledge.

Harris, Anita. 2008. "Young Women, Late Modern Politics, and the Participatory Possibilities of Online Cultures." *Journal of Youth Studies* 11 (5): 481–495.

Haughney, Christine. 2012. "Seventeen Vows to Show Girls 'as They Really Are,'" *New York Times*, July 3. Accessed August 21, 2016. https://mediadecoder.blogs.nytimes.com/2012/07/03/after-petition-drive-seventeen-magazine-commits-to-show-girls-as-they-really-are/.

Keller, Jessalynn. 2012. "Virtual Feminisms: Girls' Blogging Communities, Feminist Activism, and Participatory Politics." *Information, Communication & Society* 15 (3): 429–447.

Keller, Jessalynn. 2015. *Girls' Feminist Blogging in a Postfeminist Age*. New York: Routledge.

Laughlin, Kathleen A., Julie Gallagher, Dorothy Sue Cobble, Eileen Boris, Premilla Nadasen, Stephanie Gilmore, and Leandra Zarnow. 2010. "Is it Time to Jump Ship? Historians Rethink the Waves Metaphor." *Feminist Formations* 22 (1): 76–135.

Levy, Ariel. 2006. *Female Chauvinist Pigs: Women and the Rise of Raunch Culture*. New York: Simon and Schuster.

McKenney, Sarah and Rebecca S. Bigler. 2014 "Internalized Sexualization and its Relation to Sexualized appearance, Body Surveillance, and Body Shame Among Early Adolescent Girls." *Journal of Early Adolescence* 36 (2): 1–27.

McRobbie, Angela. 2009. *The Aftermath of Feminism: Gender, Culture and Social Change*. London: Sage.

Morozov, Evgeny. 2009. "The Brave New World of Slacktivism." *Foreign Policy* 19 (05).

Moscatello, Caitlin. 2014. "So . . . are you a Feminist?" *Seventeen* 73 (4): 122–123.

Orenstein, Peggy. 2014. "The Battle Over Dress Codes," *New York Times*, June 13. Accessed August 21, 2016. https://www.nytimes.com/2014/06/14/opinion/the-battle-over-dress-codes.html?_r=0

Pomerantz, Shauna. 2007. "Cleavage in a Tank Top: Bodily Prohibition and the Discourses of School Dress Codes." *Alberta Journal of Educational Research* 53 (4): 373–386.

Raby, Rebecca. 2010. "'Tank Tops Are OK but I Don't Want to See Her Thong': Girls Engagement with Secondary School Dress Codes." *Youth & Society* 41 (3): 333–356.

Sandberg, Sheryl. 2013. *Lean in: Women, Work, and the Will to Lead*. New York: Knopf.

Sastre, Alexandra. 2014. "Towards a Radical Body Positive." *Feminist Media Studies* 14 (6): 929–943.

Szücs, Eszter. 2015. "Space for Girls: Feminism, Political Agency, and Girl Culture on the Internet." *Women's Studies* 44 (5): 657–680.

Tolman, Deborah. 2012. "SPARKing Change: Not Just One Girl At a Time," *Huffington Post*, May 10. Accessed on August 21, 2016. http://www.huffingtonpost.com/deborah-l-tolman/sparking-change-not-just-_b_1506433.html.

Zaslow, Emilie. 2009. *Feminism, Inc.: Coming of Age in Girl Power Media Culture*. New York: Palgrave.

Zeisler, Andi. 2016. *We Were Feminists Once: From Riot Grrrl to CoverGirl, the Buying and Selling of a Political Movement*. New York, Public Affairs.

6

INDIGNANT FEMINISM

Parsing the Ironic Grammar of YouTube Activism

Sujata Moorti

. . . let's face it ladies. Rape, it's your fault.

. . . when you put on a wedding ring, it means that the guy that gave you the ring can do whatever he wants to you and it's automatically your fault.

The quotes above are from two YouTube videos produced in India and North America respectively, which use humor to mock stereotypes pertaining to sexual assaults. The two YouTube videos are symptomatic of contemporary social media productions which build on a long legacy of feminist reliance on the media to publicize and challenge the pervasiveness of gender-based violence. Bypassing mainstream media, feminists have created their own outlets—newspapers, magazines, radio stations, zines and so on—to articulate their vision of how to contest gender-based violence in colonial and postcolonial contexts, in the developed world, and across the color line. Over the past century, new media technologies have altered the form and content of these feminist media productions.

Social media platforms have recently become one of the most fertile sites from which feminist arguments about gender-based violence are articulated (Horeck 2014; Losh 2014; Loza 2014; McLean and Maalsen 2013). Culling from a larger project where I examine the feminist socialites enabled by digital technologies, in this chapter I hone in on two YouTube videos addressing sexual assault: The 2013 "Rape: It's Your Fault" video (henceforth "Rape") was produced by a comedy group in India to challenge prevalent rape myths, and the 2014 "Ray Rice Inspired Makeup Tutorial" video (henceforth "Ray Rice") which showcases Canadian comedian Megan MacKay's critique of professional athletic organizations' anemic responses to intimate partner violence. Both videos were seen by millions of viewers within the first year of their posting and were recirculated by other media, such as newspaper articles, television programs, and a variety of digital platforms. The two videos use humor and irony to articulate what I identify as an indignant feminism, an emergent feminist stance that argues forcefully for a feminist challenge to existing institutional structures and cultures of misogyny and sexism. In addition to spelling out the contours of indignant feminism, in what follows I tease out the visual grammar and aesthetic devices these YouTube videos deploy in order to make their messages relevant to local and global audiences. In particular, I isolate social media's capacity to telescope the local into the global and evaluate the usefulness of such a strategy to address gender-based violence. Overall, I argue that indignant feminism has become a critical means of contesting prevalent attitudes toward sexual assault in local and global arenas.

Scholarship on social media often oscillates between lavishing praise on their communicative possibilities and condemning them for their inability to ensure long-term social change (Fuchs 2014; Gladwell 2010; Novak 2016). My assessment in this chapter highlights the potentials and limits of forging a millennial feminism without borders through YouTube videos. I use the term millennial to signal a temporality of the new millennium, and to underscore the digital technologies feminists have mobilized. As a response to the forces of globalization, Chandra Mohanty (2003) argued for a feminism without borders. I extend this insight to the technological affordances of YouTube, which permit a millennial feminism to be staged globally. As I delineate later in this chapter, the globally circulating YouTube videos, however, do not engage with or respond to contemporary conditions of globality. Mapping the modalities through which these videos navigate the particularities of local and global feminisms I argue that social media offer a productive site for the articulation of an indignant feminism, a form of activism that aims to cultivate a transnational community of sentiment, a term I will return to later in the chapter.

The indignant feminism I single out in this chapter shares features with both the feminist politics and the postfeminist sensibilities that other chapters in this book investigate. However, indignant feminism, as I argue later in this chapter, is distinctive in its insistence on the need for a feminist engagement with a variety of issues, especially those pertaining to sexual violence and sexism in general. Indignant feminism reiterates the validity of feminist claims and does not lend itself to a discussion about who or what is to blame for sexual assaults. Significantly, indignant feminism revitalizes a transnational feminism and also replicates key features of neoliberal governmentality that are antithetical to feminism as a political project. The two videos I analyze gesture toward long-term structural changes but most of their energies are directed at individual solutions to address the problem of gender-based violence.

Working through these paradoxical energies of YouTube videos, this essay offers some insights into the forms of feminist socialities and solidarities that predominate in millennial understandings of gender-based violence. I contend that indignant feminism strategically deploys humor and parody not to gloss over but to speak across the radically different gender scripts that prevail around the world and takes into account the unequal geopolitical terrains in which the videos circulate. Indignant feminism taps into the participatory networks of social media to offer local communities fresh avenues from which to challenge understandings of gender and to mobilize a broader global audience to echo local feminist claims. Indignant feminism marks a move away from postfeminist sensibilities and yet it remains enmeshed within neoliberal drives, especially those that posit private solutions to structural concerns.

Mediated Feminisms

Feminist media scholars have documented the plurality of modes through which mass media have engaged with feminism. Over the last five decades, media representations have co-opted feminist ideas in the service of commodity culture, thereby producing a commodity feminism (Goldman et al. 1991). Choice, agency, and empowerment are the dominant tropes of commodity feminism, but they are each emptied of their political significance. At some moments, as Susan Faludi (1991) has documented eloquently, media products have become the site for the articulation of a virulent backlash against feminism, feminists, and feminist ideas. Since the 1990s, a postfeminist sensibility has dominated (McRobbie 2004; Gill 2009). The introduction to this book outlines carefully the signature features of postfeminism while other chapters have elaborated on the limits to using this term, especially in non-Western media contexts. As I illustrate in my analysis of "Rape" and "Ray Rice," the indignant feminism I document shares a familial resemblance with postfeminist sensibility but it is markedly different as well. I locate indignant feminism within a broader array of terms that have emerged to characterize the granular details of postfeminism: enlightened sexism, lean-in feminism, neoliberal feminism, empowerment feminism, and so on. Simultaneously, indignant feminism remains committed to a political practice.

Susan Douglas (2010) has coined the term enlightened sexism to describe the ways in which sexist humor has been revitalized in contemporary media culture. Douglas contends that a central premise of much contemporary television programming is that feminist ideals have already been so well established in U.S. society that sexism no longer signifies structural disparities, but could be deployed as a punchline to humorous effect. Highlighting a different angle of postfeminist practice, Sarah Banet-Weiser (2015) has documented the increasing prevalence of an empowerment feminism wherein media content incorporates some of the dominant critiques of 20th-century feminisms, addresses its blind spots, and attempts to fold in intersectional ideas in the service of commodity culture. Moving beyond media representations to workplace politics in the U.S. lean-in feminism, which is attributed to Sheryl Sandberg's (2013) book of the same name and the online communities it has mobilized, acknowledges the incomplete accomplishment of feminist goals. But lean-in feminism calls for individual, privatized solutions to redress structural inequalities. Each of these narrowly defined understandings of contemporary feminism parse the ways in which postfeminist ideology manifests itself in and through the media.

As Angela McRobbie (2004) has described postfeminism, these iterations rest on a taken-for-grantedness of feminist ideas even as feminist politics are undermined. The indignant feminism I document in this chapter takes for granted feminist ideas and feminist claims. From within this vantage point, indignant feminism highlights the continued prevalence of sexism and misogyny as they are evinced in gender-based violence. However, in a shift from postfeminist attitudes which may have glossed over the persistence of gender-based violence, indignant feminism captures the seemingly contradictory ideas about women and sexual violence that are vying to emerge at this historical juncture. It uses irony and satire to provoke anger and to mobilize renewed interest in attaining feminist goals (also see Lawrence and Ringrose, this volume). It seeks empowerment for marginalized and oppressed groups (victims of gender-based violence in this instance), but does not offer prescriptive solutions.

Most significantly, indignant feminism does not seek to convince people of the validity of feminist claims but rather cultivates a community of sentiment by inciting an indignation at continued inequities. Anthropologist of globalization Arjun Appadurai (1996) uses the term community of sentiment to designate a group that begins to imagine and feel things together. These are communities that could potentially move from shared imagination to collective action. Working from this conceptualization of a transnational community of sentiment that is generated by YouTube videos, I hone in on the forms of feminism they enable with respect to gender-based violence. The indignant feminism I delineate in the chapter is generated in the affective response YouTube videos produce in viewers, an emotional response that has the potential for producing activism. Teresa Brennan (2004) has discussed affect as a charge that precedes emotion and action; affect also contains an evaluation and judgment. The YouTube videos I analyze here contain this potential for action, inciting an emotional response, evaluation, and judgment.

Like other social media, YouTube has become a productive platform for feminists to facilitate a new set of conversations and exchanges about gender-based violence. The DIY (do-it-yourself) aspect of YouTube enables feminists a degree of control over the messages they wish to communicate. Yet, the global sites in which these videos circulate sharply limit their legibility; local gender scripts sometimes obscure the relevance of the message and at other moments the humor fails to translate. Despite these limitations inherent to the transnational circulation of videos, I argue that the indignant feminism articulated in them helps forge a transnational community of sentiment. While postfeminism was largely confined to Western media and texts, the transnational address and appeal of indignant feminism is markedly different. In what follows, I first rehearse some general information about YouTube as a social media platform. I then analyze the "Rape" and "Ray Rice" videos and integrate feminist theories of humor and irony to map out the possibilities of a millennial feminism without borders.

YouTube Feminism

Now a decade-old technology, YouTube has shifted direction and morphed from a social networking site designed to share amateur videos to one where media producers circulate their products.[1] The platform's history has been well documented by scholars who contend that when it was launched in 2005, YouTube was primarily conceptualized as an alternative to television, revolutionizing "the experience of lean-back television into lean-forward interactive engagement and pitted user-generated content against professionally generated content" (van Dijck 2013). But after Google acquired it in 2006 conventional media producers became responsible for the majority of YouTube content. These transformations are registered in the ways in which YouTube has identified itself. In 2005, its slogan was "your digital video repository". In the years after Google's purchase the slogan shifted to "Broadcast Yourself." Today, YouTube has no slogan. These shifts indicate the ways in which the platform's constituency has altered as a result of both corporate practices and audience use (Strangelove 2010). From a do-it-yourself site the platform now serves as an ancillary distribution site for media industries. Therefore, the two videos I analyze in this chapter as well as the arguments I make about indignant feminism reference a very small minority of YouTube videos. Both of the videos I examine could be considered as partially amateur productions; I elaborate later as to why I qualify the amateur status of the videos in this manner. Thus, the arguments I put forward here are not about the platform but rather about the forms of (transnational) socialities and feminisms that could be engendered by social media.

Today's YouTube functions like mainstream media soliciting advertising revenues. The most significant difference lies in the global reach and connectivities associated with social media. The platform proclaims that 80 percent of its viewers are from outside the U.S. and that it is available in 88 different languages. As I indicate in the analysis that follows, YouTube videos circulate transnationally; thus, a video made in India can obtain the same kinds of global audiences as one made in the U.S. In addition, the participatory aspect of YouTube makes it a valuable component of the contemporary feminist toolkit. However, once uploaded, the producers have little control over how the videos circulate. As Jean Burgess and Joshua Green (2009) remind us, YouTube videos populate websites, they are embedded in blogs, discussed on mainstream media and other places. Their spreadability, as Henry Jenkins (Jenkins et al. 2013) terms it, and the interconnectivities they facilitate are the key features I focus on in assessing its usefulness to a feminist project.

YouTube as a technology enables a communal simultaneity through the shared experience of watching a video. However, as Carol Vernallis (2013) points out, YouTube videos are polysemic. They generate different meanings depending on how and with whom you experience them. There is some variability in the reception of the two videos I analyze, but the indignation they generate is structured in the videos' narrative. "Rape" and "Ray Rice" are directed at viewers who are familiar with feminist understandings of gender-based violence. In their global circulations, the videos engender conversations about local concerns rather than about the Indian or U.S. event discussed per se. The videos incite a shock of recognition and familiarity which are integral to the "imagining and feeling things together" that are central to the formation of a community of sentiment (Appadurai 1996, 8). As the comments section reveals, the videos also draw viewers who "misread" the irony or contest the feminist claims. It is the tension produced by the connectivities YouTube enables and the misreadings that ensue, as well as the potential for multiple conversations, that make this social media site productive for articulating an indignant feminism.

Raising Consciousness

In December 2012, a woman was gang-raped in New Delhi and the violence inflicted on her and the ensuing protests elicited global attention. Unlike in contemporaneous cases, there was no video-recording of the incident; nevertheless the rape became a flashpoint for activism within India. Television and print media covered the activism and the plight of the survivor extensively (Rao 2013). The woman, whom the media named Nirbhaya, died a week later from injuries sustained during the rape attack.[2] In the immediate aftermath of the rape and her death, people in many cities across India organized massive street protests. They condemned the government and the state for their indifference to the violation of women's bodies. Even in the face of police blockades and tear gas attacks, people in New Delhi continued to take to the streets to seek justice and accountability from the state. The protests produced a curious juxtaposition of people with posters seeking the death penalty for the accused rapists and feminists who sought long-term cultural change, rather than carceral solutions for gender-based violence.

On a national level, the rape provoked a wide-ranging set of conversations about the status of millennial India. Unsurprisingly, some politicians and public leaders blamed women's new freedoms—working outside the home, going to the movies in the evening, socializing with men—for the violence. The gang rape became a site from which people rehearsed anxieties pertaining to globalization processes and the shifts in gender roles they had entailed. Others pointed out flaws in the archaic laws pertaining to gender-based violence, such as narrow definitions which excluded marital rape. Feminists in India, who had long worked on this issue, reinvigorated conversations on how the intersections of caste, class, and religious identity shaped understandings of sexual violence and criminality (Kapur 2014). They simultaneously drew attention to the ways in which the state, especially the police and judiciary, were complicit in maintaining structures of violence.

Amidst this cacophony of voices, observers wondered why Nirbhaya had become the catalyst for protests. They suggested primarily that the woman, an aspiring physiotherapist who worked at a call center, represented the aspirational model of citizenship central to contemporary India's goals of being a key player in the global economy. Notwithstanding all the problematic reasons of global capital that enabled Nirbhaya to become a flashpoint of Indian gender justice, Anupama Roy (2014) has argued that we should conceptualize the Delhi gang rape as an "event" which assumed criticality by becoming a part of an incremental accumulation of memories of gendered violence. December 2012 became a point of "convergence for discrete memories of violence which, while located in different temporalities, became momentous by acquiring simultaneity, contemporaneity and historical coevalness in the present" (240).

Events, as Veena Das (1995) has pointed out, become critical when they "institute a new modality of historical action which was not inscribed in the inventory of that situation" (5). The Delhi gang rape became momentous through the unleashing of new modalities of action, built through a convergence of forces, which were drawn from the past and reverberated through the present. Earlier rape cases, including custodial rapes, took on new valence in light of the Delhi gang rape as did all of the feminist activism against rape since at least 1972 (Kumar 2002). Within India, media coverage tended to gloss over the antecedents to this case as well as the feminist activism which had engaged with gender-based violence for at least four decades. On a global level, this event drew sustained media coverage that tended to highlight the brutality involved and recast India in familiar, Orientalist tropes (Bhowmick 2013; Burke, 2013).

Months after the "event," a Delhi-based comedy group, All India Bakchod (AIB), released a YouTube video called "Rape: It's Your Fault." The all-male comedy group AIB started in 2012 and in the absence of a robust standup circuit in India had been largely sustained through their YouTube channel. AIB regularly uploads videos on their channel addressing any of a number of issues such as corruption and Bollywood tropes; satire is the primary mode through which they address social issues. Their parodies and comedic routines have gained its YouTube channel over 1.5 million followers. Today, AIB has added a repertoire of live performances as well as a weekly cable television show. AIB's YouTube channel fits neither in the category of media industry production nor amateur. Their videos rely on the minimalist aesthetics of amateur productions even as they have come to bear the imprimatur of mainstream media productions.

As mentioned previously, in the immediate aftermath of the December 2012 gang rape, politicians and other public figures speculated on the causes of rape.

Apart from resuscitating discredited rape myths, the debates in India also drew on some vernacular understandings of female sexuality. I elaborate on these below. "Rape" was conceived as a response to the victim-blaming that became the official line of the political class (which was in strong contrast to the accountability demanded by the protesters). On its YouTube channel, AIB avers that "(e)very sexual assault case in India inspires a string of stupid and hateful remarks against women. This is our response to those remarks." It is important to note that none of the founders of AIB has any formal alliance with feminist organizations, but like the actors who star in the video, the group claims allegiance to a broadly defined set of feminist principles.

The 3:35 minute video, which was posted in September 2013, features actor Kalki Koechlin, who has cultivated a star persona as a cross-over actor. Koechlin has won awards for her roles in mainstream Hindi films such as *Zindagi Na Milegi Dubara* (Akhtar 2011) and in independent films such as *Margarita With a Straw* (Bose 2014) as well as in alternative theatre. In "Rape" Koechlin is accompanied by Juhi Pandey, who was then a popular VJ on the music cable channel, Channel V. In the carefully measured tones characteristic of a television news anchor, Koechlin begins with the question, "Ladies, do you think rape is something men do out of a desire for control, empowered by years of patriarchy? You have clearly been misled by the notion that women are people, too. Because, let's face it, ladies. Rape, it's your fault." Koechlin first appears on-screen in a sleeveless dress, sitting outdoors. Wearing light makeup, she smiles directly into the camera. Subsequently, Koechlin and Pandey take turns appearing against a plain white background. Initially the women appear smiling and seemingly docile. Shifting through a variety of outfits, casual and formal, and with varying degrees of makeup the two actors intone the various "scientific" causes of rape politicians had proffered and each cause is punctuated by the refrain, "It's your fault." But as they enumerate each "fact," Koechlin's and Pandey's faces and bodies are increasingly brutalized by disembodied hands, initially a pair and then groups of hands (Figure 6.1). In one scene, Pandey appears resplendent in bridal jewelry and a lavish silk outfit. Even as she speaks deprecatingly about women's desire to work outside the home, a pair of hand first snatches her jewelry, and then smudges her elaborate makeup. As Pandey intones "It's your fault," a hand yanks her head by her hair. Viewers do not see the person or people who inflict the violence.

Operating in the idiom of a public service announcement, the video creates the space for the re-articulation of some key feminist ideas about sexual violence. The video makes no reference to Nirbhaya but it makes sense only within the context of the 2012 gang rape. The video's title riffs on the feminist mantra "It's Not Your Fault" to underscore the ways in which patriarchy limits and structures the ways in which violence against women is rendered invisible. "Rape" received over a million views in the first week; it has since sustained over 6.2 million views from around the world.[3] The video elicited shoutouts from

FIGURE 6.1 Author screenshot from YouTube video, "Rape: It's Your Fault" (All India Bakchod 2013)

Ms. Magazine, Al Jazeera, *The Guardian,* blog sites such as *Jezebel, Racialicious* and *Huffington Post.* As is the constitutive nature of YouTube, the video was recirculated through a number of Internet sites as well as among activist groups. It is this shared culture that is central to YouTube or what Jean Burgess and Joshua Green (2009) term as the "YouTubeness" of YouTube. They argue that what distinguishes YouTube from other social media is its capacity to enable exchanges between its users, the agglomeration of casual viewers, regular contributors, corporate entities and core users.

In "Rape" the smiling Koechlin and Pandey recite the different excuses Indian politicians and functionaries offered as the cause of rape: provocative clothing, which in the Indian context refers to jeans or any outfit that could be characterized as Western, as well as the burqa or a spacesuit; the refusal of male protection through marriage; the consumption of chowmein; the use of cell phones; and so on. Familiar rape myths jostle with ideas that are endemic to the Indian political climate. The rise of the Hindu fundamentalist political party, the Bharatiya Janata Party (BJP), as well as India's rapid immersion in global capitalism have resuscitated revanchist ideas about Indian culture and tradition as well as gender roles. These are reflected in the reasons political functionaries offered as the causes of sexual violence. Some politicians believed that the consumption of chowmein (which was a standin for all "foreign" food) resulted in hormonal imbalances leading to rape. The politicians never clarified who consumed chowmein and suffered hormonal imbalances, the rape victim or the rapist. But, Chinese food was presented in these discourses as not just foreign, but as inducing criminal behavior (Figure 6.2). Similarly, women's use of cell phones was singled out as a cause of rape, as this technology was seen as expanding women's sphere beyond the home. The politicians' focus on foreign food and new technologies is akin to the logics of moral panics (Cohen 2002). Other politicians characterized gender-based violence as a "Western" import which was prevalent in urban centers but absent in traditional, rural India, Bharat. They urged women to seek male protection by hailing their assailants as brothers. The call of filial duty would eliminate sexual assaults, they reasoned.

"Rape" mocks each of these vernacular explanations for rape and rape prevention strategies by enumerating them even as the visuals depict the two actors' increasingly brutalized faces. Throughout, the smiling faces of Koechlin and Pandey performing standard femininity highlights the absurdity of the cultural scripts of gender. It is the disjuncture between the visible and the aural texts that produces humor and shock. The two women appear with prosthetic bruises but the bloody bandages covering fake wounds do not detract from the power of their performance. Similarly, the refrain "Ladies, it's your fault" seems to address women exclusively although the intended audience for the video is broader.

The video draws on a feminist grammar analogous to the one used by the Guerrilla Girls in the 1980s. It kidnaps patriarchal images of the feminine and re-narrates them to stage an oppositional politics while generating an uncomfortable

FIGURE 6.2 Author screenshot from YouTube video, "Rape: It's Your Fault" (All India Bakchod 2013)

laughter that helps raise consciousness about rape myths. By enumerating the absurd "facts" politicians mobilized to explain away sexual violence, the video incites derisive laughter (Douglas 2010). This laughter short-circuits any discussion of the validity of gender-based violence or feminist responses to it. Instead, the video fuels a call for action. By aggregating various causes of rape, each one more absurd than the other, the video enables what Linda Hutcheon (1994) has described as instrumental irony: "the literal meaning is not completely negated. It remains alive and kicking as one calls it into question . . . it helps breathe fresh and witty life into familiar political statements, slogans and sentiments" (58). The video insists that we pay attention to politicians' statements and challenge them rather than ignore them. The derisive laughter it generates sets the stage for critique, debate, and discussion.

"Rape" works in transnational and local circuits because of the shock of recognition it elicits as evidenced in the comments section, where several viewers compared women's rights in India, Australia, the UK, and the U.S. The video does not flatten differences to produce a totalizing or universal subject for feminism. Instead it insists on the specificity of the local, which is simultaneously legible and alien in global spaces. The video serves as a launching pad to think through the specificities of local patriarchies. For instance, writing in *The Independent*, Rachel Roberts (2013) addressed the video not to present India as alien but to foreground the prevalence of sexual assaults in the UK and the absence of state accountability. The indignant feminism of "Rape" does not seek to write back to patriarchy, but rather the video stages a writing to and a talking to a transnational community of feminists.

In its global circulations, the video's legibility lies not in the immediate translation of vernacular rape myths but rather on the ways in which it recapitulates key feminist insights and mobilizes laughter. In her canonical essay "Laugh of the Medusa," Hélène Cixous (1976) signals the importance of laughter to craft not just a resistance to patriarchy but to constitute a new, anti-patriarchal language. Luce Irigaray (1985) similarly notes that laughter can be the first stage of liberation from subjugation. She insists:

> One must assume the feminine role deliberately, which means already to convert a form of subordination into an affirmation, and thus to begin to thwart it. Whereas a direct feminine challenge to this condition means demanding to speak as a (masculine) subject . . . To play with mimesis is, thus, for a woman, to try to recover the place of her exploitation by discourse, without allowing herself to be simply reduced to it. It means to resubmit herself . . . to ideas, in particular to ideas about herself, that are elaborated in/by a masculine logic, but so as to make it visible, by an effect of playful repetition, what was supposed to remain invisible: the cover-up of a possible operation of the feminine in language.

(76)

Humor can shift away from or disrupt patriarchal language and move towards a language in which women (as themselves or as a class) can speak. "Rape" with its repeated intonation of "It's your fault" exemplifies some of these resistance strategies. As Irigaray instructs, both Koechlin and Pandey mimic earnest and sincere femininity. They assert that women are to blame for rape unconditionally because, even if men were responsible for the actions, because women give birth to men, "ladies, it's your fault." Such claims even as the two actors perform a docile femininity helps makes the humor of this video legible locally and globally. Postfeminist scholarship suggests that women perform normative femininity in order to achieve individual success and recognition in public and private spheres. In this instance, I contend that there is a political charge to the actors' performance of normative femininity. Their seemingly docile appearance allows them to be heard and to activate viewers' indignation.

After rehearsing the different ways in which public figures reinforce rape myths, the video turns to the institutional impediments to gender justice. Towards the conclusion of the video, Koechlin suggests that "if you are tired of being humiliated by rape, you can go to the cops and be humiliated by them instead." On screen, she is shown speaking to a uniformed police officer; her by-now battered and bruised body reinforces the complacent femininity of her voice which shifts into a lower and quieter register. The police officer asks her whether there were any boys with her when she went out. When she says no, he questions her on her decision to be out late at night alone. Koechlin's character quickly clarifies that she was with some boys, at which point the police officer ripostes that "you were with boys that night, so what will happen?" And Koechlin confesses to the officer that it's her fault. The video ends with a range of women appearing in close up and speaking into the camera, "It's my fault." This series of voices helps locate this discussion outside the narrow confines of elite circles and introduces a plurality of experiences. After the credits, the video enjoins viewers, "Stop blaming the victim."

The AIB video was made by a small group of comedians as a response to the prevalent "rape culture." It does not seek to represent Indian women. Rather, through its parody it holds all viewers accountable to challenge rape myths. It is this aspect which lends "Rape" its affective charge. The video has the potential to jolt feminist viewers into action, to evaluate and offer judgment. It is through the shared sense of recognition and desire for change that the video cultivates a transnational community of feminists. The second video I analyze in this chapter shifts our attention to the West and adopts a different approach to parody and the ways to tackle gender-based violence.

Tackling Football

Makeup tutorials have gained a significant following on YouTube, especially among a female-identified audience. These videos exemplify how the technology of YouTube has breathed new life into social practices that appeared to have lost traction in the new millennium. YouTube makeup tutorials exemplify the enlightened sexism Douglas has documented and which I referenced earlier in the chapter. The videos have helped revive a feminine culture that seems to hark back to a prefeminist time and yet are lodged firmly in a postfeminist performance of normative femininity. Makeup tutorials focus on using cosmetics to create the illusion of perfection and adhere to narrowly defined beauty norms. In the characteristic tone of postfeminism, the videos operate as though the cosmetics industry is divorced from cultures of sexism and objectification. On YouTube, makeup tutorials are positioned as sites of empowerment, entrepreneurship, and arenas where individuals assert their agency in a feminine idiom.

Beauty gurus such as Michelle Phan, Zoella, and Marian Castrejon, are a few of the people who routinely populate the most subscribed YouTube channel lists.[4] Their tutorials have helped them catapult their careers as beauty industry entrepreneurs. Irrespective of the amateur or professional status of the beauty guru, this feminized genre of video combines deftly the functional—how to apply makeup, an assessment of cosmetic products and skincare routines, and so on—with entertainment. Notwithstanding the country where these videos are created, they share a common grammar and signature visual strategies (Fischer 2014; Wotanis and McMillan 2014). The tutorials are recorded in a bedroom or bathroom, or a place staged to look like one, and are often produced by the guru herself. The beauty guru sits in front of the camera or monitor, which takes the place of a mirror, and speaks directly to the viewer, offering step-by-step instructions and she typically displays the product that is being used and its specifications (often in a close-up shot) before applying it. Similarly, the guru displays the color of a product by applying it to the back of her hand to show its effect on skin. These videos document the transformation of a person's appearance and include aesthetic assessments about normative beauty standards. YouTube beauty tutorials are vehicles through which hegemonic norms of femininity are reinforced and women are urged to invest in consumer culture.

Much like the actors in "Rape," beauty gurus adhere to cultural scripts of gender, both in appearance and their approach to the tutorial. While most of the videos in this genre are sincere tutorials, a few gurus have used the format to articulate an indignant feminism. Megan MacKay, a Canadian comedian with a YouTube channel, deploys the grammar of the makeup tutorial to produce satire. She uses the step-by-step format to offer a feminist critique of current affairs. For instance, in 2014, the private corporation Hobby Lobby successfully appealed to the Supreme Court that it should be exempted from offering insurance coverage for contraception on the grounds of religious freedom. MacKay produced a makeup tutorial for "Christian extremists" where she was able to infuse a feminist critique of the religious exemption clause as well as of gender scripts in fundamentalist communities.

I have isolated one video she made in September 2014, "Ray Rice Inspired Makeup Tutorial," to illustrate the indignant feminism these faux tutorials articulate. Early in 2014, professional football player Ray Rice and his fiancée Janay Palmer were arrested following an altercation in Atlantic City, New Jersey. Subsequently, a celebrity website circulated surveillance footage which showed Ray Rice assault his fiancée, knock her unconscious, and drag her out of an elevator. While the police and legal system addressed the assault, the National Football League (NFL), the governing athletic body, described it as a "serious matter." A grand jury indicted Rice with assault but instead of a prison sentence asked him to perform community service. Initially, the NFL suspended Rice for two games in the 2014 season. His team, the Baltimore Ravens, terminated his contract in September and the NFL suspended him from the league only to reverse their decision. The Ray Rice incident became one of several instances where the NFL's approach to intimate partner violence seemed insufficient.

MacKay addressed this perceived indifference to intimate partner violence in her 3-minute long video created in "honor of this vicious and horrific act of violence." Following the grammar of makeup tutorials, MacKay begins with a foundation called NFL which she claims she really likes because "it will literally cover up anything, just to save face." She proceeds through every step of the makeup process inserting acerbic remarks about the NFL and Ray Rice. She declares that her eye shadow is #27, because it was Ray Rice's jersey number for the Baltimore Ravens or was his former jersey number: "It is so hard to get used to people getting fired for doing bad things." Her feminist critique is integrated with the instructions she offers. For instance, in a step describing the use of eyeliner, she suggests it should be applied all around the eye as though it were a wedding ring. "And think about it, when you put on a wedding ring, it means that the guy that gave you the ring can do whatever he wants to you and it's automatically your fault," she adds.

Throughout the video, MacKay adopts the earnest tone and gestures which are the norm for makeup tutorials, displaying the colors she is using and the precise ways in which she uses different cosmetics. After satirizing the NFL and Ray Rice for the majority of the video she concludes with a call to activism. She recommends the use of a lipstick called "We can do better." She ends the video in a somber voice, "Millions of North American women are violently or verbally assaulted by their domestic partner, and we find reasons not to help them . . . Remember there is always an alternative to covering up violence. You don't have to be like the NFL." More than "Rape" MacKay's video taps into the connectivities that are constitutive of YouTube. Her site includes information about a number of organizations that address spousal abuse and intimate partner violence; her site also uses a number of tags that permit users to watch other videos that address similar issues. Through the insertion of factual information, MacKay's video uses YouTube technology differently than AIB does.

She does not rouse people to take action as much as she uses parody to make information available to her audience. Her YouTube channel taps into what Vernallis (2013) calls the technology's "baroque obsessiveness." MacKay indicates to viewers that she is aware of the issues she has ignored in her video but by permitting links to other videos she broadens the conversation pertaining to gender-based violence.

Since it was first published in September 2014, the video has received over 3 million views. It was also circulated on news sites such as *Huffington Post* and *Ms. Magazine*. MacKay's use of the beauty tutorial is at some distance from the postfeminist sensibility characteristic of the genre. Instead of instructing viewers on how to cultivate normative beauty ideals, MacKay's video offers a stinging critique of social norms. MacKay manages to focus her attention on the NFL and its practices rather than on an individual player; the Ray Rice incident becomes a hook for her critique of professional sports organizations. The notion of the transformation of the self is central to makeup videos. MacKay uses this conceit as the staging ground for a critique of the structures and institutions that maintain silence on intimate partner violence. The hyperbolically feminine persona required by makeup tutorials also allows her to carve out a space from which she can articulate an indignant feminism.

In all of her fake makeup tutorials, MacKay presents herself as an unruly woman, someone who does not conform to codes of feminine beauty. Her acerbic humor further thwarts expectations of the makeup tutorial. In interviews MacKay has pointed out that the step-by-step format of the makeup tutorial offers the perfect setup for her punchlines. "Good satire takes a bad thing and says, 'This is bad'. Great satire takes a bad thing, pulls it apart and points out all of the specific reasons why the thing is bad," she concludes (Chance 2014).

Conclusions: Feeling Feminism Together

Megan MacKay, as well as the actors in "Rape," are representative of the unruly woman who transgresses, troubles, and makes a mockery of the disciplinary norms of femininity. Their seemingly docile feminine persona helps them launch a scathing critique of contemporary institutions and practices. They manage to simultaneously address local and global audiences, paying attention to granular details even as they limn the broad cultural elements that sustain gender-based violence. The indignant feminism in these videos becomes the staging grounds for the confrontation of differences (not their reconciliation) and humor becomes a key modality through which these differences are acknowledged and not domesticated. The two videos I have analyzed in this chapter use humor to enable a transnational community of sentiment, groups that imagine and feel feminism together.

Like Jessica McLean and Sophia Maalsen (2013), I contend that these YouTube videos revitalize feminism in new spaces. Their indignant feminism helps the proliferation of feminist principles on social media. These feminist ideas are not geared exclusively at a national audience, but also toward a global community to enable a feminism without borders. They speak to these two audiences quite differently but incite a feminist consciousness about gender-based inequities and consequences. In particular, they reassert the need to address gender-based violence thoughtfully and carefully. But they do this through satire and humor. Anger and outrage are recalibrated through irony as a key mode of combatting attitudes toward gender-based violence.

Both videos hail a feminism without borders through different registers. In "Rape," the diversity of women at the end declaring "It's my fault" hails a broader audience than the protagonists. Similarly, the McKay video, by listing the range of services available, draws into the fold of its critique mechanisms for resistance. The indignant feminism of these videos revitalizes a transnational feminist awareness of gender-based violence and its different manifestations, and points to the ways in which emergent feminisms are highlighting structural concerns and demanding a change not of the self, but in others.

Notes

1 On its website, YouTube continues to proclaim that it is a site to upload original videos even as it advertises itself as a forum for "people to connect, inform, and inspire others across the globe and acts as a distribution platform for original content creators and advertisers large and small." See www.youtube.com/yt/press (accessed on June 29, 2016).
2 Indian law prohibits the media from divulging a rape victim's name even if the person agrees to it.
3 Jean Burgess and Joshua Green (2009) caution against using views as a measure of a YouTube video's popularity. In this instance, I spell out these numbers to hint at the wide-ranging audience it drew rather than to make any claims about its success or popularity.
4 I use the term amateur cautiously for once individual beauty gurus have gained a significant audience, their tutorials are sponsored by the beauty industry and the do-it-yourself production aspects are ceded to professionals.
   It is important to note that makeup tutorials constitute a segment of the over 45,000 YouTube channels devoted to fashion and beauty videos. The majority of these videos are produced by women and illustrate what they buy and how they wear clothing and makeup as part of their daily routines.

Works Cited

AIB, https://www.youtube.com/watch?v=8hC0Ng_ajpY
Akhtar, Zoya. 2011. *Zindagi Na Milegi Dubara*. Excel Entertainment.
Appadurai, Arjun. 1996. *Modernity at Large: Cultural Dimensions of Globalization*. Minneapolis: University of Minnesota Press.
Banet-Weiser, Sarah. 2015. "Feminism in an Age of Empowerment: Popular Media, Gender, and the Economy of Visibility," Paper presented at the Society for Cinema Studies. Montreal, Canada, March 26.

Bhowmick, Nilanjana. 2013. "The Real Shame: India's Patriarchy Roars Back after Delhi Gang Rape," *Time*, January 18. http://world.time.com/2013/01/18/the-real-shame-indias-patriarchy-roars-back-after-delhi-gang-rape/

Bose, Shonali. 2014. *Margarita With a Straw.* Viacom 18 Motion Pictures.

Brennan, Teresa. 2004. *The Transmission of Affect.* Ithaca: Cornell University Press.

Burgess, Jean and Joshua Green. 2009. *YouTube: Online Video and Participatory Culture.* Cambridge: Polity Press.

Burke, Jason. 2013. "Delhi Rape: How India's Other Half Lives," *Guardian.* September 10. https://www.theguardian.com/world/2013/sep/10/delhi-gang-rape-india-women

Chance, Rebecca. 2014. "YouTube's Soaring Social Justice Comic: An Interview with Megan MacKay," *Flounce*, September. http://theflounce.com/youtubes-coming-sketch-comic-interview-megan-mackay/

Cixous, Hélène, translated by Keith Cohen and Paula Cohen. 1976. "The Laugh of the Medusa," *Signs* 1 (4): 875–893.

Cohen, Stanley. 2002. *Folk Devils and Moral Panics: The Creation of the Mods and the Rockers,* 3rd ed. New York: Routledge.

Das, Veena. 1995. *Critical Events: An Anthropological Perspective on Contemporary India.* New Delhi: Oxford University Press.

Douglas, Susan J. 2010. *Enlightened Sexism: The Seductive Message that Feminism's Work is Done.* New York: Times Books.

Faludi, Susan. 1991. *Backlash: The Undeclared War Against American Women.* New York: Crown.

Fischer, Tianna. 2014. "Makeup, YouTube, and Amateur Media in the Twenty-First Century." *Crash/Cut* 3: https://issuu.com/ucfilmsociety/docs/crashcut_3

Fuchs, Christian. 2014. *Social Media: A Critical Introduction.* London: Sage.

Gill, Rosalind. 2009. "Supersexualize Me!: Advertising and the 'Midriffs'." In *Mainstreaming Sex: The Sexualization of Western Culture*, edited by Feona Atwood, 93–99. New York: I.B. Tauris.

Gladwell, Malcolm. 2010. "Small Change: Why the Revolution Will not be Tweeted." *New Yorker*, October 4. https://www.newyorker.com/magazine/2010/10/04/small-change-malcolm-gladwell

Goldman, Robert, Deborah Heath and Sharon Smith. 1991. "Commodity Feminism." *Critical Studies in Mass Communication* 8 (3): 333–351.

Horeck, Tanya. 2014. "#askThicke: 'Blurred Lines', Rape Culture, and the Feminist Hashtag Takeover." *Feminist Media Studies* 14 (6): 1105–1107.

Hutcheon, Linda. 1994. *Irony's Edge: The Theory and Politics of Irony.* New York: Routledge.

Irigaray, Luce. 1985. *The Sex Which is Not One.* New York: Cornell University Press.

Jenkins, Henry, Sam Ford and Joshua Green. 2013. *Spreadable Media: Creating Value and Meaning in a Networked Culture.* New York: New York University Press.

Kapur, Ratna. 2014. "Brutalized Bodies and Sexy Dressing on the Indian Street." *Signs* 40 (1): 9–14.

Kumar, Radha. 2002. *The History of Doing: An Illustrated Account of Movements for Women's Rights and Feminism in India, 1800–1900.* New Delhi: Kali for Women.

Losh, Elizabeth. 2014. "Hashtag Feminism and Twitter Activism in India." *Social Epistemology Review and Reply Collective* 3 (12): 10–22.

Loza, Susana. 2014. "Hashtag Feminism, #SolidarityIsForWhiteWomen, and the other #FemFuture." *Ada: A Journal of Gender, New Media, and Technology* 5: doi: 10.7264/N337770V

McLean, Jessica and Sophia Maalsen. 2013. "Destroying the Joint and Dying of Shame? A Geography of Revitalised Feminism in Social Media and Beyond." *Geographical Research* 51 (3): 243–256.

McRobbie, Angela. 2004. "Post-Feminism and Popular Culture," *Feminist Media Studies* 4 (3): 255–264.

Mohanty, Chandra. 2003. *Feminism Without Borders: Decolonizing Theory, Practicing Solidarity*. Durham: Duke University Press.

Novak, Alison. 2016. *Media, Millennials, and Politics: The Coming of Age of the Next Political Generation*. Maryland: Lexington Books.

Rao, Shakuntala. 2013. "Covering Rape: The Changing Nature of Society and Indian Journalism." *Center for Journalism Ethics*, March 19. https://ethics.journalism.wisc.edu/2013/03/19/covering-rape-the-changing-nature-of-society-and-indian-journalism/

Roberts, Rachel. 2013. "India's Parody Rape 'It's Your Fault' Video Sends a Message to us all about the Ways Victims are Blamed." *Independent*, September 25. http://www.independent.co.uk/voices/comment/indias-parody-rape-its-your-fault-video-sends-a-message-to-us-all-about-the-ways-victims-are-blamed-8838787.html

Roy, Anupama. 2014. "Critical Events, Incremental Memories, and Gendered Violence." *Australian Feminist Studies* 29: 238–254.

Sandberg, Sheryl. 2013. *Lean In: Women, Work and the Will to Lead*. New York: Knopf.

Strangelove, Michael. 2010. *Watching YouTube: Extraordinary Videos by Ordinary People*. Toronto: University of Toronto Press.

van Dijck, José. 2013. *The Culture of Connectivity: A Critical History of Social Media*. New York: Oxford University Press.

Vernallis, Carol. 2013. *Unruly Media: YouTube, Music Video, and the New Digital Cinema*. New York: Oxford University Press.

Wotanis, Lindsey and Laurie McMillan. 2014. "Performing Gender on YouTube." *Feminist Media Studies* 14 (6): 912–928.

7

FROM PRO-EQUALITY TO ANTI-SEXUAL VIOLENCE

The Feminist Logics of Title IX in Media Culture

Sarah Projansky

> No person in the United States shall, on the basis of sex, be excluded from participation in, be denied the benefits of, or be subjected to discrimination under any education program or activity receiving federal financial assistance.
>
> *(Title IX, Education Amendments of 1972)*

> Sexual harassment of a student can deny or limit, on the basis of sex, the student's ability to participate in or to receive benefits, services, or opportunities, in the school's program. Sexual harassment of students is, therefore, a form of sex discrimination prohibited by Title IX.
>
> *(Revised Sexual Harassment Guidance, 2001, Office for Civil Rights, U.S. Department of Education)*

> A number of different acts fall into the category of sexual violence, including rape, sexual assault, sexual battery, and sexual coercion. All such acts of sexual violence are forms of sexual harassment covered under Title IX.
>
> *(Dear Colleague Letter, 2011, Office for Civil Rights, U.S. Department of Education)*

As is evident from the first quotation above, Title IX is about access to all aspects of education in the United States. Nevertheless, until as recently as 2013, media outlets defined Title IX as virtually synonymous with women's and girls' access to sports.[1] Coverage of the growth of, for example, girls' afterschool soccer leagues (see Longman 1999) and NCAA women's basketball (see Dick 1996) illustrates this connection, as does a chain of online and retail stores selling women's sports clothing named Title Nine.[2] In the academy, too, decades of feminist scholarship address the phenomenal impact Title IX has had on women's sports participation (see Blinde 1989; Francis 1993; Lopiano 2000; Kennedy 2010).

As others have argued (McDonald 2000; Heinecken 2016), much of this media and some of the scholarly coverage is celebratory, engaging a postfeminist ethos of "just do it" to champion the phenomenal athletic achievements of both everyday girls and sports super stars, and to define those achievements as evidence not only of girls' and women's physical capabilities, but also of their academic, professional, and heteronormative familial success (Vande Berg and Projansky 2003; Harris 2004). In short, the quintessentially postfeminist equation goes: "Title IX + sports = girls' and women's social equality and success."

In 2011–2013, however, the meaning of Title IX shifted dramatically in the public imaginary. No longer primarily associating it with the "can do" (Harris 2004) athletic girl/woman, media now depict Title IX as a tool to fight campus sexual assault, and they discuss how universities are (or are not) meeting the Department of Education's Office for Civil Rights' (hereafter, OCR) Title IX expectations. As I discuss in this chapter, this wide-ranging media coverage includes *The Hunting Ground*, a CNN documentary about the pervasiveness of campus sexual assault and young activists' use of Title IX to hold universities responsible for responding to and preventing that assault; and a nearly year-long discussion across various news outlets of Emma Sulkowicz and her feminist performance piece, "The Mattress Performance (Carry That Weight)"—during which time everywhere she went on campus she carried a mattress much like the one on which she was raped as part of her demand that Columbia University adhere to Title IX.

The association between Title IX and sports is simple and direct: sports are an aspect of education and therefore if someone is denied access to sports on the basis of sex, they do not have equal access to education. The association between Title IX and sexual violence, defined by the OCR as a type of sexual harassment, however, is indirect and requires several feminist logical moves to produce. Specifically, as I discuss below, the current governmental,[3] judicial, and activist interpretation of Title IX asserts that sexual violence is a form of sexual harassment, and that because sexual harassment creates a hostile environment, it impedes equal access to education. Title IX therefore holds educational institutions responsible not only to provide equal access to sports, academics, and all other aspects of education, but also to ensure that access is available by reducing sexual harassment/violence and responding quickly to mitigate its interference when it does occur.

In this chapter, I argue that this recent interpretation of Title IX as prohibiting sexual violence draws on emergent feminist discourses that contrast to earlier postfeminist media representations of the individual can-do girl/woman who has benefited from her Title IX-guaranteed access to sports. Strikingly, these feminisms emerge not only in student activism but also in government and judicial policy that defines the pervasiveness of campus sexual assault as a structural factor that limits equal access to education, media representations that accept and normalize this structural logic, and media celebration of organized, wide-reaching feminist activism leading to both policy and practice change on U.S. college campuses.

In the analysis below I ask: How did we get from "equal access" to sports to preventing sexual violence? And, what are the strengths and weaknesses of the mediated feminisms that emerge in this context? In order to answer these questions, I first discuss the Title IX policy developments related to sexual violence and identify the feminist logics therein. Then, I look at how mainstream commercial media mobilized and embraced feminist understandings of sexual violence as structural and collective activism as necessary. Finally, I turn to two short case studies of media depictions—first of the feminist activist figure, particularly as she appears in *The Hunting Ground*, and second of Sulkowicz and "The Mattress Performance (Carry That Weight)"—looking more closely at both the possibilities and the problematics in these emergent feminisms.

A History of Title IX and Sexual Harassment/Violence Policy

In 1977, five years after Title IX was enacted, a group of Yale University students filed a lawsuit asserting "that Yale's failure to adequately protect female students from sexual harassment and to provide an adequate reporting system amounted to violations of Title IX" (Suran 2014, 280). While the suit failed, Emily Suran argues that it "established the foundation for all future sexual harassment lawsuits against schools" (275). Subsequently, a series of 1990s Title IX cases definitively established that sexual harassment violates Title IX. For example, in *Gebser v. Lago Vista Independent School District* (1998), "The Supreme Court established the liability of an educational institution under Title IX for teacher-student sexual harassment if . . . an appropriate person 'who at minimum has authority to institute corrective measures, has actual notice of, and is deliberately indifferent to,' the sexual harassment" (Ahmed 2004, 367); and, in *Davis v. Monroe County Board of Education* (1999) the court ruled that a school "can be held liable in a private cause of action for student-student sexual harassment because the school board 'exercises substantial control over both harasser and context in which known harassment occurs'" (Ahmed 2004, 365). In the midst of these influential cases, the OCR released a Sexual Harassment Guidance document (1997, revised 2001) unequivocally asserting that Title IX protects against sexual harassment: "The Office for Civil Rights has long recognized that sexual harassment of students engaged in by school employees, other students, or third parties is covered by Title IX. OCR's policy and practice is consistent with . . . United States Supreme Court Precedent and well-established legal principles that have developed under Title IX."[4]

By the beginning of the 21st century, then, both case law and OCR documents firmly established that sexual harassment violates Title IX. The interpretation was not yet expansive enough, however, to include sexual violence. Nevertheless, during this time period the federal government was increasing attention to sexual violence in other contexts, giving a clue to how the OCR arrived at its 2011 interpretation of Title IX as protecting against sexual violence. For example, the 1992 Campus Sexual Assault Victim's Bill of Rights "deals specifically with the creation and communication to students of institutional programs, policies, and procedures designed to prevent sexual violence and to respond to it properly once it occurs" (Cantalupo 2010, 55). In addition, in 2007 the Department of Justice commissioned a report on campus sexual assault in which the authors found that "19% of undergraduate women reported experiencing attempted or completed sexual assault since entering college," the source (as I discuss below) of the widespread claim that "1 in 5" women will experience sexual violence before graduation.[5]

During the first decade of the 21st century, activists too were increasingly using OCR complaints to establish that Title IX protects against sexual harassment/violence. In her analysis of all resolved OCR Title IX complaints 1994–2014, Celene Reynolds shows that since 2006, the number of sexual harassment complaints has risen steadily, with a significant uptick starting in 2009 and then an even more significant increase in 2013 (Reynolds 2016, 24, 37). In fact, "by 2014, sexual harassment complaints approached parity with athletic and academic filings" (2016, 37). While Reynolds has not yet identified whether these sexual harassment complaints involved sexual assault, sexual violence, sexual battery, or rape, given the fact that the OCR includes these four violations under the umbrella of sexual harassment,[6] and given that, as Reynolds suggests, "growing social movement activity around the issue of sexual assault on college campuses might have contributed to the recent rapid rise in sexual harassment complaints," (38) it seems fair to assume that at least some (if not most) of the sexual harassment complaints since 2006 were cases of sexual violence, in particular.[7]

Arguably, the confluence of actual Title IX cases and feminist activism led to the 2011 OCR Dear Colleague Letter (DCL) in which the federal government—for the first time—explicitly articulated that Title IX prohibits sexual violence. In making this move, the document "fundamentally changed the way colleges and universities [would] treat sexual harassment cases" (Block 2012, 61–62). Specifically, first, this document is entirely about "sexual violence," including "rape, sexual assault, sexual battery, and sexual coercion," and defines "all such acts of sexual violence [as] forms of sexual harassment covered under Title IX," thereby requiring schools to rethink their sexual harassment and sexual violence policies. Second, the document introduces a number of new expectations for schools, including disseminating the campus sexual harassment policy; ensuring that the campus has a Title IX coordinator; addressing activity at "any location that is somehow related to the school" (e.g., off-campus fraternity houses or bars) (2012, 65); protecting against "retaliation as a whistle-blower" (Suran 2014, 297); and shifting to "a preponderance of evidence, or 'more likely than not' standard, a lower burden than 'clear and convincing'" (Block 2012, 67). Third, the document includes the frequently cited claim that "about 1 in 5 women are victims of completed or attempted sexual assault while in college," thus emphasizing how pervasive and arguably implicitly sanctioned campus sexual violence is. In short, from the federal government's perspective, in complainant and activist arguments and actions, and (as I discuss below) in media coverage, Title IX now indisputably protects against sexual violence. In the next section, I ask: What are the feminisms inherent in this protection?

The Feminisms of Title IX Policy

Title IX has always been a feminist law, in that it calls for freedom from discrimination, regardless of sex. The initial application of the law to college admissions and sports relied on the principle of equality and was relatively straightforward in that admission to a university or to that institution's sports program is *a priori* required for access. In this context, if an individual woman brings a Title IX case claiming a school denied her access, implicitly she is claiming that the institution excluded women in general. Thus, in relation to admissions and sports, Title IX's feminism is about equal access for women as a group, a legally protected class.

Title IX's feminism in relation to sexual harassment and sexual violence, however, is more complex, requiring that the courts and the OCR make several feminist interpretive moves to get from lack of access to education to sexual harassment to sexual violence. First, generally it is not sexual harassment/violence itself that denies access to education (as exclusion from a particular educational program would), but rather the hostile environment—created by the sexual harassment/violence—that excludes. For example, sexual harassment might make a woman feel uncomfortable in a particular class, or while playing on a predominantly male sports team, and therefore—because of that hostile environment— she cannot fully access those aspects of her education. This logical move is necessary because Title IX prohibits exclusion from education on the basis of *sex*, but it does not explicitly prohibit *sexual* harassment.

A second feminist interpretive move required for the application of Title IX to sexual harassment/violence cases is the fact that individuals, in addition to women as a class, can use Title IX to claim sex discrimination as a result of sexual harassment/violence. In other words, unlike sports programs that exclude women as a whole, sexual harassment/violence cases generally (although not always) involve an individual harassing a second individual. Nevertheless, under Title IX the school would be held responsible for not ensuring that the individual target of the sexual harassment/violence had access to education free from a hostile environment. I call this application of Title IX feminist because it links individual cases to an understanding of sexual harassment as a social problem for which the institution is responsible. Thus, in this context an institution not only must respond appropriately to an individual case of sexual harassment/violence (e.g., hold disciplinary hearings), but it must also address the context that made it possible for that harassment to occur, considering whether, for example, the culture of a sports team implicitly condones the harassment/violence and how harassment/violence directed toward a particular student might impact other students as well. As the 2001 Revised Sexual Harassment Guidance document states: "if a student, group of students, or a teacher regularly directs sexual comments toward a particular student, a hostile environment may be created not only for the targeted student, but also for others who witness the conduct." In short, the feminist logic goes, individual cases of harassment/violence occur in and are manifestations of an institutionalized culture of harassment/violence that impedes equal access and must be addressed in that context.

Third, Title IX's feminism has become more complex and arguably more powerful in its application to sexual harassment/violence because the word "sex" now has two meanings and therefore broader application. In the first meaning, "sex" continues to function as a synonym for gender, in that sexual harassment/violence disproportionally impacts women (and transgender people),[8] just as exclusion from admissions and sports disproportionally impacted women when Title IX was enacted in 1972. While feminist theory has thoroughly critiqued the cultural use of sex and gender as synonyms, shown them to be non-binary, and illustrated that both are social constructs (see Butler 1989; Fausto-Sterling 2000), nevertheless the application of Title IX to sexual harassment/violence as a type of sex/gender discrimination is a form of feminism that can be activated by people of many genders in order to seek social justice. Importantly, however, "sex" also now has a second meaning of "sexual activity," in this case sexual harassment/violence. In fact, in the 2001 Revised Sexual Harassment Guidance, the OCR uses a painfully anti-feminist example of "sexual orientation" to help explain this more wide-reaching interpretation, stating: "Title IX does not prohibit discrimination on the basis of sexual orientation," but rather only applies to "actions . . . of a sexual nature." Thus, "physical sexual advances" toward a "gay student" would count as sexual harassment prohibited by Title IX, "just as it would if the victim were heterosexual," but "if students heckle another student with comments based on the student's sexual orientation (for example, 'gay students are not welcome at this table in the cafeteria'), but their actions do not involve conduct of a sexual nature, their actions would not be sexual harassment covered by Title IX."

This clarification was simultaneously feminist and anti-feminist: the OCR accepted the feminist argument that "sex" has multiple meanings and that sexual harassment/violence is a form of institutionalized discrimination on the basis of sex/gender, but it resisted—and in fact worked against—the feminist argument that sex and gender are not only fluid and non-biological but also intersectional with sexual identities that exist on a continuum.[9] Nevertheless, I would argue that by loosening the meaning of sex in relation to both gender and sexual activity and by defining sexual harassment/violence as an institutional problem that is a form of discrimination, the OCR opened its logic up in a feminist way such that by 2016 it was able to reverse itself and define violence based on the fluidity of gender, not necessarily linked to sexual activity, as prohibited by Title IX. Specifically, as of this writing the most recent (May 2016) DCL states: "Title IX . . . and its implementing regulations prohibit sex discrimination in educational programs and activities operated by recipients of Federal financial assistance. This prohibition encompasses discrimination based on a student's gender identity, including discrimination based on a student's transgender status."[10]

Media Coverage of Title IX and Sexual Violence

How, then, have media dealt with what I am arguing are the complex, insistent, powerful, and still-growing feminisms in the now matter-of-fact relationship between Title IX and sexual violence? In this section, I argue that, like the government's treatment of this relationship, mainstream media coverage of Title IX evolved throughout the 1990s and into the 2000s, increasingly acknowledging the pervasiveness of sexual violence and eventually embracing feminist perspectives on that violence. My argument here is not that all media coverage was feminist; in fact, some of it was explicitly anti-feminist (see Pope 2012; Taranto 2014).[11] Rather, my interest is in exploring the kinds of feminism that did emerge in the media during this time.

1999 marks the first explicit mass media discussion of Title IX's relevance to "sexual assault." In her *Ms.* article about the then-ongoing *Davis* case, Annys Shin not only mentions that the assailant pled guilty in juvenile court to sexual battery, but also ends the article with a quotation from Marcia Greenberger, founder of the National Women's Law Center: "'If the court rules against the Davises in this case, school systems will have a green light to ignore sexual harassment and *sexual assaults* that occur on school property'" (Shin 1999, 33, emphasis added). It was not until five years later, however, that mass media engaged sustained discussion of sexual violence as a violation of Title IX. In the 2004 "Colorado scandal" case, Katie Hnida, a rare female university football kicker, spoke publicly of having been raped by a fellow player; and, following her public statement, additional women reported related assaults. Overall, coverage of this case implicitly assumes that the assaults did happen. For example, on CBS's *The Early Show* (2004, February 19), Harry Smith asks his co-host "do you get the sense that the athletic department doesn't get it?" Furthermore, the coverage explains and reiterates the feminist logic necessary to apply Title IX to sexual violence cases, sometimes quoting the 2001 Revised Sexual Harassment Guidance: "Sexual harassment of a student can deny or limit, on the basis of sex, the student's ability to participate in or to receive benefits, services, or opportunities in the school's program . . . (and) is, therefore, a form of sex discrimination prohibited by Title IX" (e.g., Brady 2004, C2).

With time, media coverage not only accepted this logic but also began to criticize universities and the OCR itself for not applying the law powerfully enough. For example, on NPR's *All Things Considered* (2010, February 26) Joseph Shapiro reports on an Indiana University case, stating that although a student, Margaux, filed a Title IX, and although the OCR "opened an investigation," not only did the OCR "conclude[] that Indiana University did not need to expel the man," but "between 1998 and 2008 the Office for Civil Rights ruled against just five universities out of 24 complaints."

Despite holding two major social institutions—universities and the federal government—responsible for preventing sexual violence, the report also uses Margaux and her story as an object of fascination rather than, for example, as a feminist agent of change. Specifically, the report ends with this ominous image: "Margaux is trying to get her life back on track. She's enrolled in a college in Chicago. As for the man found responsible for attacking her, he dropped out of Indiana University, too. Now, he's going to school in Chicago as well; he lives not far away. Margaux still startles when she sees someone on the street who resembles him." Heightening this sense of vulnerability, around this time media began to repeat the government-circulated statistic that "1 in 5 college women will become a victim of rape or attempted rape."[12] Of course, findings of the high prevalence of college rape are not new, nor is the "1 in 5" statistic surprising or revelatory for those of us who have long been working in this area (see Gardner 1995). Yet media *represented* this statistic as new and therefore contributed to the idea that campus sexual assault is a growing epidemic and a real and serious problem.

In short, over the last ten years or so, media coverage of the relationship between Title IX and sexual violence collectively offers a series of well-established feminist perspectives on rape: (1) sexual assaults do happen (i.e., women are not lying) and those assaults are in fact institutionalized and pervasive, (2) in this context Title IX is a tool against sexual violence, and (3) the government and universities are responsible for taking action. More recently, a fourth feminist representation has emerged: (4) the character of the activist college woman whose organized use of Title IX brings about these positive changes. Specifically, media have stopped emphasizing vulnerability following sexual assault, as in the case of NPR's Margaux, and have started showcasing action. I turn now to a case study of Annie Clark, Andrea Pino, and *The Hunting Ground* to illustrate this characterization in more depth.

The Activist College Woman: Annie Clark, Andrea Pino, and *The Hunting Ground*

By 2013, media suggest that activist women frequently bring about Title IX sexual violence cases, for example, defining a case at the University of North Carolina at Chapel Hill as "the latest in a series of . . . allegations against high-profile colleges and universities" (Pérez-Peña 2013b). Two activist women in particular became quite prominent in the coverage of the UNC case: Annie Clark and Andrea Pino. Both now UNC alumni, they met at UNC and worked with others to file the Title IX complaint. Media coverage depicts Clark and Pino not as victims (although both did experience sexual assault at UNC), but as activists, using Title IX to seek to improve UNC's response to sexual assault and activating social media, such as Twitter and Facebook, to build a national coalition of anti-rape college activists who "[learn] largely from one another" how to use Title IX and to "[go] public" to pressure their schools to improve and to "create a space for people to talk" (Pérez-Peña 2013a). The visual that accompanies this *New York Times* article shows Clark and Pino sitting together on a blanket featuring a repeated image of the U.S. flag, staring unsmilingly into the camera (Figure 7.1). Behind them a map of the United States shows dots for all the schools with Title IX complaints: "PENN STATE, NOTRE DAME, OXY, YALE, HARVARD," and others. Another image shows a close up of their ankles on the same blanket, displaying matching tattoos of "IX" just above

Andrea Pino, left, and Annie Clark filed a Title IX complaint with the federal government against the University of North Carolina at Chapel Hill for its handling of sexual assault cases on campus.
Thomas Patterson for The New York Times

FIGURE 7.1 Feature image from the *New York Times* story, featuring Annie Clark and Andrea Pino. Author screenshot from the *New York Times*, photo credit: Thomas Patterson

their heels. Thus, the article and the accompanying images make clear that these women are serious, that they are involved in a growing national movement, and that they are deeply committed to their cause, choosing to document their activist tool permanently on their bodies.

The Hunting Ground emphasizes Clark and Pino's activism, as well. The documentary—released in theatres in large metropolitan areas and then aired on CNN—defines college campuses as profoundly dangerous. The film opens with a montage of teenagers celebrating as they open emails notifying them of their admission, followed by a credit sequence over images of students and families on move-in day, as well as clips of inspiring convocation speeches. After establishing this collective joy, the film abruptly shifts. It provides frightening graphics, such as "more than 16 percent of college women are sexually assaulted while in college" and "less than 8% of men in college commit more than 90% of sexual assaults," as well as partial dramatizations of individual horrific stories of sexual assault and a montage of interviews with multiple women (and one man) who add that their university took no action and blamed them for the assault. The film confirms that universities are indifferent, for example stating that in 2012 45% of U.S. colleges reported zero rapes and interviewing former college administrators who state that colleges purposefully under-report sexual assaults. The film also addresses the institutionalization of sexual violence in fraternities and sports cultures. Using specific cases, the film claims that in fraternities a man's "behavior of being sexually aggressive gets rewarded by his brothers," and that sports programs sometimes offer an opportunity to sexually assault as a reward or a form of recruitment.

The film establishes college campuses as dangerous "hunting grounds" in less than 30 minutes, and continues to return to it throughout its 105-minute run time. In addition, however, in the midst of setting up this context, the film introduces Clark and Pino as the heroes of the film. Specifically, the film details how the two came together to research Title IX, to use social media to reach out to sexual assault survivors across the country, to file their Title IX complaint, and ultimately to educate activists at other campuses on how to file additional Title IX complaints. In interviews, they recount their use of Twitter and Facebook (and images show them using Skype) to connect with other sexual assault survivors and activists, leading not only to more and more individual stories but also to public protests, several of which appear in a montage toward the end of the film. As one interviewee states and the film suggests, "there is a revolution happening on college campuses across the country."

In *The Hunting Ground*, then, Pino and Clark are not just heroes, but feminist heroes, fighting sexual violence through collectivity and a savvy use of social media that connects activists nationwide. This depiction of the feminist hero-activist is now pervasive, with the extensive media coverage of Sulkowicz and "The Mattress Performance (Carry That Weight)" the most recent (as of this writing) example. I turn now to a case study of Sulkowicz in order to reflect more fully on the implications in the media's production of this feminist hero-activist figure.

Emma Sulkowicz and "The Mattress Performance (Carry That Weight)"

In April 2014, Emma Sulkowicz, then a Columbia University junior, spoke publicly about having been raped "on the first day of her sophomore year" (Warren 2014, 2). Within a month, the *New York Times* published a cover story about the case, including Sulkowicz's description of the assault, the fact that she reported the rape to the university after discovering that two other women had been sexually assaulted by the same man, the fact that the university found the man "not responsible" in all three cases, and the fact that Sulkowicz was one of twenty-three students who subsequently filed a Title IX complaint against Columbia and Barnard; and the cover story also detailed Sulkowicz's connection to "a new network of activists [that] makes shrewd use of the law and the media" (Pérez-Peña 2014, A1). Overall, this cover story depicts Sulkowicz as an activist both for speaking publicly and for participating in the Title IX complaint, stating for example that "Ms. Sulkowicz has channeled some of her frustration into action, appearing with Senator Gillibrand last month to speak out, and joining in the federal complaint against Columbia" (A1).

The next week Sulkowicz was in the *New York Times* again when a flyer listing names of "sexual assault violators on campus" was distributed around Columbia. While the article reports that Sulkowicz did not know "who was behind" the flyer, it also states that "she was glad that the names were now public." Then, on May 16, *Time* published an article written by Sulkowicz (2014) in which she describes her experience during Columbia's misconduct proceedings and her resultant trauma (including being "afraid to leave [her] room"), and holds Columbia responsible. Her article ends with: "The Columbia administration is harboring serial rapists on campus. They're more concerned about their public image than keeping people safe." In short, in April and May of 2014, media characterized Sulkowicz, like Clark and Pino, as an activist using Title IX to produce social change.

By the fall of 2014, however, coverage of Sulkowicz's activism stopped addressing the Title IX complaint. Instead, attention turned to Sulkowicz's senior thesis project, "The Mattress Project (Carry That Weight)." Initially, media took the performance piece seriously as feminist art, emphasizing its complexity and defining it as "powerful, indelible" (Grigoriadis 2014, 28). A *Time* article explains that the project is about the "burden that sexual assault survivors carry with them," and quotes Sulkowicz saying that the memory of rape is "everywhere I go" (Trianni 2014). In interviews, Sulkowicz also talks about how the project connects her to others when they help carry the mattress. In this context, she engages in "conversations with three [the number required to make the mattress easy to carry] people I've never met before who are all really interested in the same things I'm interested in and passionate about these same things as well."[13] In December 2014, even before the performance was completed, art critic Jerry Saltz (2015) named "The Mattress Project (Carry That Weight)" the top of the "Ten Best Art Shows of the Year," writing that "Sulkowicz's gesture is clear, to the point, insistent, adamant . . . This work is pure radical vulnerability" (110). In short, media coverage defines the project as feminist art, adding Sulkowicz's identity as artist to her characterization as an activist.

Throughout this 2014 coverage, media depict Sulkowicz as credible. Even when using the term "alleged" rapist, coverage includes details of the assault that make clear he used force, as well as details of the misconduct hearing that make clear that at least one administrator was ill-equipped to judge the case, coupled with the repeated mention of the "1 in 5" statistic[14] and connections between Sulkowicz and other campus activists who seek to address the "epidemic." As Vanessa Grigoriadis (2014) puts it in her *New York* magazine cover story (Figure 7.2), Sulkowicz, as well as Clark and Pino, are involved in "the most effective, organized anti-rape movement since the late 70s" (26), including public demonstrations that include "cover[ing Columbia's] Alma Mater's mouth with red tape and dragg[ing] dozens

FIGURE 7.2 Cover image of *New York Magazine* (September 22–October 5, 2014), featuring Emma Sulkowicz. Author screenshot from the *Columbia Spectrum* website

of mattresses onto the steps" of the library . . . "For nearly three hours, survivors—females and males, straight and LGBTQ—talked about their experiences" (116). On MSNBC a panelist says to Sulkowicz: "I just want to applaud you for your courage" and the host says "thank you for your courage on campus."[15]

By April 2015, however, when Paul Nungesser, the man who Sulkowicz identified as having raped her, filed a suit against Columbia University claiming that "Columbia failed to protect him from a 'harassment campaign,'" media reported the suit and began to depict Nungesser's version of the story alongside Sulkowicz's (Kaplan 2015). At first the coverage is matter-of-fact, depicting both Nungesser and Sulkowicz as credible. Concomitantly, however, the discussion of Sulkowicz's performance piece becomes more often about her art as personal, rather than activist. For example, a *Washington Post* article ends with a quotation from Sulkowicz: "It's ridiculous that [Nungesser] would read ['Carry That Weight'] as a 'bullying strategy,' especially given his continued public attempts to smear my reputation, when really it's just an artistic expression of the personal trauma I've experienced at Columbia. If artists are not allowed to make art that reflects on our experiences, then how are we to heal?" (Kaplan 2015). In addition, some media began to call Sulkowicz "mattress girl," and to describe her performance piece as "hauling around a 50-pound mattress" (Siemaszko 2015), which compared to earlier depictions of her as "courageous" and "activist" is particularly belittling. By the time Sulkowicz took the mattress to a graduation ceremony as the last day of her performance piece, the coverage was quite mixed, sometimes saying that she "def[ied] school officials" by bringing the mattress,[16] although at other times reporting that "the keynote speaker, Mayor Eric Garcetti of Los Angeles, alluded approvingly to Ms. Sulkowicz's protest" (Taylor 2015, A23). While some media stories still define Sulkowicz as the "face of a national movement" (Taylor 2015, A23) and state that "the mattress protest resonated far beyond Columbia's campus and inspired student activists" (Izadi 2015), others report on "#RapeHoax posters" that claim Sulkowicz lied about what happened to her and include details about other criticisms of her project and her decision to bring the mattress to the graduation ceremony (e.g., Miller 2015). In this *Washington Post* article, Sulkowicz is no longer a leader of a national movement but instead simply engaged in a "one-woman protest." Over time, then, mainstream media became much more ambivalent about Sulkowicz's activism.

Conclusions: Minding the Gaps in Emergent Feminisms

Overall, mainstream media coverage of Title IX's applicability to sexual violence produces a progressive narrative moving from shocking statistics about the occurrence of campus sexual violence to activism led by college women who seek to change those statistics and get justice. Media make clear that Title IX is a tool available to these women, and they expand from there to other forms of activism, including the use of performance art and 21st-century social media. As others have argued, social and mobile media can be incredibly powerful tools against sexual violence, connecting women to each other, documenting moments of street harassment (Rentschler 2014), and providing a space in which women can voice their experiences and social critiques (Keller et al. 2016). Yet, others have pointed out that social media can lead to virulent discursive assaults, including death and rape threats. And, in fact, this happened to Sulkowicz fairly soon after the media began covering "The Mattress Performance (Carry That Weight)," which seemed to decrease significantly her willingness to speak to the media (Miller 2015).

In this chapter, I have explored the feminisms available in Title IX policy as applied to sexual violence, as well as in media coverage of that application. The trajectory of the media coverage of Sulkowicz and "The Mattress Project (Carry That Weight)"—from overwhelming acceptance of Sulkowicz's perspective and celebration of her involvement in both collective activism and socially meaningful performance art to later depictions of Sulkowicz as untrustworthy and engaged in a personal vendetta—reminds me, however, to look for the gaps in these emergent feminisms. In terms of Sulkowicz, the attention to one case opened up the possibility of discrediting that case, regardless of how iron-clad her story appeared at first glance. At least when the coverage is of an individual case, then, it moves away from attention to the institutionalization of sexual violence and collective social activism to a "he-said/she-said" scenario that makes it impossible to sustain a feminist commitment to ending rape rather than a journalistic investment in reporting" "both sides" of a story and pursuing "facts."

Nevertheless, that feminist commitment does appear in much contemporary coverage of the use—by the government, educational institutions, and activists—of Title IX to fight sexual violence, and this is worth pausing over. Previous research on media depictions of sexual violence generally does not find those depictions to be feminist, including, for example, my own argument that late 20th-century depictions of sexual violence are overwhelmingly postfeminist in the way "women's independence [is] limited to their relationships to family and/or to an abstract equality with men" (Projansky 2001, 94), and Martha McCluskey's (1997) and Helen Benedict's (1997) arguments that media express "fear of feminism." Thus, the coverage of Title IX and sexual violence I discuss in this chapter certainly seems to illustrate a significant shift in media's support of feminist perspectives on rape, buttressed by remarkably feminist government interpretations of Title IX. The question remains, however, if a focus on one particularly powerful tool for fighting institutional sexual violence—Title IX—is vulnerable to the same discrediting that Sulkowicz faced.

Notes

1 In the Proquest Newsstand database, between 1988–2012, over 70% of Title IX media coverage addressed sports; whereas less than 20% addressed sexual assault/violence/harassment, and/or rape, with most years falling below 10%. Conversely, since 2014

over 50% of the Title IX coverage has addressed sexual assault/violence/harassment, and/or rape. In 2016, Title IX coverage addressing sports dropped to 17%.

2 https://www.linkedin.com/company/title-nine (accessed February 14, 2017).

3 I completed this essay before Donald Trump was elected, and thus before Betsy DeVos was appointed Secretary of Education and Candace Jackson was appointed Acting Assistant Secretary of the Office for Civil Rights. In a future project, I plan to examine how various forms of media are grappling with the abrupt ideological and policy shifts regarding Title IX and sexual violence that have been taking place since January 2017.

4 http://www2.ed.gov/about/offices/list/ocr/docs/sexhar00.html (accessed February 14, 2017).

5 https://www.ncjrs.gov/pdffiles1/nij/grants/221153.pdf (accessed February 14, 2017). The report continues: "Half (52.7%) of our sample had experienced less than 2 years of college. . . . The data show that . . . 26.3% of seniors [who are theoretically in their last year of college] reported experiencing attempted or completed sexual assault since entering college." Hence, based on this report, as some media suggest, "1 in 4" (not "1 in 5") college women experience sexual assault.

6 The OCR defines sexual violence as a subset of sexual harassment, and prior to 2009 did not separate these two issues. In 2009 the OCR created a code "Sexual Harassment (sexual violence)," but it still does not distinguish among types of sexual violence. Reynolds is currently working to identify the percentage of sexual harassment cases that are specifically sexual violence (personal conversation with the author).

7 Also see Pérez-Peña 2013a.

8 https://www.ovc.gov/pubs/forge/sexual_numbers.html (accessed February 11, 2017).

9 Unfortunately, I do not have sufficient space here to address the complexity of these feminist arguments. See Fausto-Sterling (2000), Rich (1980), and Crenshaw (1991).

10 https://www2.ed.gov/about/offices/list/ocr/letters/colleague-201605-title-ix-transgender.pdf (accessed February 14, 2017).

11 Repeated media criticism of the use of Title IX in sexual violence cases include concerns about due process for accused assailants and assumptions that college administrators are ill-equipped to handle such cases.

12 E.g., *All Things Considered*. 2011. NPR, April 6.

13 *Melissa Harris-Perry Show*. 2014. MSNBC, September 6.

14 Ibid.

15 Ibid.

16 *Good Morning America*. 2015. ABC, May 20.

Works Cited

Ahmed, Farah S. 2004. "Title IX of the 1972 Education Amendments." *Georgetown Journal of Gender and the Law* 361: 361–375.

Benedict, Helen. 1997. "Blindfolded: Rape and the Press's Fear of Feminism." In *Feminism, Media, and the Law*. Ed. Martha A. Fineman and Martha T. McCluskey, 267–272. Oxford: Oxford University Press.

Blinde, Elaine M. 1989. "Participation in a Male Sport Model and the Value Alienation of Female Intercollegiate Athletics." *Sociology of Sport Journal* 6 (1): 36–49.

Block, Jason A. 2012. "'Prompt and Equitable' Explained: How to Craft a Title IX Complaint Sexual Harassment Policy and Why It Matters." *College Student Affairs Journal* 30 (2): 61–71.

Brady, Eric. 2004. "Title IX Covers Harassment," *USA Today* May 26: C2.

Butler, Judith. 1989. *Gender Trouble: Feminism and the Subversion of Identity*. New York: Routledge.

Cantalupo, Nancy Chi. 2010. "How Should Colleges and Universities Respond to Peer Sexual Violence on Campus? What the Current Legal Environment Tells Us." *National Association of Student Personnel Administrators (NASPA) Journal about Women in Higher Education* 49: 49–84.

Crenshaw, Kimberle. 1991. "Mapping the Margins: Intersectionality, Identity Politics, and Violence against Women of Color." *Stanford Law Review* 43 (6): 1241–1299.

Dick, Patrick. 1996. "SEC Tournament Rivals Final Four's Intensity: Schools Have Built Winning Tradition." *USA Today* March 11: F8.

Fausto-Sterling, Anne. 2000. "The Five Sexes, Revisited." *The Sciences* (July/Aug): 18. Reprinted in *Women's Voices: Feminist Visions: Classic and Contemporary Readings*. Fifth edition. Ed. Susan M. Shaw and Janet Lee. New York: McGraw Hill, 2012. 121–125.

Francis, Leslie P. 1993. "Title IX: Equity for Women's Sports." *Journal of the Philosophy of Sport* 20 (1): 32–47.

Gardner, Carol Brooks. 1995. *Passing By: Gender and Public Harassment*. Berkeley: University of California Press.

Grigoriadis, Vanessa. 2014. "How to Start a Revolution." *New York Magazine* September 22: 26+.

Harris, Anita. 2004. *Future Girl: Young Women in the Twenty-First Century*. New York: Routledge.

Heinecken, Dawn. 2016. "Empowering Girls through Sport?: Sports Advice Books for Young Female Readers." *Children's Literature in Education* 47 (4): 325–342.

Izadi, Elahe. 2015. "Columbia Student Protesting Campus Rape Carries Mattress during Graduation." *Washington Post*, May 20.

Kaplan, Sarah. 2015. "Columbia University Sued by Male Student in 'Carry That Weight' Rape Case." *Washington Post*, April 24.

Keller, Jessalynn, Kaitlynn Mendes, and Jessica Ringrose. 2016. "Speaking 'Unspeakable Things': Documenting Digital Feminist Responses to Rape Culture." *Journal of Gender Studies*. Accessed October 24, 2017. http://www.tandfonline.com/doi/full/10.1080/09589236.2016.1211511.

Kennedy, Charles. 2010. "A New Frontier for Women's Sports (Beyond Title IX)." *Gender Issues* 27 (1/2): 78–90.

Longman, Jere. 1999. "Pride in Their Play, and in Their Bodies." *New York Times*, July 8: D1+.

Lopiano, D.A. 2000. "Modern History of Women in Sports: Twenty-Five Years of Title IX." *Clinics in Sport Medicine* 19 (2): 163–173.

McCluskey, Martha T. 1997. "Fear of Feminism: Media Stories of Feminist Victims and Victims of Feminism on College Campuses." In *Feminism, Media, and the Law*. Ed. Martha A. Fineman and Martha T. McCluskey, 57–71. Oxford: Oxford University Press.

McDonald, Mary. 2000. "The Marketing of the Women's National Basketball Association and the Making of Postfeminism." *International Review for the Sociology of Sport* 35 (1): 35–47.

Miller, Michael E. 2015. "#RapeHoax Posters Plastered around Columbia University in Backlash against Alleged Rape Victim." *Washington Post*, May 22.

Pérez-Peña, Richard. 2013a. "College Groups Connect to Fight Sexual Assault." *New York Times*, March 19.

Pérez-Peña, Richard. 2013b. "Students Initiate Inquiry into Harassment Reports." *New York Times*, March 7.

Pérez-Peña, Richard. 2014. "Fight against Sex Assault Holds Colleges to Account." *New York Times*, May 4: A1.

Pope, Justin. 2012. "Title IX Tackles Campus Sex Assaults: Colleges Are Applying the 40-Year-Old Federal Gender-Equity Law to Isolated Cases—but Some Object to Its Expanding Role." *Los Angeles Times*, April 29: A12.

Projansky, Sarah. 2001. *Watching Rape: Film and Television in Postfeminist Culture*. New York: New York University Press.

Rentschler, Carrie A. 2014. "Rape Culture and the Feminist Politics of Social Media." *Girlhood Studies* 7 (1): 65–82.

Reynolds, Celene. 2016. "The Mobilization of Title IX in Colleges and Universities, 1994–2014." *Social Science Research Network* April 20. Accessed May 20, 2016. http://papers.ssrn.com/sol3/papers.cfm?abstract_id=2767797&download=yes Also forthcoming in *Social Problems*.

Rich, Adrienne. 1980. "Compulsory Heterosexuality and Lesbian Existence." *Signs: Journal of Women in Culture and Society* 5 (4): 631–660.

Saltz, Jerry. 2015. "The Ten Best Art Shows of the Year." *New York*, December 15: 110.

Shin, Annys. 1999. "Testing Title IX." *Ms.*, April/May: 32–33.

Siemaszko, Corky. 2015. "Cap and Gown and Mattress." *New York Daily News*, May 20: 19.

Sulkowicz, Emma. 2014. "My Rapist Is Still on Campus." *Time*, May 15. Accessed October 30, 2017. http://time.com/99780/campus-sexual-assault-emma-sulkowicz/

Suran, Emily. 2014. "Title IX and Social Media: Going Beyond the Law." *Michigan Journal of Gender and Law* 21: 273–309.

Taranto, James. 2014. "The Other Side of Title IX: A Warning to Higher-Education Administrators." *Wall Street Journal*, April 28. Accessed October 30, 2017. https://www.wsj.com/articles/best-of-the-web-today-the-other-side-of-title-ix-1398707892

Taylor, Kate. 2015. "Columbia Act of Protest Extends to Graduation." *New York Times*, May 20: A23.

Trianni, Francesca. 2014. "Columbia Student Pledges to Carry a Mattress Every Day Until Alleged Rapist Leaves Campus." *Time*, September 3. Accessed October 30, 2017. http://time.com/3259455/columbia-student-pledges-to-carry-a-mattress-every-day-till-alleged-rapist-leaves-campus/

Vande Berg, Leah R., and Sarah Projansky. 2003. "Hoop Games: Narrativizing Identity in Televised Coverage of U.S. Professional Women's and Men's Basketball." In *Case Studies in Sports Communication*. Ed. Robert S. Brown and Daniel J. O'Rourke, 27–49. Westport, CT: Greenwood.

Warren, James. 2014. "Gilly Targets Campus Rape." *New York Daily News*, April 9: 2.

8

BLACK "RANTINGS"

Indigenous Feminisms Online

Verity Trott

> Aboriginal children; 95% of the incarcerated population in NT, 44 times more likely to be imprisoned in NSW #handsoffaboriginalkids
>
> *(Lui 2016)*

> Please, the only narrative most progressive sources were selling until today was an erasive one.
>
> *(Liddle 2016)*

In July 2016, the hashtag #handsoffaboriginalkids started trending on the microblogging site Twitter, accompanying physical rallies that were happening around Australia to protest the brutal treatment of Aboriginal and Torres Strait Islander kids in police custody. Indigenous Australian feminist writer Nakkiah Lui posted and shared tweets, adding to the online discussions and raising awareness about the issue. She also shared photos, documenting her own and others' experiences of being at the protests, showing solidarity with those affected by the police brutality and those who came out to make a stand. Many of the tweets encapsulate a few key sentiments that surround the issue of police brutality against Indigenous Australian children and challenge the postracial attitudes that are prevalent in Australian politics. The tweets made the distinction that while this is an issue Indigenous peoples face, it cannot be dismissed as one of Indigenous people's making, but instead a problem of structural inequality and racism.

Also in July 2016, the Yolngu woman Magnolia Maymuru was the first Northern Territory woman to make the finals of the beauty pageant Miss World Australia. Numerous mainstream media outlets also reported that she was the first Indigenous woman to be featured in the finals and had been "challenging the ideals of beauty" and "created a conversation" as one of the most talked-about contestants of the year.[1] However, Indigenous Australian feminist writer Celeste Liddle picked up on this incorrect reportage and took to Twitter to call them out for erasing the narratives of the two other Indigenous contestants who had made the finals in the Miss World Australia pageant that year, as well as the three Indigenous women who had made the finals the previous year. Liddle suggested the reason these women were overlooked (unlike Magnolia) was because only some Indigenous women are deemed fit to recognize. Magnolia played well into the role of a "traditional" Indigenous woman, one who would not wear a bikini and expressed cultural reasons for not showing her legs. In this case, Twitter provided Liddle an alternative platform to present a counternarrative that challenged the postracial and postfeminist discourse that led to the erasure of five Indigenous Australian women from mainstream media reporting.

This chapter examines the ways in which Indigenous Australian feminist writers use Twitter to develop and circulate feminist critiques of postfeminist sensibilities. With the proliferation of intersectional hashtags created by women of color, Twitter has been identified as an important tool in the effort to develop "a sustained critique of white feminism" (Daniels 2015, 27; Loza 2014). While social media sites have been praised for providing alternative and liberating spaces for marginalized feminist voices (Boler & Nitsou 2014; Halavais & Garrido 2014; Radsch & Khamis 2013; Shaw 2012), there remains a racial disparity between the voices that are elevated online and those that aren't (Nakamura 2002), with white feminists often given more attention and engagement. This chapter asks, how are Indigenous Australian feminist writers challenging aspects of postfeminism and postracism online, and what are the prevailing counternarratives about women, indigeneity, and feminism that they advance?

In order to do so, I explore how whiteness informs postfeminist narratives and illustrate how Indigenous writers are problematizing the whiteness inherent in much of the dialogue surrounding feminism in Australia today. While Rosalind Gill's (2007; 2009) analysis of postfeminist sensibilities is helpful, she acknowledges that her critique of postfeminism is developed from an Anglo-American perspective and further research into how postfeminism "recenters both heterosexuality and whiteness" (25) is required. This chapter aims to fill this void by examining how Indigenous Australian writers use digital media to critically intervene in postfeminist discourses and by modelling a form of resistance that mobilizes an explicit anti-racist critique. For this study, I conducted a discourse analysis of 800 tweets posted by Indigenous Australian feminist writers Celeste Liddle and Nakkiah Lui on Twitter to provide an understanding of what postfeminist narratives they encounter and challenge online. I initially collected 200 tweets from each user using the software NodeXL, which limits the collection of tweets to the most recent 200. A month later, I collected another 200 tweets from each user to make up 400 tweets from each feminist writer, and 800 tweets in total. Collecting tweets over the course of a few weeks was beneficial for providing a broader insight into the types of topics and conversations the writers engaged with and ensured that the results were not skewed by any particular event that might dominate conversation on Twitter at the time of data collection. However, this was nonetheless a purposive sample and not designed to reflect the entirety of their network but rather to shed light on some of the issues Indigenous feminist writers engaged with, the postfeminist narratives they encountered, and the ways in which they promoted their own experiences online.

This chapter begins by outlining the context of racial politics in contemporary Australia. It illustrates the tension between the Indigenous Australian community and the Australian government, as well as between Indigenous women and white feminism. It then goes on to highlight the inherent whiteness amongst online discourse and documents the ways Liddle and Lui challenge the hegemony of whiteness, drawing attention to some of the prevalent concerns Indigenous women face. Furthermore, the chapter analyzes how Liddle and Lui, as Indigenous feminist writers, challenge and complicate specific tenets of postfeminism identified by Gill.

Racial Politics in Contemporary Australia

Postracial narratives are at the core of ongoing heated political debates surrounding the call for Aboriginal and Torres Strait Islander peoples to be recognized within the Australian Constitution. The fight for statutory recognition has long been a struggle for Indigenous peoples and there are complex structural issues embedded in the law and public perception that inhibit and limit social and cultural recognition by the State (Povinelli 2002). The Recognise movement notes that the issue of recognizing Indigenous people within the Constitution has been debated for over 20 years and that the Constitution is written in a way that depicts Australia's national story as only beginning with the arrival of British settlers.[2]

The dominant postracial narrative, which opposes the Recognise movement, positions the explicit acknowledgment of Indigenous Australians within the Constitution as in itself racist, separating Indigenous Australians from white Australia in its distinction. Opposition to the Recognise movement argues that racial equality is no longer an issue and we need to move beyond race and unite as one nation. The denial of the recognition of cultural history, the belief that racial equality has been achieved, and the assumption that race is, as Ralina L. Joseph (2009) described, an individual, personal trait, ultimately work to re-enact colonial processes of assimilation cloaked in postracial and postfeminist narratives.

Joseph (2009) effectively outlines postracism and its link to postfeminism in the contemporary United States. She describes this ideology of post-race as the prevailing thought that the civil rights movement eradicated racism and that we can now move beyond identity categories of race and gender. She effectively debunks this "post-identity" ideology in her analysis of the racialized and gendered critiques that African-American television personality and former model Tyra Banks endured from tabloid media. She argues that in the U.S., race and gender are perceived as personal and individual traits or characteristics as opposed to "structural, institutional, and historic forces" (237). Post-race and postfeminist thought ignore the realities of how gender and race inform and shape our lives and experiences from an institutional level (249). Melissa Lucashenko (1994), in an article about the tension between Aboriginal women and Australian feminism, makes it clear that black women cannot separate or detach their Indigenous identities in the name of a broader female solidarity, and points out how doing so would be "assimilation by another stratagem" (23). The same can be said for the problem of Indigenous peoples remaining unrecognized in the Constitution and the postracial expectation that Indigenous people should detach themselves from their Indigenous identity to become united with the broader (white) Australia.

Addressing the issues that Aboriginal women face involves recognizing a multitude of factors that are at play. As Penelope Andrews (1997) discusses in her article focusing on the problem of violence against Aboriginal women in Australia, we must address an array of interrelated issues, including: "race, gender, the after effects of colonialism, the minority status of Aboriginal people, the unequal access to societal resources, the consequent unequal development of Aboriginal communities" (918). The reverberations of how these variables complicate women's issues for Indigenous Australians have not been addressed by mainstream feminism. Indeed, while the feminist movement has made some impressive accomplishments at a legislative level for white women, which are foundational to postfeminism's claim that feminism is now no longer needed, Andrews illustrates how these gains do not necessarily translate into successes for Aboriginal women. The focus of the feminist movement, Andrews identifies, has often revolved around reproductive and sexual rights, workplace equity, child-care services, and the condemnation of sexual harassment and violence. However, these issues have affected Aboriginal women in often racially different and sometimes even contradictory ways. For one, the child-care and reproductive rights pursued by the feminist movement do not take into account Aboriginal women's experiences of and struggles with forced sterilization and the removal of children from Aboriginal families (Andrews 1997, 930). It is in this way that gender does not act alone; rather, it is intertwined with the experiences of racism and colonialism that have intersected to develop the multilayered oppression that Aboriginal women have had to confront.

Interrogating Whiteness Online

In her analysis of "The Trouble with White Feminism," Jessie Daniels (2015, 5) identifies some of the ways whiteness is embodied in online feminist discourse.

Whiteness, she determines, is "socially constructed and actively maintained through social boundaries." She illustrates whiteness as "shape-shifting" and describes how it often has a quality of invisibility as it is often adopted as the default and allows those who are deemed to be white to be thought of as "simply human, individual and without race" (see also Dyer 1997). Whiteness has been, as Nado Aveling illustrates in her article about the challenges of learning to be a "White Ally," "simultaneously ignored and universalized and thus is both opaque and transparent" (2004, 2). Often, as Aileen Moreton-Robinson (2000) reveals, whiteness is unspoken, represented as the "norm" or thought of as "natural," the context from which to compare difference, and has remained unquestioned. Daniels argues that in order to become adept at critically analyzing whiteness, we need to begin addressing race and recognizing that white people have race. She contends that as it stands, race is nearly always pointed out by a person of color. With this in mind, we can turn to Indigenous feminist writers and learn from them as to how they are challenging whiteness, as well as how they interrogate race in online discourse. For example, Indigenous Australian feminist writer Celeste Liddle constructs her identity online as a "black feminist ranter" and continually refers to herself as an Aboriginal woman in many of her tweets. Liddle also explicitly labels whiteness when she speaks about people who are not Aboriginal: "white media folks," "white people," and "white dudes" are just a few of the mentions. Indigenous Australian feminist writer Nakkiah Lui, who is known for her wit and the comedy show *Black Comedy*, also explicitly invokes race when she constructs her own identity by using terms like "black." It is interesting to note that Lui often uses the phrase "non-Aboriginal people" rather than "whites" or "white people." This is indicated in her tweet: "Having non-Aboriginal people acknowledge the injustices and violence perpetrated against us does help. Thank you." However, she does use the term "white" in a few instances. This can perhaps be attributed to the complexities of intersectionality, especially given Lui's biracial heritage.

Daniels (2015) outlines key critiques of white feminism in her analysis of feminism online, and the rhetoric Daniels pinpoints within three case studies of white feminist campaigns helps illustrate the nature of digital whiteness and how it might present problems in a feminist context. Firstly, she highlights the basic tenets of liberal feminism as being focused around achieving equal access to opportunity for women and granting women the same representation in public spaces as men. She states that this type of dominant liberal feminism is based around the model woman as "white, cisgender, heterosexual, married or about to be, middle or upper-middle class, and working in corporations" (14). This is obviously problematic as it excludes and erases all women who do not fit such a model. Whiteness often remains invisible to white women and consequentially feminism has been instead framed by differences and positions of class, sex, age, gender, and ability. Lui emphasizes the pervasiveness of whiteness and challenges its normalization when she tweets, "The default human isn't White.

When applying your value systems to someone else, question what dominant experience are your values." Lui challenges her followers to become aware of the inherent whiteness that shapes dominant values and experiences, and provokes us to recognize the normalization and assumed white model that is so often taken for granted. Aileen Moreton-Robinson argues that the very epistemology by which postfeminism is constructed is intertwined with the "values and assumptions that make whiteness invisible, unnamed and unmarked to white people in society" (2000, 42). Instead, we need to begin recognizing that there are other forms of knowledge that have not been legitimized by white society. We need to interrogate and critique the assumptions contemporary postfeminism is based on and how it might be complicit in denying Indigenous women's experiences, concerns and culture.

Janell Hobson (2008) traces the ways in which whiteness is associated with "'progress,' 'technology,' and 'civilisation'," while blackness is situated "within a discourse of 'nature' and 'primitivism'" (113). Hobson illustrates the dominant scripts that continue to portray black females as reduced to their "'illicit' black body," and argues that power dynamics which exist offline are reproduced online by dominant media (112). Further, she argues that new media are perpetuating old ideologies and that this undermines the concept of a cyberspace in which we can transcend race, gender, and other perceived differences (112). Hobson develops a more nuanced discussion of the discourses of the "digital divide" that goes beyond simple issues of access. She identifies how the Eurocentric notions of "progress" and "civilisation," combined with colonial conquest and scientific racism, have worked to discredit and dismiss other forms of knowledge, silencing women and communities of color (113). By recognizing and exposing these power structures, she argues we can acknowledge the ways in which marginalized people are positioned as "outside technology" and can begin to reimagine their existence within technological narratives (114).

Further research must examine not only whiteness, but the ways in which it is articulated within online contexts to begin the process of making it visible. Hobson eloquently argues, "digital divides reinforce underdeveloped 'primitive blackness' while 'digital whiteness' reigns supreme in all its cyber-glory" (2008, 123). However, Hobson provides some optimism in relation to challenging these narratives. She documents how artists of color and African–American bloggers are reimagining and promoting counternarratives that portray women of color as embracing digital technology. While Hobson's research has a U.S. focus, the trends she identifies are relevant in Australia, which has a rich community of feminist bloggers. Much like the African–American bloggers Hobson describes, Indigenous Australian feminist writer Celeste Liddle also began carving out a space for her counternarratives on her blog, *Black Feminist Ranter*, from which she rose to prominence, before also utilizing the microblogging site Twitter. By turning to these spaces carved out by marginalized peoples, we can also begin identifying and racializing whiteness to enable a better critique and proper recognition of how whiteness shapes the postfeminist narratives in broader society. This in turn will help us recognize the complexities of intersectionality and how race inextricably interplays with gender, as well as class, ability, sexuality, age, nationality, and other axes of identity. Furthermore, an intersectional understanding of how race cannot be divorced from gender can begin to acknowledge and prioritize the issues experienced by Indigenous women.

The Sexualization of Culture

Social media sites have often been hailed for granting exposure to voices of the marginalized that may have never been previously heard and consequentially broadening the debate around feminist concerns (Radsch & Khamis, 2013; Shaw, 2012). As Amber Kinser (2004) argues, digital media technologies lend power to the "multi-voiced intonations" of feminism, which can enable a greater awareness of the complexities and diversity of women's concerns. However, these sites are not entirely liberated spaces, which is evident in Celeste Liddle's experiences of posting about Indigenous cultural narratives. Facebook in particular embodies white cultural attitudes and values which fosters tension with, and the oppression of, alternative cultural expressions. One of the white cultural attitudes that are perpetuated by Facebook stems from what Gill (2007) labels the sexualization of culture.

One of the tenets of postfeminism, the sexualization of culture, is closely tied to two other traits of a postfeminist sensibility: femininity as a bodily property, and a shift from objectification to subjectification. Firstly, Gill identifies an intense focus on women's bodies and the ways in which femininity is defined as an actual bodily property as opposed to a social structure. The "sexy body" is considered to be a primary source of a woman's identity and a source of power, empowering females with the charge of responsibility for all sexual relationships, and for men's needs and self-esteem. Furthermore, girls and women are given agency only insofar as they construct and present themselves as subjects that resemble the heterosexual male fantasy frequently found in media culture.

The sexualization of culture shapes the ways in which social media content is interpreted and policed. For example, Liddle posted a picture of an ancient Aboriginal ceremony that depicted two Aboriginal women from a community in remote Central Australia performing a public ritual semi-naked with their breasts uncovered, an image which accompanied the speech she had made for International Women's day.[3] Facebook banned and suspended users for posting or sharing the image because they deemed it to breach "community standards" of nudity. Liddle accused Facebook of only having a problem with female "nudity" when it is not sexualized. The hypocrisy of the Facebook "community standards" becomes apparent when there are many exploitative images of young women circulating with no consequences, while images of breastfeeding women or Aboriginal elders performing a traditional ceremony are banned.[4] The sexualization of the image documenting the sacred ritual clearly illustrates the pervasiveness of the postfeminist sensibility. It reveals that the presentation of the nude female body is considered unacceptable if it steps outside the bounds of the heterosexual male fantasy found in pornography as described by Gill.

Social media sites such as Facebook thus embody white attitudes through the enforcement of community policies that are developed and sustained within a cultural and social context in which a post-identity ideology is dominant. Twitter, on the other hand, has a significantly more hands-off approach to regulating content, which can both be further liberating for Indigenous women but also oppressing (Lewis et al. 2016). Twitter was documented as the most commonly used social media for feminist debates by a 2016 study that examined the online abuse of feminists as an emerging form of violence against women (Lewis et al. 2016). However, the same study reported that the most abuse was also experienced on Twitter. There have been countless documentations of torrents of abuse aimed at female Twitter users and, in particular, self-proclaimed feminists (Lewis et al. 2016; Matias et al. 2015; Ronson 2015). Twitter has remained impassive and distant in responding to its users' complaints. On the other hand, due to the open access of Twitter compared with other social media sites, it has become a platform from which users can speak out when experiencing censorship or regulations from other outlets. Liddle turned to Twitter to voice her discontent and challenge the censorship she experienced on Facebook: "My page is being targeted by fascists & MRAs again. Just received another frivolous @facebook warning. Going public in case I get banned again." Twitter becomes an alternative avenue that assists in elevating Liddle's voice and her counternarratives that challenge the post-identity politics Facebook embodies, as well as a space in which she can connect to and receive support from her online community.

Individualism, Choice, and Empowerment

Angela McRobbie (2004) outlines what she labels a "double entanglement" of feminist and anti-feminist ideologies that constitute postfeminist narratives. One particular tenet of the postfeminist sensibility McRobbie critiques is the centrality of women's perceived choice and agency. She argues that women are granted choice in so far as they utilize their feminist freedom to "choose" a role more aligned with traditional femininity. Within postfeminist discourse, choice is presented in isolation of any social, political, or historical context. Liddle and Lui challenge this postfeminist notion of choice and empowerment in various ways on Twitter. For instance, Liddle uses Twitter to promote an article she has written that analyzes the ways in which women's choice is a myth and how it works to enable the gender pay gap: "My latest article – It's time to dispel the myth that women's choices cause the gender pay gap."

Published on the *Sydney Morning Herald's* website on September 8, 2016, Liddle's article pushes against the statement made by the former Prime Minister of Australia John Howard who claimed that women play a "caring" role in society and thus it is unlikely for women to make up half of the government. Howard's statement is indicative of the postfeminist sensibility that suggests women choose to take on care work and he emphasized women's freedom and agency to deflect from addressing and improving female representation within Australian politics. Liddle is critical of Howard's postfeminist narrative that the gender gap is purely because women "choose" to do particular types of jobs, and that to fix this problem, the responsibility is shifted onto women to choose work in higher-paid industries. Instead, Liddle puts forward a counternarrative that legitimizes the gender pay gap and reveals the structural oppressions that have led to such a gap. Liddle quotes findings from the Workplace Gender Equality Agency and the Equal Pay Alliance that demonstrates the constant undervaluing of the industries deemed "women's work" and the discrepancies between the starting wages for men and women. At the end of her article, Liddle further challenges the postfeminist sensibility revolving around choice by considering why the disparity is greater for non-white women and begins to outline how we might approach the gender pay gap from an intersectional standpoint. Liddle's argument reveals how much of the overemphasis on individuality embodied by a postfeminist sensibility is actually shaped by the model of a middle-class, heterosexual, white woman. Some of Liddle and Lui's tweets therefore work to problematize and challenge the postfeminist narrative of individuality from a racial and intersectional standpoint.

Lui also challenged the overemphasis postfeminist and post-identity narratives place on empowerment when she posted a series of tweets responding to the controversial political cartoon by Bill Leak that was published by the *Australian* in August 2016. Leak's political cartoon illustrates a police officer holding up an Aboriginal boy saying, "You'll have to sit down and talk to your son about personal responsibility," and an Aboriginal man with a beer can replying, "Yeah righto what's his name then?" The cartoon essentially portrays an alcoholic Aboriginal man not remembering his son's name and implies Aboriginal people take little responsibility in raising their children. The contentious political cartoon was published on Aboriginal and Torres Strait Islander Children's Day. The postracial narrative that stems from the cartoon is one that overemphasizes personal agency and empowerment and, as Gill (2007) and McRobbie (2004) argue, critiques this agency in isolation of history, politics, and sociality. Lui challenges this postfeminist and postracial narrative of empowerment and personal agency when she draws attention to the history and experiences of Indigenous people during colonization in a series of tweets:

> Where was our self determination and "personal agency" in 1788 when the British invaded and murdered us? #WhiteExcuses #billleaksyoulose,

> Where was our self determination and "personal agency" when you stole our land and forced us into slavery? #WhiteExcuses #billleaksyoulose,

> Where was our self determination & "personal agency" when you forced us onto missions & stole our children? #WhiteExcuses #billleaksyoulose,

> Where was our "personal agency" when you didn't consider us human and wouldn't allow us into public spaces? #WhiteExcuses #billleaksyoulose,

> Where was our self determination and "personal agency" when you invaded the NT & took away our civil rights? #WhiteExcuses #billleaksyoulose.
>
> (Lui 2016)

With these tweets, Lui reminds her audience that personal agency and empowerment should not be judged in isolation of experience and history, and challenges the erasive narratives of postracism and postfeminism by recounting the trauma of the past. Lui argues that the shift to this focus on self-determination and personal agency is a way for white people to deflect accountability in relation to the contemporary issues Indigenous communities struggle with that are inextricably tied to colonialism.

Liddle also uses Twitter to engage in the debate surrounding the Bill Leak cartoon. Liddle's tweets in relation to the wider debate help reveal the diversity and varied beliefs within the Indigenous community and work to challenge the postracial and postfeminist narratives that homogenize Indigenous communities. Liddle is a self-proclaimed progressive and responds to comments about the cartoon made by conservative and right-wing Indigenous men. In a series of tweets, she emphasizes her identity as an Aboriginal feminist and the twofold struggle she faces from a racial and gendered intersection, not just from white men and women, but also from Indigenous men:

> The continual claim by certain members of the indig right that the indig left are trying to preserve traditional culture to the determent [sic]

> 2. of Aboriginal women would be hilarious if it weren't so dangerous. Self determination and the right to culture is not about preserving

> 3. harmful practices. It's about our rights to autonomy and respect. I hardly think myself, as an avowed feminist and marriage abolitionist

4. is going to be standing up for the right to "promised" brides or be okay with culturally-excused rape any time soon. When I say "smash

5. the patriarchy" I actually mean, all the patriarchy. It's really not that difficult to understand. So why doesn't The Australian get it?

(Liddle 2016)

Liddle's tweets capture the pressures of assimilation under the guise of gender equality, and the dismissal of the impacts racism and colonialism have had in the continued oppression of Aboriginal women. Her tweets challenge the overemphasis placed on individuality and empowerment when she makes it clear that Aboriginal women are still fighting for their personal agency and autonomy. She also confronts the postfeminist notion of choice and agency when she foregrounds how the right to culture is an issue of autonomy and its denial is an act of oppression.

Another element of the post-identity politics that ties into McRobbie's notion of a "double entanglement" relating to the overemphasis of individuality and personal agency is the refusal to recognize racial difference, causing the reduction of racial identities and the homogenization of Indigenous people. Joseph (2011) describes how a post-identity ideology allows women of color agency only insofar as they are representing the success and freedom of a post-race world. The body of color is held up as a symbol of progress and achievement of equality, whilst difference and structural inequalities are silenced by post-identity sensibilities (Joseph 2011). Stemming from this postracial narrative is what Bronwyn Fredericks labels "casual accommodation" as well as the issues of tokenism (2010, 547). Indigenous women are often invited to attend events, to be a guest speaker, or to contribute some work that highlights aspects of Indigenous culture. Both Liddle and Lui express frustration at the expectations and responsibilities they are charged with when asked to speak at events or frequently asked questions about Indigenous culture. Fredericks argues that the invitations offered to Aboriginal women to speak to and participate within the realm of Australian women is an attempt to "accommodate" as opposed to genuine "inclusion" (2010, 546). Indigenous women are often asked to speak, in the guise of making space for them, to provide white people answers about their culture. Lui echoes the reality of this experience when she tweets, "Non-Aboriginals! If you have a q abt [sic] Aboriginal community/culture, try Google? Don't contact random Aboriginals & expect them to answer for you!" What can be drawn from this tweet is the issue surrounding how Aboriginal women are tasked with the responsibility of educating white people about their racism and Indigenous culture, further removing accountability from white people and shifting the burden onto Indigenous peoples.

Aboriginal women are charged with the responsibility of speaking for all Indigenous women by the broader society. Accompanying the postracial homogenization of Indigenous people is the expectation that Aboriginal women must represent and embody the exotic elements of Indigenous cultures, which are pleasing to white Australians. White people are often interested or curious about the spiritual or exotic elements of Aboriginal culture, or what Fredericks labels the "pretty business" (2010, 546). Celeste Liddle echoes this, highlighting how people are often not so much interested in hearing about her experiences and reality as an Indigenous woman, as they are theoretically curious about the exotic, "pretty" elements that make up Aboriginal culture. She draws attention to this when she sarcastically tweets, "I'm intrigued with white people and find their culture fascinating. Can anyone recommend any books I can read to learn more?" Liddle challenges the reductive and romanticized perception of Indigenous culture promoted by postfeminist narratives.

Celeste Liddle's above tweet also draws attention to the ways in which humour is employed as a tactic to challenge dominant postfeminist narratives (see also Lawrence and Ringrose, this collection). This is also evident in the comedy television series *Black Comedy* co-written by and featuring Nakkiah Lui. Gill discusses how irony is a characteristic of a postfeminist media culture and is used to distance oneself from a particular belief at a time where it is deemed "uncool" to be passionate about something (2007, 20). However, this same technique is re-employed to combat and challenge postfeminist narratives as we can see by both Liddle's tweets and the skits that feature on *Black Comedy*. Audrey Bilger, in her book *Laughing Feminism* (2002), argues that comedy and humour can both be used for subversive ends whilst also being utilized for conservative ends to preserve the status quo. She contends that humour can be a vehicle for delivering radical or alternative ideas in a more palatable manner to an audience that might otherwise be offended. This becomes strikingly apparent in Lui's show *Black Comedy*, as it delivers counternarratives that depict the reality of Indigenous people's experiences while revealing and laughing at everyday racist actions that often go unquestioned in broader Australia.

Lui also employs irony when she tweets, "I've been told all my life that as an Aboriginal person I must get everything for free because "Aboriginals get so many benefits" (we don't) . . . Since ppl [sic] think I get everything for free bc [sic] I'm Aboriginal, I should try to! Next year, I'm going to try and live entirely off White Guilt." In this example, Lui is drawing on the absurdity of the ignorant judgments she encounters and challenges the accompanying postracial narrative by recontextualizing it within the wider history of colonialism. In her book, Bilger also describes how humour can be employed by women as a psychological survival skill as well as an emancipatory strategy (2002, 10). She draws on Gloria Kaufman's argument that underlining feminist humour is an attitude that embodies a revolutionary; it is a way for women to ridicule the system as well as a means to build a foundation for political solidarity amongst other women (10). While Lui's tweet works to challenge postfeminist and postracial narratives, it also operates as a "knowing wink," a way to connect and express solidarity with other Indigenous women.

Humour not only works as a way to build solidarity but also a means for expressing one's identity. In an attempt to rebel against the type of representation that comes from the "casual accommodation" described earlier, Fredericks suggests Australian Aboriginal women are trying to re-empower themselves through the naming of what Aboriginal identity means and the various ways in which it manifests. One of the ways in which Aboriginal women are fighting against postfeminist and postracial narratives is by speaking out about their stories and illustrating that Aboriginality comprises a multitude of experiences, rights, identities, values, and responsibilities. Lui and Liddle spend time constructing their identities and providing information about their experiences as Indigenous women. Lui's pinned tweet at the time of data collection says, "This is my dad Jack. Im [sic] so lucky to have such an amazing dad love me and be there throughout my life #Indigenousdads" and includes three photos of her across a range of ages with her father. In the face of dominant narratives about deviant Aboriginal fatherhood (as discussed earlier), Lui provides a counternarrative that documents her experiences and illustrates a more positive reality and representation of Aboriginal people.

Conclusions: Mapping Digital "Herstories"

There is little research into Indigenous feminisms online, and this chapter aims to fill this gap by examining how Indigenous feminist writers have challenged various tenets that constitute a postfeminist sensibility alongside postracial discourses. It first introduces the context and current climate of racial politics in contemporary Australia and draws on Ralina L. Joseph's conceptualization of postracism, and its connections to Rosalind Gill's postfeminist sensibility, to describe the dominant ideology in Australian political and racial narratives. It goes on to outline the historical tensions between white feminism and Indigenous Australian women and then probes further into the embedded whiteness of contemporary digital narratives. A textual analysis of Indigenous feminist writers Celeste Liddle and Nakkiah Lui's Twitter feeds illustrates how they are challenging postfeminist and postracial narratives online at an everyday level and draws attention to the counternarratives and experiences they fight to have heard. Twitter in particular is a valuable platform to examine because it is an increasingly popular site for feminist discourse (Lewis et al. 2016) and also provides an avenue for the writers to not only post stories that were censored by other media outlets, but also provides a space for them to critique other media platforms.

From the analysis, it becomes apparent that Liddle and Lui use a range of techniques to challenge the narratives that constitute postracism and a postfeminist sensibility. Firstly, they both draw attention to a postracial colorblindness by recognizing and emphasizing whiteness as a race when it is commonly assumed to be a deracialized default. They use racial identifiers and address white people with the terms "white folks" and "white people" and refer to themselves as "black" and "Aboriginal" to firmly claim their identity. They also fight to re-establish the historical and political contexts for the contemporary struggles that a post-identity ideology erases. A postfeminist sensibility acknowledges previous successes and firmly situates struggles of inequality within the past. In response to this narrative, Liddle and Lui contend that many modern-day struggles faced by Indigenous people are intertwined with the effects of colonialism, thus working to reposition the past as relevant to today's debates.

Celeste Liddle also encountered what Gill (2007) identifies as the sexual-ization of culture. Liddle fights the sexualization of the depiction of a sacred ceremony and turns to Twitter to challenge the community standards that are upheld by Facebook, questioning the inherent structural whiteness that has led to the banning and censorship of the Indigenous ritual but not the removal of exploitative, sexualized images of young women. Both Liddle and Lui repeatedly fight against the overemphasis postfeminism places on individuality and personal empowerment, underlining the homogenization of indigeneity and the "double entanglement" McRobbie (2004) pinpointed as existing behind women's per-ceived agency. Finally, from the analysis of Indigenous women's use of Twitter to challenge postracial and postfeminist narratives, it has become clear that simply telling their stories and illustrating the heterogeneity of indigeneity challenges post-identity discourses. Aileen Moreton-Robinson has discussed the power and politics of the personal in relation to Indigenous women's life writing. She argues that writing about one's life makes "visible dimensions of the hidden," and can work to re-humanize the position of Indigenous women by re-animating their histories (2000, 2). Twitter has become an avenue that enables Indigenous femi-nist writers to express their stories and experiences even when other platforms such as Facebook censor and inhibit them. Developing representations and nar-ratives of Indigenous women by Indigenous women can provide insight into the multitude of experiences and cultures that challenge the stereotypical and postracial representation of Aborigines. They will add to the development of what Moreton-Robinson calls "herstories" (2000, xvii).

Notes

1 For reference see the *Northern Territory News*: http://www.ntnews.com.au/news/north ern-territory/territory-beauty-magnolia-maymuru-wows-at-miss-world-australia-pageant/news-story/bec9eee7a709b07d719ed65ee6b3b16c, the *Sydney Morning Herald*: http://www.smh.com.au/lifestyle/fashion/fashion-news/magnolia-maymuru-to-be-first-aboriginal-woman-to-represent-nt-at-miss-world-australia-20160512-gotyal, the *Telegraph*: http://www.telegraph.co.uk/news/2016/06/01/aboriginal-teen-model-makes-history-after-making-miss-world-aust/ and *New Idea*: https://www.newidea.com.au/article/practical-parenting/meet-magnolia-the-first-aboriginal-to-run-for-miss-world-australia. ABC coverage can be found here: http://www.abc.net.au/news/2016-07-23/miss-world-australia-magnolia-maymuru/7646052.

2 "The "Recognise" movement was established in 2012 after the call for a "properly resourced public education and awareness program." It operates to provide and cam-paign for an understanding of Indigenous Constitutional perspectives. More informa-tion can be found here: http://www.recognise.org.au/about/.

3 For more information, her speech "Looking Past White Australia and White Feminism" can be read here: https://newmatilda.com/2016/03/09/looking-past-white-australia-and-white-feminism/.
4 Further critique of the issues surrounding Facebook's "community standards" around women's nudity can be read at http://www.dailylife.com.au/news-and-views/dl-opinion/facebooks-ban-of-aboriginal-activist-celeste-liddle-reveals-its-censorship-double-standards-20160314-gniycj.html.

Works Cited

Andrews, Penelope. 1997. "Violence Against Aboriginal Women in Australia: Possibilities for Redress within the International Human Rights Framework." *Alb. L. Rev.* 60: 917–941.

Aveling, Nado. 2004. "Critical Whiteness Studies and the Challenges of Learning to be a White Ally." *Borderlands: E-journal* 3 (2). Accessed September 8, 2016. researchrepository.murdoch.edu.au/id/eprint.8494

Bilger, Audrey. 2002. *Laughing Feminism: Subversive Comedy in Frances Burney, Maria Edgeworth, and Jane Austen.* Detroit: Wayne State University Press.

Boler, Megan, and Christina Nitso. 2014. "Women Activists of Occupy Wall Street." In *Cyberactivism on the Participatory Web*, edited by Martha McCaughey, 232–256. New York: Routledge.

Daniels, Jessie. 2015. "The Trouble with White Feminism." In *The Intersectional Internet*, edited by Safiya Umoja Noble and Brendesha M. Tynes. New York: Peter Lang.

Dyer, Richard. 1997. *White.* London: Routledge.

Fredericks, Bronwyn. 2010. "Reempowering Ourselves: Australian Aboriginal Women." *Signs: Journal of Women in Culture and Society* 35 (3): 546–550.

Gill, Rosalind. 2007. "Postfeminist Media Culture: Elements of a Sensibility." *European Journal of Cultural Studies* 10 (2): 147–166.

Gill, Rosalind. 2009. "Mediated Intimacy and Postfeminism: A Discourse Analytic Examination of Sex and Relationships Advice in a Women's Magazine." *Discourse & Communication* 3 (4): 345–369.

Halavais, Alexander, and Maria Garrido. 2014. "Twitter as the People's Microphone: Emergence of Authorities During Protest Tweeting." In *Cyberactivism on the Participatory Web*, edited by Martha McCaughey, 117–139. New York: Routledge.

Hobson, Janell. 2008. "Digital Whiteness, Primitive Blackness: Racializing the 'Digital Divide' in Film and New Media." *Feminist Media Studies* 8 (2): 111–126. doi: 10.1080/00220380801980467

Joseph, Ralina L. 2009. "'Tyra Banks is Fat': Reading (Post-)racism and (Post-)feminism in the New Millennium." *Critical Studies in Media Communication* 26 (3): 237–254.

Joseph, Ralina L. 2011. "'Hope Is Finally Making a Comeback': First Lady Reframed." *Communication, Culture & Critique* 4 (1): 56–77.

Kinser, Amber E. 2004. "Negotiating Spaces for/through Third-Wave Feminism." *NSWA Journal* 16 (3): 124–153.

Lewis, Ruth, Michael Rowe, and Clare Wiper. 2016. "Online Abuse of Feminists as an Emerging Form of Violence Against Women and Girls." *British Journal of Criminology* 57 (6): 1462–1481.

Liddle, Celeste. 2016. "It's Time to Dispel the Myth That Women's Choices Cause the Gender Pay Gap." *Sydney Morning Herald*, September 8. Accessed September 12, 2016. http://www.smh.com.au/lifestyle/news-and-views/opinion/its-time-to-dispel-the-myth-that-womens-choices-cause-the-gender-pay-gap-20160907-grb9bd.html

Loza, Susana. 2014. "Hashtag feminism, #SolidarityIsForWhiteWomen, and the other #FemFuture." *Ada: A Journal of Gender, New Media, and Technology* 5. Accessed September 8, 2016. http://adanewmedia.org/2014/07/issue5-loza/

Lucashenko, Melissa. 1994. "No other Truth? Aboriginal Women and Australian Feminism." *Social Alternatives* 12 (4): 21–24.

Matias, J. Nathan, Amy Johnson, Whitney Erin Boesel, Brian Keegan, Jaclyn Friedman, and Charlie DeTar. 2015. "Reporting, Reviewing, and Responding to Harassment on Twitter." Accessed July 29, 2016. Available at SSRN 2602018.

McRobbie, Angela. 2004. "Post-Feminism and Popular Culture." *Feminist Media Studies* 4 (3): 255–264.

Moreton-Robinson, Aileen. 2000. *Talkin' Up to the White Woman: Aboriginal Women and Feminism.* Queensland: University of Queensland Press.

Nakamura, Lisa. 2002. *Cybertypes: Race, Ethnicity, and Identity on the Internet.* New York: Routledge.

Povinelli, Elizabeth A. 2002. *The Cunning of Recognition: Indigenous Alterities and the Making of Australian Multiculturalism.* Durham: Duke University Press.

Radsch, Courtney C., and Sahar Khamis. 2013. "In Their Own Voice: Technologically Mediated Empowerment and Transformation Among Young Arab Women." *Feminist Media Studies* 13 (5): 881–890.

Ronson, Jon. 2015. *So You've Been Publicly Shamed.* Riverhead Books (Hardcover).

Shaw, Frances. 2012. "'HOTTEST 100 WOMEN': Cross-platform Discursive Activism in Feminist Blogging Networks." *Australian Feminist Studies* 27 (74): 373–387.

Ambivalences

9

THE *NEW* AFRO IN A POSTFEMINIST MEDIA CULTURE

Rachel Dolezal, Beyoncé's "Formation," and the Politics of Choice

Cheryl Thompson

The August 2015 issue of *Allure* magazine featured a "how to" piece, titled "You (Yes, You) Can Have an Afro." Modelled by white actress Marissa Neitling, the editorial instructed readers on how to achieve a curly, loose Afro. The article made no mention of the hairstyle's black politics, most notably, its link to the 1960s Black Power movement when the Afro became a symbolic aesthetic of sociopolitical change. After public outcry from African American hair bloggers, hairstylists, and cultural critics, Chris McMillan, the hairstylist responsible for Neitling's temporary Afro, told *Huffington Post* on August 3, 2015 that Barbra Streisand in *A Star Is Born* (1976) inspired his take on the Afro for white women. The *Allure* piece came on the heels of the racial "outing" of Rachel Dolezal, a civil rights activist, Africana Studies instructor, and president of the National Association for the Advancement of Colored People (NAACP) chapter in Spokane, Washington who became fodder for media outlets when photographs circulated showing her childhood self (a white, blonde-haired girl) alongside her adult self (darkened skin and a curly, loose Afro). Dolezal became a symbol of cultural appropriation after it was revealed that she was, in fact, not black as she had been claiming for years. Critics accused her of racial theft while others said her racial "passing" was an act of violence against black people. Like *Allure*'s "how-to" guide, Dolezal's curly, loose Afro became a floating signifier for the *new* Afro.

Unlike the *old* Afro, as depicted by and through radical black activism, the *new* Afro in contemporary media culture appears as a race-neutral choice for white women. "Yes We Can," the slogan attached to Barack Obama's 2008 presidential campaign also became a single for Black Eyed Peas frontman will.i.am, "Yes We Can" (2008). The "we" in these two examples denoted a collective America, but on a connotative level, both were a "knowing wink" to black America that unprecedented levels of political capital were now possible. With this in mind, *Allure* magazine's "how-to" guide was not just about hair; by removing the "we" (*blackness*) and replacing it with "you" (*whiteness*), editors signalled that the Afro, with all its latent blackness, was now available to white women as mere style. The *new* Afro, in this sense, is similar to the *new* racism because it has become a symbol of complicated, ambivalent racial representations that circulate within a contemporary media culture where radical movements like Black Lives Matter seem to care more about structural changes than activists' strict adoption of a uniform black aesthetic.

Patricia Hill Collins asserts that the *new* racism, a new strain of racism, is pervasive but harder to recognize than the old kind of overt racism because it is subtle (2004, 121). Just as the *new* racism uses coded language and race-neutral rhetoric to mask its presence, the *new* Afro is embedded in coded language around choice and post-raciality; its discourse also centers on white women appropriating black culture. Yet, interestingly, the *new* Afro presents a challenge to postfeminism because it re-centralizes race, raising key questions about choice and gender, questions that critiques of postfeminism have yet to fully explore. At the same time, the *new* Afro also debunks the logic of a post-racial America because, while it reflects a desire to deracialize a collective *black* aesthetic by depoliticizing individual *white* choices marked by the pronoun shift in media discourse from "we" to "you," in the visual landscape, it is always encoded as "black."

Using the cases of Rachel Dolezal and Beyoncé's "Formation" music video, where the pop singer appears wearing several blonde hairstyles (an aesthetic of whiteness), this chapter explores the slipperiness of racial identity in contemporary media culture. The questions underpinning this chapter are threefold. First, how does Dolezal's *new* Afro, an embodiment of blackness, evoke an unruliness and disobedience associated with black bodies, and therefore, diminish her white skin and blonde hair, as ideal embodiments of whiteness? Stated otherwise, is the controversy that surrounds her about her adopted blackness or is it her disavowed whiteness that angers so many people? Second, how does the *new* Afro challenge the discourse on postfeminism, especially as it relates to choice and "authentic" white feminine subjectivity and black womanhood? Third, if Beyoncé can play in *whiteness* but Dolezal cannot live in *blackness*, what politics around choice have yet to be fully explored within contemporary media culture? In order to contend with these questions, I first explain how the *new* Afro challenges current critiques of postfeminism.

The *New* Afro as a Challenge to Postfeminism: Troubling Transformation Narratives

Feminist media scholars have pointed to the fact that the self-transformation narrative in postfeminist media representations often appears as compulsory for hegemonic white femininity, so much so that audiences are often encouraged to forget that the transformation happened in the first place. In her examination of films like *Sweet Home Alabama, The Wedding Planner*, and *How to Lose a Guy in 10 Days*, Samantha Senda-Cook (2009) found that each film encouraged the audience to see female self-transformation as natural and inevitable. In most cases, the transformation narrative in films adopting a postfeminist sensibility depicts a woman who exhibits idealized gender traits—namely kindness, obedience and humility (Marston 2012). Scholars have also noted that postfeminism, like neo-liberalism, advances a myth of individual success and the ability to self-regulate foregrounds discourses of choice and agency (Arthurs and Gill 2006). Thus, part of the critique of postfeminist media texts has focused on choice and agency as compulsory for contemporary hegemonic femininity. What happens, however, when the self-transformation is not about romantic heterosexual courtship, self-regulation, idealized femininity, about *freely* choosing, but is premised almost entirely on blurring the boundaries of race and racial identity? For Homi Bhabha, the performance of race is a colonial imposition on the identity of the colonized, which aims to show them as imperfect and flawed or "almost the same, but not white" (1994, 86). If white women have, historically, had the power to play in "darkness" because it was understood as play to be put on and taken off when they so desired, what if one's racial *choosing* is not for play but for *real*? If whites who "choose" to become *black* always "satiate a fascination with both an existence and way of being that does not belong to them," as blogger Sincere Kirabo argued, to whom does *blackness* belong? What and/or who is arbiter of an authentic blackness and white femininity?

The *new* Afro presents a challenge to the scholarship on freely choosing white feminine subjectivity. This scholarship has not sufficiently addressed the politics of choice, and the racialized boundaries of embodiment that surround acts of choosing. As Janell Hobson (2012, 8) observes, "far from reflecting a world in which race or gender no longer restricts the upward mobility of certain bodies . . . the global scope of our media-reliant information culture insists on perpetuating raced and gendered meanings that support ideologies of dominance, privilege, and power." On the one hand, the *new* Afro aligns with the discourse on post-feminism as "individualistic in focus" and "lifestyle"-driven. On the other hand, it debunks one of the core tenets scholars who critique postfeminist media culture often fail to problematize; namely, the hyperfocus on "white, heterosexual, and middle-class women's issues" that are then "generalized to all women, including those whose identities include none of these traits" (Vavrus 2012, 226). By pitting the *new* Afro's blackness against the whiteness of blonde hair, this chapter aims to demonstrate the slipperiness of identity in contemporary media culture, and the ways in which choosing is not singularly an individualized act, as it has been framed by many feminist media scholars, but is *always already* a racialized act as well. For example, Angela McRobbie makes the claim that the fashion and beauty industries are central to postfeminist femininity, and women are encouraged to "choose" to adhere to the norms directed by them in order to mark oneself as an ambitious, empowered, and a desirable subject (as quoted in Keller 2014). Since black women have historically been excluded from the fashion and beauty industries, they have rarely, if ever, been encouraged to "choose" how they appear. If anything, these industries have forced black women to opt out of choosing altogether.

The scholarship on postfeminism has often failed to fully interrogate the politics of choice and the social politics of race in America. As Rosalind Gill (2007, 72) aptly notes, "we urgently need to complicate our understandings of choice and agency if we are to develop a meaningful feminist critique of neoliberal, postfeminist consumer culture." Where feminist critiques of postfeminism have noted that the contemporary culture applies no breaks to the fantasies of rearrangement and self-transformation, such that "we are constantly told that we can 'choose' our own bodies" (Bordo 1993, 297), how does race complicate the parameters of the self-transformation narrative? Rachel Dolezal and Beyoncé's "Formation" are two contemporary examples of the challenge hair choice presents to contemporary media culture, revealing an ambivalence around racial representations that require unpacking. The *new* Afro on a white woman's body, and blonde hair on a black woman's body, problematizes postfeminist ideas about choice, demanding us to explore how white and non-white women alike "adopt, internalize, negotiate, and challenge hegemonic postfeminist conceptions of race, gender, and sexuality" (Butler 2013, 49).

Media Reporting on Dolezal's "Choosing" and How She Became *Black*

According to a June 16, 2015 editorial in the New York Times, in 2004, when Dolezal moved into her uncle's basement in the largely white town of Coeur d'Alene, Idaho, she was blonde, "pale-skinned," and identified as a white woman. When Dolezal appeared on NBC's *Today Show* to address accusations of "pretending to be black," she was darker skinned, her hair styled in a curly, loose Afro (Figure 9.1). In her interview with host Matt Lauer, Dolezal stated, "I identify as black." When asked when she started "deceiving" people about her racial identity, Dolezal pushed back, "It's a little more complex than me identifying as black, or answering a question of, 'Are you black or white? Well, I definitely am not white. Nothing about being white describes who I am." At some point in the 1990s her parents, Larry and Ruthanne, adopted four black children – Ezra, Izaiah, Zachariah, and Esther. Dolezal claims that her black siblings played no role in her *black* identity; instead, she asserts that it was "always there," a subconscious yet conscious feeling that she was "different" from whites in her community. In an interview with *Vice* on December 7, 2015, Dolezal stated that even though she went to an all-white school, she paradoxically experienced a form of racial cognitive dissonance as a child: "In terms of drawing myself, my self-portrait, I instinctively felt my skin color was brown. That looked better in the picture."

FIGURE 9.1 Rachel Dolezal on NBC's *Today Show*. Author screenshot from television segment

Dolezal told *Vice* that after graduating high school, her sense of self was transformed when she read *More Than Equals: Racial Healing for the Sake of the Gospel*. In it, authors Spencer Perkins, an African American scholar, and Chris Rice, a white Christian, proposed that white people should move into a large house in a black neighbourhood in order to learn how to live together. "It struck a chord with me," she said, adding that she was so moved by the authors that she got in touch with Perkins, who was living in Jackson, Mississippi, and asked if he could become her mentor if she went to school at nearby Belhaven University. Perkins agreed, and shortly thereafter, Dolezal moved to Mississippi, and enrolled in the private, predominately white, Christian university. As she recalls, "I wasn't white! It's so hard to explain this to people: I don't feel white. I didn't hang out with anybody white in Mississippi." Dolezal's explanation of her *blackness* coincides with the postfeminist narrative around authenticity, especially as it relates to black women. In her analysis of Tyra Banks, for example, Jessalynn Keller (2014) argues that Banks positions her hair straightening ("relaxing") practices as a matter of personal choice, encouraging black women to make their own individualized hair choices, divorced from the broader political and social implications that these decisions may imply. For Banks, *authenticity* was affirmed by, and through, her ability to "crossover" into mainstream (read: *white*) America not by "selling out" her culture but by interpellating other black women to come along with her (Keller 2014). At Dolezal's own admission, she ascribed an *authentic* blackness to the choices she made while living in Mississippi because she was permitted to *become* black. Her choosing was sanctioned by *real* black women; therefore, in her mind, it was authentic.

When Ruthanne and Larry told a local Idaho newspaper that their daughter was indisputably white, her story began to attract the interest of the mainstream media. "It is very disturbing that she has become so dishonest," said Ruthanne, in a phone interview with the *Coeur d'Alene Press* on June 11, 2015. Larry also told the newspaper by email that they were "saddened she has chosen to misrepresent her ethnicity." Her second "outing" occurred a few days later when local Spokane TV station KXLY4 reported that she was the biological daughter of Ruthanne and Larry. In that news story, the "before and after" photographs of Dolezal were used. For Melissa Luck, a white woman and KXLY4 Assistant News Director, Dolezal's racial identification matters. In an editorial piece on the station's website Luck wrote, "Our community was misled," adding, "We trusted this voice to speak for those without a voice. We trusted her to teach our students. We stood by her when she said she and her family were targeted and afraid. We're a trusting community and she broke that trust." The "our" in this instance, denotes a collective black community for which "we" (white people) granted Dolezal the right to speak because she "looked" *black*.

Alternatively, Allison Samuels, an African American journalist, concluded in an editorial for *Vanity Fair* on July 19, 2015 that "Dolezal is still unapologetically identifying as a black woman . . . her cover is blown, but that turned out not to matter. It was never a cover to her, anyway." For Samuels, Dolezal committed an act of racial theft for which she should apologize to *all* black people. Where Dolezal's racial crossing signified to white people that she could not be trusted, for black people, Dolezal needed to admit her lie and also be punished for it. As *Ebony* magazine argued on June 26, 2015, "Rachel Dolezal is a white woman who laid false claim to . . . blackness. She is not . . . [a] white savior who came to love and save black people, and then save the world from racial categorization." Despite her community-building with *real* black people, African American media refused to give Dolezal a "pass." In order to contend with her choosing and the resulting media discourse that she wrongfully crossed a line *into* blackness, we must consider the history of racial passing in America.

The media's representation of Dolezal's self-transformation reflects the historical issue of not contending with images whose content, as Bordo once noted, "is far from arbitrary, but instead suffused with the dominance of gendered, racial, class, and other cultural iconography" (1993, 297). To focus solely on her bodily transformation into *blackness* without contending with the history of *black-to-white* and *white-to-black* racial passing is to interpret Dolezal's act of transgression along one line (race) when in fact her choice reflects what David Delaney has called, "the racialization of space and the spatialization of race" (2002, 8). Marcia Alesan Dawkins (2012, 154) argues that while passing can be traced back to a "colonized, segregated and biracial world, it crossed over from that world and into the worlds of gender, sexuality, age, class, caste, ability, religion, technology, language, and citizenship." Whether *black-to-white* or *white-to-black*, all passing presumes that there is a duality and ambiguity to one's identity, meaning that because racial passing lacks visual "proof" of the transformation, it is more destabilizing to widely held cultural beliefs about race than, say, gender-identity transformations. Transition-focused media representations of trans women, for instance, always seem to follow the same format, which includes discussions of all the medical procedures involved in one's gender transition, and the requisite before-and-after shots following the transformation (Serrano 2007, 41). By capturing trans women *in the act* of becoming, the audience is given the impression that their *femaleness* is an artificial mask or costume (41). Conversely, because the racial pass is never *seen* in the process of transition but only "discovered" after the fact, once the passer has successfully "crossed" over, it has often been framed as more transgressive. It threatens the notion of a "white" and "black" America, which, I would argue, is more destabilizing than the notion of gender or sexual ambiguity. When it comes to the *new* Afro, it challenges the post-racial logic of postfeminist media culture, raising questions about the histories and legacies of racial (embodied) passing and crossing of believed-to-be rigid racial lines.

Reverse Racial Passing and the Embodied Boundaries of Race

The African American colloquialism for passing, "crossing the line," means to transgress the social boundary of race, to "cross" or thwart the "line" (both real and imagined) of racial distinction that has been a basis of racial oppression and exploitation in the United States since the seventeenth century (Wald 2000, 6). In *A Chosen Exile*, Allyson Hobbs (2014, 29) posits that "white skin functioned as a cloak in antebellum America" in that when attached to the "appropriate dress, measured cadences of speech, and proper comportment, racial ambiguity could mask one's slave status and provide an effectual strategy for escape." For African Americans, there was sociopolitical intent behind racial passing. In the antebellum and post-bellum reconstruction period, tactical or strategic passing— i.e. passing temporarily with a particular purpose in mind—was born out of a desire for freedom. In the twentieth century, passing allowed racially ambiguous men and women to get jobs ("nine-to-five passing"), to "travel without encumbrance, and to attend elite colleges" (29). This form of passing was born out of a desire for social mobility. Thus, *black-to-white* passing has historically marked the symbolic boundaries of race (i.e., an enslaved person "passing as free") and of citizenship (i.e., a black person "passing as white" could gain rights denied black people). Conversely, *white-to-black* racial passing has historically carried different sets of meanings.

The term "reverse racial pass," according to Philip Brian Harper (1998, 382), is "any instance in which a person legally recognized as white effectively functions as a non-white person in any quarter of the social arena." There have been several books written about reverse racial passing, most notably *Black Like Me* (1961) by John Howard Griffin, and *Soul Sister* (1969) by Grace Halsell. The significance of their books lay in the fact that a white man (Griffin) and white woman (Halsell) darkened their skins to "register as black in the primarily visual economy of racial classification" (Harper 1998, 383). "In their narrative disclosure as such, in the publication of the books by which we became aware of Griffin's and Halsell's having passed in the first place" (383), we *know* they transgressed the spatial boundaries of race for valid reasons. Stated otherwise, they "outed" themselves as performing an artifice of blackness (they were not "outed" by the media) to aid in the advancement of American society-at-large, not, as the contemporary argument goes, for their own individual gain. The reverse racial pass, then, drawing upon the same binaristic logic of racial identification as the racial pass, demonstrates even more clearly that what is at stake within the logic of race in America is the definition of whiteness itself, against which blackness functions as the oppositional sign under which all racial Others are organized and subsumed (Harper 1998). *White-to-black* passing can therefore be more destabilizing to the binaristic logic of race in America because it displaces white skin as the natural locus of racial superiority.

After Dolezal made international headlines, Eastern Washington University barred her from campus, declining to renew her quarterly adjunct professor contract; the Spokane NAACP chapter for which she sat as president forced her to resign; the Spokane City Council voted to remove her from a volunteer position as Police Ombudsman Commission, and an #AskRachel meme appeared on Twitter, posing questions intended for African Americans. In an interview with *Vanity Fair* on July 19, 2015, Dolezal was adamant, "It's taken my entire life to negotiate how to identify, and I've done a lot of research and a lot of studying." She added, "If people feel misled or deceived, then sorry that they feel that way, but I believe that's more due to their definition and construct of race in their own minds than it is to my integrity or honesty." Many of her critics have accused Dolezal of being a cultural appropriator akin to Carl Van Vechten, the white American writer who, in the 1920s, in his voyeuristic novel, *Nigger Heaven*, purported to expose the literary, art, music of Harlem to the world (i.e., white people) by co-mingling and taking in the music, culture, and aesthetics of black people.

In response to Dolezal's second appearance on *Today* on April 12, 2016 where she revealed she was writing a book about racial identity titled *In Full Color: Finding My Place in a Black and White World* (2017), and that she had no regrets about how she identifies, blogger Sincere Kirabo penned an article on *thehumanist.com* titled "The Myth of Transracial Identity." In his lament, Kirabo argued that like Van Vechten, Dolezal shamelessly satiates a fascination with both an existence and way of being that does not belong to her. "Both acts are cousins to cultural appropriation in that both involve members of a dominant group exploiting the culture of a less privileged group with no concern for the social context that framed the latter's history, marginalization, and traditions," he argued. The term "transracial" commonly refers to a child of one racial or ethnic group, placed with adoptive parents of another racial or ethnic group. It also denotes changing one's physical appearance to "look" like another race or to undergo a self-transformation where you take on or adopt the corporeal aesthetics of a particular racial group. In Dolezal's case, she adopted a black hairstyle, darkened (tanned) her skin, and lived as a *black* woman. To her defense, she has never claimed the term "transracial." Instead, she has maintained that she "identifies" as *black*.

The discourse on Dolezal's passing, her "crossing the line," raises questions about racial transgression and the metaphoric geography of race—that is, the spaces where one crosses, or passes over, the color line dividing white and black (Kawash 1996). The very notion of "crossing" a line connotes a space that is already segregated, bounded, and imbued with homogeneity, but one that is also porous and malleable (Delaney 2002). As Baz Dreisinger (2008, 14) aptly writes, "recognizing the potency and the longevity of . . . white passing . . . is thus crucial to our understanding of how whites and blacks look upon each other, whether with awe, fear, desires—or all three." Even though Dolezal located herself in *black* spaces—she attended college in Mississippi, a state with a significant black population, and she obtained a master of fine arts from the historically black Howard University in Washington, D.C.—if her crossing over into black spaces was OK some would argue that her choice of an embodied crossing into *blackness* should be, as well. As Steve Pile (2010, 26) argues, "Certain bodies can 'assume' certain identities, while others cannot." Rather than position Dolezal's Afro and tanned (darker) skin as automatic racial theft her case should ask us to probe the politics of embodiment that make it a symbolic crime to "cross" that line that is, in reality, invisible. The freely choosing white woman is exalted in contemporary media culture, but why is Dolezal's choice unforgiveable?

For example, in her reading of the films *Knocked Up*, *Waitress*, and *Juno*, Pamela Thoma writes that one of the markers of an "authentic" modern (white) feminine subjectivity is choice. "The banner feminism of these films," she writes, "is constructed as a politics of the past that no longer warrants articulation with the lives of today's more sophisticated, already liberated young women who need only make the correct individual consumer choices to achieve professional success and an affluent lifestyle" (2009, 412). Before we automatically vilify Dolezal, we should also consider the fact that her narrative follows a similar ahistorical trajectory; that is, instead of recognizing the history of *white-to-black* passing, she locates her choices in an individual narrative similar to other white women in contemporary media culture. For example, even though the postfeminist film *Waitress* is set in Mississippi, it is populated by an overwhelmingly white cast, an act that either removes people of color from the world the film is supposed to represent or emulates the segregation for which the state has been infamous (2009, 412). At least Dolezal located herself firmly in Mississippi's black communities, openly embracing people of color and crosses the segregated line invisible in postfeminist films like *Waitress*.

It is also important to dispute the claim that Dolezal's *blackness* is akin to blackface. As Dreisinger (2008, 24, 25) observes, "Whites who blacked up were not *becoming* black but *performing blackness*. . . . Even in blackface, minstrels were clearly and essentially white; passers were not." At no point has Dolezal performed a caricatured *blackness* by adopting an African American Vernacular English; she has never worn a costume that she has subsequently taken off and put on; nor has she publicly mocked any aspect of African American culture. We can however question why she darkened her skin (with or without the use of a tanning product), when, since the antebellum period, hair has typically served as a better indicator of one's racial identity than skin color because of the institutionalized pattern of rape during slavery (Davis 1983). Is the totality of her bodily transgressions, however, an act of cultural appropriation? I contend that Dolezal's case illustrates that white racial transgressions are always fixed and immutable (viewed as exertions of power over the Other) in the spatialization of race, but black racial transgressions in the racialization of space reflect lines that can *always* be crossed (viewed as expressions of agency). The racial transgression has been largely ignored in critiques of postfeminist media texts. Beyoncé's "Formation" stands as further example of a racial crossing; it represents a (re)claiming of power through the embodiment of a white aesthetic that also challenges the parameters of choice in postfeminist media culture.

Black-to-White Crossings in Beyoncé's "Formation"

"Formation," the first single from *Lemonade* (2016), is set in contemporary New Orleans, but also in Louisiana's past. As the video starts, Beyoncé sits atop a New Orleans police car partially submerged in flood waters from Hurricane Katrina (c. 2005). In the scenes that follow, the camera pans through black neighbourhoods, private black spaces, a black pastor standing at his pulpit, and then back to Beyoncé atop the police car. This sequence frames Beyoncé as firmly located in, and within, *authentic* black spaces. As the video progresses, the viewer is moved inside the interior of a nineteenth-century plantation home. Beyoncé and her dancers wear modernized corseted dresses with "leg-o-mutton" sleeves, a style popular in the 1890s, and for all intents and purposes, this interior scene encodes Beyoncé as a "lady" (Figure 9.2).

In the nineteenth century, black women could become a "proper" lady provided that they could demonstrate a proximity to a white progeny (Brody 1998). It is no coincidence that in this scene Beyoncé sings, "My daddy Alabama, Momma Louisiana/You mix that negro with that Creole/make a Texas bama/I like my baby heir with baby hair and Afros/I like my negro nose with Jackson Five nostrils." Her lyrics speak to a Creole (of white and black) ancestry, which in the nineteenth century was not exactly white or black and not exactly

FIGURE 9.2 Beyoncé donned blonde hair extensions for her album *Lemonade*. Author screenshot from music video

free or enslaved. New Orleans, as Dawkins explains, "operated in a three-tiered system with whites at the top, Creoles in the middle, and blacks at the bottom" (2012, 57). Given the Creole in-between-ness, "Many Creoles may have passed without even knowing it, for every time s/he was mistaken for white, s/he passed (Blay 2010, 43)." To be Creole in Louisiana is to disrupt the binaristic logic of race in America; Creoles embody a racialized space where lines can (and are expected to) be crossed. Thus, the first minute of "Formation" presents an immediate challenge to the logic of postfeminism because it declares that race is not only immutable but in the context of America, it is *always already* a bricolage. Even though Beyoncé's hair, captured in various braided hairstyles, is blonde in "Formation," she is permitted to blur the lines of *whiteness* and *blackness* in the encoded bricolage space of Louisiana because her body, symbolically and culturally, *belongs* there.

In *Time*'s April 25, 2016 review of *Lemonade*, Omise'eke Natasha Tinsley noted that Beyoncé is "Crowned in braids, a bejeweled headdress and a triangular silver bra, she's Nefertiti, the powerful Egyptian queen-deity whose name means 'The Beautiful One Has Come'." She made no mention of her blondeness. In an article she penned for *Ms.*, appearing on April 29, 2016, Janell Hobson also noted, "The black-and-white cinematography of the Louisiana plantation alludes to the work of artist Carrie Mae Weems' 'Louisiana Project,' while the surrounding landscape evokes the aesthetic treatment of black feminist films like

Julie Dash's *Daughters of the Dust* and Kasi Lemons' *Eve's Bayou*." Hobson said nothing of her racial in-between-ness. For these African American cultural critics, Beyoncé's *blackness* is so authentic that it prevents her body, Louisiana, and her Creole identity from being subsumed by the *whiteness* of blonde hair. Similar to Nicki Minaj who defends "her right to identify as a Barbie *and* as a 'bad bitch,' distancing herself from contemporary constructions of femininity" (Butler 2013), Beyoncé similarly moves through the complex terrain of postfeminism by choosing *not* to choose; stated otherwise, she owns her in-between-ness as both black and white, free and enslaved, white feminist and black feminist, never claiming or being put in a position to claim her *choices*. She is neither post-racial nor post-feminist; she is post-choice.

Beyoncé's ability to never explain her choosing challenges how feminist media scholars have historically debated postfeminist choosing because it signals both to a past when black people were not *free* and a present when the "we" of "Yes, We Can" has widened the boundaries of blackness in America. "Formation" demonstrates that where Beyoncé is "free" to play in *whiteness* – her blonde hair to be put on and taken off when she so desires – Dolezal reveals that white women are never "free" to play in *blackness*, even if their "play" encompasses the totality of their biography. If whites can *become* black, the very "being" of *blackness* as the oppositional lesser to whiteness becomes less true. If critiques of postfeminist media culture are to contend with choice, they must first acknowledge that not *all* bodies are freely choosing how they appear (and are seen) in contemporary media culture. The freely choosing postfeminist subject is a fallacy that even the most ardent of postfeminist critics have yet to problematize.

Conclusions: Destabilizing Postfeminist Whiteness

If we are to think relationally about postfeminist representations of women as freely choosing, we must recognize the intersectional processes through which racial tropes, discursive spaces, and media texts combine, influence, and shape such choosing. As Steve Pile (2010, 28) observes, whiteness has been "ontologized as mobility, agency and responsibility, yet seemingly removed from the 'fact' of having white skin (or not)." If postfeminist critiques are to account for race, they must first recognize the social construction of whiteness. For example, the media reporting on Dolezal went to great lengths to probe her personal narrative, her choosing, and the reasons why she *became* black without ever contending with her whiteness in the first place. If an Afro and darker skin are the only signifiers for racial pretense, by that measure, more media scrutiny should be levied against other white women whose appearances have "crossed the line" into *blackness*. For example, Kim Kardashian, like Dolezal, married and had children with a black man, has engaged in self-transformations such as enlarging her lips and allegedly her buttocks, has adopted black hairstyles, such as braids and cornrows, and yet, few have accused her of "pretending to be black." The *new* Afro is a challenge to postfeminism because it puts into question the construction of whiteness, destabilizing a universal and seemingly "authentic" white feminine subjectivity that is privileged within postfeminist media culture.

Second, the postfeminist discourse on choice has failed to problematize the politics of choosing. As Nadine Ehlers (2012, 9) aptly observes, "because all racial subjects are formed through the compelled and never-ending recitation of norms associated with particular categories of race, racial identity in general operates as a pass that is a *becoming*, one that never assumes the fixed status of 'being.'" To "pass," therefore, is to illuminate "that race is, essentially, a scopic regime because it relies on the ability to identify difference as the means by and through which to delineate subjects. If the subject cannot be visually coded as black, then the possibility of regulating this subject within black subject status becomes compromised" (61–62). Dolezal reminds us that racial identity is mutable and fluid. Her permutable blackness—Afro and darker skin—ultimately symbolizes the unstable fragility of whiteness. What are the contemporary politics of race if whiteness, like blackness, can be *un*chosen? Critiques of postfeminism must begin to contend with the variability of whiteness and not presume it as *always already* there. Blonde hair, for example, might be a floating signifier for whiteness but it can also function as a veil onto which we place the difference(s) of white bodies so that the surface of the skin becomes immune to a racial "outing." To think about race as a continuum would displace whiteness as superior in the same way it would deposition blackness as inferior.

If masculinity and whiteness, as Sally Robinson (2000, 1) once wrote, "retain their power as signifiers and as social practice because they are opaque to analysis, the argument goes; one cannot question, let alone dismantle, what remains hidden from view," feminist media scholars must begin to ask similar questions of femininity. The transgressive passing of Dolezal and the performative play of Beyoncé reveal that *all* women in contemporary media culture, whether they are actively choosing subjects or are acted upon by media forces, are choosing to construct their identities. Scholarly criticism of postfeminist media culture must begin to question the boundaries of female embodiment, not merely contend with the representational discourses around women's bodies. For example, Brenda Weber argues that makeover shows, as postfeminist texts, present a "true self," freed from one's past bad choices and poor bodily discipline but the authenticity of the "after-body" is never questioned and is not understood as performed, but as "natural" (as quoted in Keller 2014). Dolezal and Beyoncé demonstrate that the very notion of an *authentic* self is a fallacy; gender and racial identity is always about "play" and as such, future challenges to postfeminism must begin to deconstruct the larger question of who is *freely* choosing, which would decentralize the binaristic logic around race and women's bodies.

Works Cited

Arthurs, Jane and Rosalind Gill. 2006. "New Femininities?" *Feminist Media Studies* 6 (4): 443–451.

Bhabha, Homi K. 1994. *The Location of Culture.* London and New York: Routledge.

Blay, Yaba Amgborale. 2010. "'Pretty Color 'n Good Hair': Creole Women of New Orleans and the Politics of Identity." In *Blackberries and Redbones: Critical Articulations of Black Hair/Body Politics in Africana Communities,* edited by Regina E. Spellers and Kimberly R. Moffat, 29–52. Cresskill, New Jersey: Hampton Press.

Bordo, Susan. 1993. "'Material Girl': The Effacements of Postmodern Culture." In *Negotiating at the Margins: The Gendered Discourses of Power and Resistance,* edited by Sue Fisher and Kathy Davis, 295–316. New Brunswick, New Jersey: Rutgers University Press.

Brody, Jennifer DeVere. 1998. *Impossible Purities: Blackness, Femininity, and Victorian Culture.* Durham and London: Duke University Press.

Butler, Jess. 2013. "For White Girls Only? Postfeminism and the Politics of Inclusion." *Feminist Formations* 25 (1): 35–58.

Davis, Angela. 1983. *Women, Race & Class.* New York: Vintage Books.

Dawkins, Marcia Alesan. 2012. *Clearly Invisible: Racial Passing and the Color of Cultural Identity.* Waco, Texas: Baylor University Press.

Delaney, David. 2002. "The Space That Race Makes." *The Professional Geographer* 54 (1): 6–14.

Dreisinger, Baz. 2008. *Near Black: White-to-Black Passing in American Culture.* Amherst: University of Massachusetts Press.

Ehlers, Nadine. 2012. *Racial Imperatives: Discipline, Performativity, and Struggles Against Subjection.* Bloomington and Indianapolis: Indiana University Press.

Gill, Rosalind. 2007. "Critical respect: the difficulties and dilemmas of agency and "choice" for feminism: a reply to Duits and van Zoonen." *European Journal of Women's Studies* 14: 69–80.

Gill, Rosalind. 2007. "Postfeminist Media Culture: Elements of a Sensibility." *European Journal of Cultural Studies* 10 (2): 147–166.

Harper, Philip Brian. 1998. "Passing for What? Racial Masquerade and the Demands of Upward Mobility." *Callaloo* 21 (2): 381–397.

Hill Collins, Patricia. 2004. *Black Sexual Politics: African Americans, Gender, and the New Racism.* New York: Routledge.

Hobbs, Allyson. 2014. *A Chosen Exile: A History of Racial Passing in American Life.* Cambridge, MA: Harvard University Press.

Hobson, Janell. 2012. *Body as Evidence: Mediating Race, Globalizing Gender.* New York: State University of New York.

Hobson, Janell. 2016. "Lemonade: Beyoncé's Redemption Song," Msmagazine.com, April 29. http://msmagazine.com/blog/2016/04/29/lemonade-beyonces-redemption-song/

Kawash, Samira. 1996. "The Autobiography of an Excolored Man: (Passing for) Black Passing for White." In *Passing and the Fictions of Identity,* edited by Elaine K. Ginsberg, 59–74. Durham, NC: Duke University Press.

Keller, Jessalynn Marie. 2014. "Fiercely Real? Tyra Banks and the Making of New Media Celebrity." *Feminist Media Studies* 14 (1): 147–164.

Kirabo, Sincere. 2016. "The Myth of Transracial Identity," *TheHumanist.com,* April 18. https://thehumanist.com/commentary/myth-transracial-identity.

Marston, Kendra. 2012. "Cinderella vs. Barbie: The Battle for Postfeminist Performance in Teen Transformation Narratives." *Scope: An Online Journal of Film and Television Studies* 24: 1–18.

Pile, Steve. 2010. "Skin, Race and Space: The Clash of Bodily Schemas in Frantz Fanon's *Black Skins, White Masks* and Nella Larsen's *Passing. Cultural Geographies* 18 (1): 25–41.

Robinson, Sally. 2000. *Marked Men: White Masculinity in Crisis.* New York: Columbia University Press.

Senda-Cook, Samantha. 2009. "Postfeminist Double Binds: How Six Contemporary Films Perpetuate the Myth of the Incomplete Woman." *Rocky Mountain Communication Review* 6 (2): 18–28.

Serrano, Julia. 2007. *Whipping Girl: A Transsexual Woman on Sexism and the Scapegoating of Femininity.* Berkeley: Seal Press.

Thoma, Pamela. 2009. "Buying up Baby: Modern Feminine Subjectivity, Assertions of 'Choice,' and the Repudiation of Reproductive Justice in Postfeminist Unwanted Pregnancy Films." *Feminist Media Studies* 9 (4): 409–425.

Tinsley, Omise'eke Natasha. 2016. "Beyonce's Lemonade is Black Woman Magic," *Time.com,* April 25. http://time.com/4306316/beyonce-lemonade-black-woman-magic/

Vavrus, Mary Douglas. 2012. "Postfeminist Redux?" *The Review of Communication* 12 (3): 224–236.

Wald, Gayle. 2000. *Crossing the Line: Racial Passing in Twentieth-Century U.S. Literature and Culture.* Durham and London: Duke University Press.

10

#WOMENAGAINSTFEMINISM

Towards a Phenomenology of Incoherence

Jonathan Cohn

With the recent emergence of the various new feminist formations described elsewhere in this collection, new antifeminist and misogynistic regimes have also flared up: men's rights activists reject feminism outright and fight to reverse and repeal many of the rights gained by women throughout the 20th and 21st centuries; the conservative Washington-based Independent Women's Forum and Concerned Women for America deny the existence of pay inequity and work to repeal the Violence Against Women Act; Donald Trump won the presidency on a platform defined by misogynistic white nationalism; and #WomenAgainstFeminism (#WAF), a popular social media campaign—and the focus of this chapter—has acted as both a rallying point for many women who dislike feminism and as an archive of their messages and community. These examples all highlight how antifeminist sentiment has of late become more explicit and visible in congruence with visible emergent feminisms.

#WAF was anonymously created in 2013 as a Tumblr site, YouTube channel, Twitter feed and later Facebook page that each presented selfies of women holding up signs often declaring why they "do not need feminism" (Figure 10.1). The posts on #WAF express anger toward feminism generally for encouraging women towards careers and lifestyles that have not necessarily made them happier and toward specific feminists for not accepting these women's life choices, which range from being religious to being housewives to working in the sex trade. Many of the women who post on the blog allude to personal experiences in which they were themselves bullied by feminists or made to feel disempowered by what they see as feminism's focus on women as victims.

Collectively, these women criticize and cast suspicion on contemporary feminism and its inability to make them happier. One recent typical post included a smirking woman holding a handwritten sign stating, "I don't need FEMINISM

FIGURE 10.1 One woman explains why she doesn't need feminism as part of the #WomenAgainstFeminism campaign. Author screenshot

because modern day feminism is a hate movement that infantalizes [*sic*] women and demonizes men. ☺" (February 16, 2016). This post exemplifies a widespread trend on #WAF that demonizes feminism in a literally incoherent manner via a display of confusingly contradictory affects and a combination of factual, grammatical and spelling errors. Indeed, I use the term "incoherent" to describe the way in which the letters, words, and other aspects of the image do not seem to fit together but, rather, remain an amalgamation of barely linked objects.

One *Los Angeles Times* article on the subject referred to these women as "wilfully ignorant" and I would further this by suggesting that #WAF fosters a sense of willful incoherence that paradoxically makes the site cohere (Abcarian 2016). Rather than simply discount this sense of incoherence as an aberration or mistake, I am interested in better describing it as a central feature not just of #WAF and antifeminism, but also of postfeminism. Here, #WAF uses incoherent statements and affects to align itself with postfeminism's focus on traditional femininity and the pursuit of happiness, while defining itself against the logical reasoning and perceived anger of feminism. These women's arguments range widely, suggesting—often simultaneously—that feminism goes too far, that it has not gone nearly far enough, and/or that it has in fact achieved all its goals and is now simply irrelevant. Given the scope of these statements, #WAF is not simply antifeminist, but is also postfeminist in the ways that Diane Negra and Yvonne Tasker broadly define it as "a set of assumptions widely disseminated within popular media forms, having to do with the 'pastness' of feminism, whether that supposed pastness is merely noted, mourned, or celebrated" (Tasker and Negra 2007, 1). This definition is an attempt to create a sense of coherence from a set of highly varied and contradictory discourses and representations that together are precisely not coherent. The experiences of feminism presented on #WAF may be incoherent, but that does not mean they should not be taken seriously. Many scholars from Rosalind Gill and Christina Scharff to Hilary Radner have attempted to articulate postfeminism's many contradictions (Gill and Scharff 2011, Radner 2011). Yet, by focusing on #WAF, I am here interested in describing this sense of willful incoherence as perhaps *the* structuring aspect of postfeminism.

Much of the scholarship on postfeminism has been focused on what Angela McRobbie refers to as the "more gentle denunciations of feminism" that one finds in contemporary chick flicks, lingerie ads and the self-help industry (McRobbie 2007, 31). This chapter seeks to examine the crueller side of postfeminism and how it may inform our understanding of postfeminism more generally. Many of the women on #WAF antagonize feminists and identify specifically as antifeminists. For instance, one woman on the site referred to feminists as "the army of angry vaginas backing me" (January 4, 2016). Indeed, the virulence of this site and the politics of antifeminism which have gained visibility in recent years seem to be in direct contrast to the more apolitical sensibilities of postfeminism as described by many critics. Tasker, Negra, and others specifically push these strong denunciations and antifeminist images aside when they challenge Susan Faludi's premise that postfeminism is a clear backlash against feminism; instead, they argue that postfeminism is far too complex a set of discourses to be framed simply as a strong and adverse reaction, or what Faludi refers to as a "war on American women" (Faludi 2006). Indeed, in many ways antifeminism is a more colloquial and blunt way of describing some of the sensibilities of postfeminism. Scholarship on postfeminism has historically steered away from more aggressively antifeminist backlash representations in order to focus more on those attractive images of empowering (and far too often simplistic images of upper middle-class, white, straight, cis-gendered) women who celebrate the gains of feminism but no longer see a need for it in their own lives because they already have everything they could ever want. By presenting its antifeminist message through the guise of a postfeminist critique, #WAF pushes us to complicate our understanding of postfeminism itself.

As Trump's rise to power has painfully foregrounded, such images averted our gaze far too often from the blunter and clumsier forms of misogyny and racism in mainstream American (and global) culture that are now writ large. While Sarah Banet-Weiser (2015) argues that this "popular misogyny" has sprung forth from the recent emergence of a popular feminism, I would argue that this strand was always present within postfeminist—and feminist—culture. To think of these movements less as waves that follow one another and more as simultaneous currents that move together may allow us to look back and see how antifeminism has always been a facet of postfeminism, and even strains of feminism itself. Indeed, many of the statements on #WAF concerning how feminism is racist and only helps the white bourgeoisie could have been lifted (and decontextualized) from bell hooks, Donna Haraway or other feminists who tried to challenge the more problematic aspects of feminism from the inside. If there is a change from the mid-2000s, when many of the foundational studies on postfeminism were written and published, it is that at that point, the glass seemed half full, whereas now, in this moment when, admittedly, the wounds of the 2016 presidential election results are still raw, it does not.

Yet, while strongly worded, many of the posts on #WAF make recognizably postfeminist arguments that, as Banet-Weiser suggests, "fun-house mirror" the logic of contemporary popular feminism itself (Banet-Weiser 2015). This logic suggests that since these chick-lit heroines, lingerie models, and self-help gurus have made it, then whatever structural issues still exist in American society around sexism are no longer serious impediments and are not worth the effort it would take to correct them; if you are unable to succeed, both #WAF and postfeminist discourses argue that you have no one to blame but yourself. Such arguments obscure the suffering of others and ignore the ways feminists continue not just to fight current injustices but also stop potential future ones. Banet-Weiser argues that this popular misogyny is, in a way, a response. In #WAF's more explicit form and coming from "normal" women rather than fantastical characters and rich celebrities, these postfeminist arguments become much more unsettling and incoherent: How can they be joyous and hateful at the same time? How can they make a claim for disempowerment in such an empowering way? And how can such a message displayed in this individualized and incoherent form unite people as a community, let alone a movement?

This project draws much of its inspiration and phenomenological methodology from the work of Sara Ahmed, Vivian Sobchack, and Don Ihde. Ahmed's various examinations of embodiment and emotion in relation to feminist and queer theory continually energize much of my discussion and analysis. I suggest that we use coherence in much the same way Ahmed argues we use emotions: to align ourselves with certain communities and not others. To paraphrase her work on hate, here I examine how "signs"—or posts—of incoherence work and their relation to bodies (Ahmed 2014, 44). I also believe that postfeminist beliefs spatially orient us to the world in much the same way that Ahmed argues queerness does: in ways that make certain ideas and objects "out of reach" and ungraspable (Ahmed 2006). However, whereas queerness does this in the service of defamiliarizing social norms, postfeminism does it in the service of re-establishing them.

I describe my own and others' experiences of #WAF in order to, as Sobchack explains, "'unpack' and make explicit the objective and subjective aspects and conditions that structure and qualify that experience as the kind of meaningful experience it is" (2004, 5). In this case, I use a deep description of my own experience of #WAF to better define "incoherence" and how it structures the site. To say that #WAF is incoherent is not surprising or revelatory, but exploring this experience in detail asks us to consider the assumptions and the context that shape our experiences of postfeminism more generally. As Ihde clarifies, "We are not considering what we already know; we are considering how what we know is phenomenologically constituted" (Ihde 2012, 46). Ihde also stresses that rather than hierarchize these experiences, highlighting the most popular, important, or interesting, they should all be discussed as valid "in order to allow the full range of appearances to show themselves" (Ihde 2012, 22). While perhaps perverse, if not actively misguided, viewing the perspectives on #WAF as in some sense valid allows us to consider incoherence not just as a failure or problem, but also as a mode of articulation and to examine it for what it does and does not make possible.

Willful Incoherence

While we now think of coherence primarily in terms of consistent argumentation and logic, it has always first and foremost been a physical force. Etymologically, cohere's earliest definitions focused on the very physical, if not biological, act of sticking together as a material substance; cohesion is the force in which "the molecules of a body or substance cleave together" ("Coherence N." 2016). This physical definition makes coherence appear as an essential physical property, which may also lead to perceiving a coherent argument as an objective natural fact that one could not reasonably or rationally debate. Coherence implies logic and the sense that an argument has been arrived at via a strict sense of mathematical and systematic reasoning. Yet, there is no one system of reason and these different systems can lead to completely different arguments and results. For instance, seemingly coherent arguments and ideologies, like those for and against slavery, have gone in and out of favour throughout history and in the process, they become more or less coherent to the present moment. Indeed, coherence can obscure the historical and cultural context of an ideology and it is often only when it has become incoherent that we recognize how it was situated and shaped.

As Robert Sokolowski points out, incoherence is disruptive and alienating not because it is inconsistent, but rather because it "cannot even be tested for consistency" (Sokolowski 2000, 171). It transcends contradiction and suggests a completely foreign way of experiencing the world that those outside the incoherent discourse can neither comprehend nor be a part of. It claims to know something we cannot reach; it pushes us away. Again, Trump is a great example of this effect as many reported that his statements throughout the election made complete sense to some but were incomprehensible nonsense to others (LaFrance 2016, Parton 2016, Gearan et al. 2016). In turn, his election has been greeted as necessary by some and unthinkable by many more. Labeling something or some people as incoherent implies a desire to make them coherent; otherwise, they are just a series of unrelated thoughts, objects, or individuals.

While arguments and ideologies cohere through an internal logic, social groups cohere around the desire for commonality despite differences. Groups may cohere around a shared logic, or common (or communal) sense, but this is rarely enough. Ahmed defines coherence as that which "sticks subjects together . . . through love, which involves the desire to be 'like' an other. . . . Through love, an ideal self is produced as a self that belongs to a community; the ideal is a proximate 'we' (Ahmed 2014, 106). She goes on to describe how emotion often becomes a tool to cover over both gaps in logic and communication. According to Ahmed's logic, coherence is a normative (if not heteronormative) force that declares who is inside and outside of a community to such a degree that the two groups cannot even communicate, let alone argue, with each other.

Social coherence suggests not just similarity but also consistency in space and over time. Such consistency is a hallmark of conservative values that uphold those traditions, from religious devotion to gendered divisions of labor that postfeminist ideologies tend to celebrate. This consistency, according to Samuel Johnson, is "essential for our awareness of order, meaning, and value" (Knoblauch 1979, 236). C.H. Knoblauch argues, "coherence is something made, not something found, a mechanical contrivance less than a priori feature of the world" (Knoblauch 1979, 236). Social coherence is political and cultural; people declare what does and does not belong to a given formation and such decisions divide us into those who can be understood as rational and normal and those who cannot. For example, Americans map out these divisions strikingly in their electoral maps, separating red states from blue, not just to illustrate, but also construct where the borders between logics and worlds lie. The lines between the blue and red become not just borders, but perilous canyons. #WAF raises the question of whether and how a social group—antifeminists—can cohere around a logic that remains incoherent.

The incoherence of postfeminist discourse is particularly troubling: part of its lure is this incoherence and our desire to make sense of it. Its promise of a world in which feminism is no longer necessary is something we should all hope for, making our failure to achieve it all the more painful. If incoherence creates a communicative gap that cannot be crossed, then it allows the feminists and antifeminists to see but not understand each other—a reality especially true within our contemporary digital media culture. On #WAF, we can see their signs, but we do not understand what they mean; they read as nonsense.

The #WAF Community

#WAF began with a flurry of 29 new and shared Tumblr posts on July 3, 2013, followed by hundreds more in the weeks to come. While Tumblr blogs can be used in a wide variety of ways, their functions, including the ability to add keywords to posts, comment on them, and reblog posts on other users' sites, focus on creating communities of bloggers around shared interests. In addition, their extremely lax censorship policies have made it a hotbed for, among other things, hate groups and the sharing of pornographic material. Several of these early posts also include a link to the #WAF YouTube page. Together with the sheer number of photos immediately posted on the site, this immediate connection to YouTube suggests that #WAF was from the very beginning not just an amateur and impromptu blog but rather an orchestrated media campaign.

After a year of relative obscurity, #WAF's Tumblr site rose to prominence in mid-2014 around the same time as the U.S. Supreme Court *Hobby Lobby* decision, which allowed corporations to refuse to pay for birth control coverage (Elderkin 2014). This event galvanized not just feminists, but also antifeminists. A number of newspapers, magazines, and blogs began publishing articles that presented #WAF as a corner of the Internet full of misinformed and deeply troubling, if not outright troubled women who appeared to be fighting against their own interests for no clear reason. While the site and campaign have decreased in popularity, a handful of new and shared photos are still consistently posted, liked, shared, and reblogged from month to month. The #WAF Facebook group also continues to be active with over 38,000 "members" and adds several new posts a month that often get hundreds of likes and shares and result in lengthy discussions that largely reaffirm the collective's antifeminist beliefs, sprinkled with a few ignored voices of dissent.

Clearly, #WAF has generated a large community of antifeminists, but at the same time there is a strong sense of incoherence located not just within each post but across the site. Even at the level of the site's code and metadata, contradictions arise. For instance, the site's creators made the confounding choice of picking "Club Monaco" as their "theme" or general layout for how posts and other information are displayed. While most Tumblr themes have bland names like "Indy" or "Minimal," "Club Monaco" acts as advertising for the clothing store. The theme itself is quite plain and just features two columns of images running down the page and a small, always-present "Club Monaco" link in the bottom left-hand corner that takes users to the store's homepage. While postfeminism links female empowerment to consumerism, the explicit choice of this particularly corporate theme does not make any particular sense. Nor does it make sense why Club Monaco, a bland mid-priced retailer owned by Ralph Lauren, would want to be associated with #WAF on any level. While there is no direct connection between the company and #WAF, the well-featured name, "Club Monaco," does lend the same air of high-class fantasy to the site that it does to the clothes in its stores. Yet, this fantasy is in direct contrast with the largely low-resolution grainy photos of women who, while often attractive, do not appear to be models. Is this theme supposed to imply that these women are fantasies, or is it supposed to remind the viewer how normal these women are in contrast? While users are left to guess how these choices fit together, there is no clear, or even vague relationship between Club Monaco and antifeminism, any reason why this company would want to be related to #WAF, or any reason why #WAF would want to be related to it.

In addition to their confusing choice of theme, #WAF also uses Tumblr's tagging system to connect itself not just to antifeminists but also to those feminists that the site's posts actively disavow. The vast majority of #WAF posts are tagged as not just #antifeminist but also #feminist, and often also #Men's Rights as well as #patriarchy. These terms make such posts visible to those both for and against feminism. Anyone searching for these topics on Tumblr would see the connected posts. These tags illustrate how #WAF uses these tags not simply to appeal to those sympathetic to antifeminism, but also to those critical or disgusted by it.

Four Smiley Faces

The very first #WAF post features a grainy image of a smiling woman with long brown hair in front of a plain white wall holding a paper on which she has written in large letters, "This is what an Anti-Feminist looks like" followed by a smiley face (July 3, 2013) (Figure 10.2). In her discussion on "Selfies and Self-Writing," Kimberley Hall places great importance on the role of handwriting in these photos because, among other things, they suggest an indexical relationship between the person and the text: "as if we are able to access the producer's innermost thoughts via the handwritten document, owing in part to the aesthetic connections to diary and letter writing" (Hall 2015, 5). Almost every post on #WAF features handwritten messages with clearly written letters, multiple colors, underlining, capitalization, and other trappings that one may demeaningly call "girly." Hélène Cixous and other feminists have made much of this handwriting, or "écriture feminine." This handwriting is a trace of the "flow of the hand, the touch of the fingers, the pulse of the blood in the arm" that allows "the body to "make itself heard" (Blyth and Sellers 2004, 34). While Cixous felt that such handwriting (and the written works that it led to) could be deeply transgressive and expose the instabilities of patriarchal thought, on #WAF, such handwriting serves to uphold such norms.

Hall describes the type of writing found on #WAF as "cue card confessions," which both reveal and discipline. Like other forms of confession, these cards project a "subjective legibility governed by visibility and consumability" that does not

FIGURE 10.2 "This is what an Anti-Feminist looks like" as part of the #WomenAgainst-Feminism campaign. Author screenshot

just describe the person, but actively makes the person what the card says she is (Hall 2015, 3). Furthermore, Hall suggests that while self-writing like this may be addressed to a public, it is not necessarily meant to engender a response. However, I would argue that in the case of #WAF, the lack of desire for a response is constitutive of its discourse. The announcement is public, but there is nothing in the message to respond to or reason with.

The very form of these antifeminist "confessions" points to an underlying—and structuring—incoherence. While there appears to be a clear indexical relationship between the writing and the woman, many aspects of the image destabilize it. For one, the image is blurry and you cannot actually see what she looks like very well. This blur is a visual incoherence that signals both the image's lack of clarity and its distance from the viewer. While the text appears to promise that the woman's body will reveal something essential about the shape of antifeminism—what it "looks" like—it does not. Indeed, as the page covers much of her body and only her shadowy face is visible, the image is surprisingly bare. The background reveals nothing about her location except that she is inside and the low resolution and low lighting obscure what she is wearing.

This #WAF post is literally an ad hominem argument that conflates the woman's body with antifeminism. It makes no attempt to create an argument with reason or logic. Nor does it appear to try to create an argument through feelings or prejudice. Instead, its incoherent blankness merely reverberates back to us whatever feelings we already had concerning antifeminism. This post is a response to the feminist social media campaigns, "Who needs feminism," which featured numerous women holding hand-written signs stating why they need feminism, and another which featured a myriad of celebrities wearing t-shirts stating, "this is what a feminist looks like." While the later campaign was designed to counter the "old canard" that feminists are ugly and angry "hirsute bra-burners," this first #WAF post suggests that antifeminists are also not ugly and angry (Valenti 2014). Yet, while there is a clear antagonistic relationship between this post and the feminist campaign, they are not arguing that feminists cannot be attractive; rather, their mirroring of the campaign message suggests that like them, antifeminists have been unfairly stereotyped as ugly. While misogyny, like other forms of hate, has often been referred to as "ugly," the physical bodies of antifeminist women have never been chided as such. Indeed, this photo and many others on #WAF go to great lengths to associate attraction and sexual availability with an antifeminist stance.

At the same time, the meaning of this objectification is completely left open to interpretation. Are we to infer that antifeminists have long brown hair, are white, or are perhaps grainy and hidden in the dark? Are they low-resolution, or perhaps irresolute? Or is the most significant aspect of this body simply her femininity? While many have commented on the whiteness and traditional femininity (as signified by the woman's long hair) of postfeminism, antifeminism is almost entirely associated with men. Re-associating antifeminism with femininity and women, who are actively harmed by antifeminist causes, is jolting. In the process, #WAF also underlines how antifeminism has become part and parcel of contemporary postfeminism at the level of the body.

#WAF enacts this confluence of postfeminism with antifeminism through a profusion of smiley faces, hearts, and stars. These symbols are related both to the feminized "girly" writing style on the site and to the emojis and emoticons endemic to digital writing. Smiley faces punctuate both posts I have mentioned and many others include heart and star motifs. When instant messaging or texting, such "emoticons" are useful for adding an emotional context and tone to what may otherwise appear to be often very terse prose. A smile may indicate sincerity while a wink often connotes sarcasm. The same logic applies on #WAF, but often result in an irreconcilable relationship between the written words and the tone they are apparently meant to be read in. In my first example, a smiley face ends a series of statements that compare feminists to demons bent on the destruction of humanity. This woman uses the smiley face to simultaneously disavow the anger in her message (an emotion #WAF often associates with feminists) and link herself more with a particular stereotypical femininity defined by bubbly emotions. This smiley face appears to soften her harsh vilifications into not just "gentle," but also deeply flippant denunciations.

In the case of the very first #WAF post, the smiley face is a synecdoche of the antifeminist herself. The smiley face takes much of the sting out of "antifeminist" and associates it more with the happy-go-lucky image of postfeminism. This emoticon and her actual smile are placed in comparison, as "this" could be referring to either of them or both. In the process, the woman's smile becomes a central detail of what makes her "look" antifeminist. According to this image, antifeminists are not just cheery, bubbly, and feminine, but they are also happy. In contrast, feminists have often been at the very least skeptical of happiness as an ideal and present it not as a goal but rather as an impediment of equality and equity. While Simone de Beauvoir opposed happiness to the feminist desire for liberty, Betty Friedan opposed it to "aliveness" (Beauvoir 1993, Friedan et al. 2013). In turn, Ahmed has argued that happiness is a logic that tends to turn social control into a social good. Ahmed asserts that "the feminist is an affect alien, estranged by happiness . . . feminists, by declaring themselves feminists, are already read as destroying something that is thought by others not only as being good but as the cause of happiness" (Ahmed 2010, 11). Feminists are deeply and rightly suspicious of the coercive effect the desire to be happy has and the ways in which it encourages the reproduction of ultimately harmful, often heteronormative social norms; for women in particular, being happy is often framed as the result of making others happy.

The belief that feminists regard happiness, which many people see as a positive value, as boring, static, and conservative, may turn off many who would otherwise "happily" associate themselves with feminism. For example, in another #WAF post, a woman holds up a notebook on which she has written, "*FUCK Feminism* . . . Because I actually enjoy cooking for my fiance [*sic*] ☺ #FeminismIsAwful" (August 17, 2015) (Figure 10.3). The woman here is hunched over in a low-lit room that appears to be a domestic space with photos and a poster in the background. She has long brown hair and wears glasses, which reflect the computer monitor that doubles as the camera. Rather than smile or smirk, she instead intensely stares down the camera/computer as if her message is deadly serious. Here, the smiley face contrasts with her composure and her writing. While it highlights the enjoyment she gets from cooking, it also makes the post appear catty and spiteful rather than "happy."

Like the other smiley faces, this one illustrates how #WAF transforms antifeminism's affect from pain and anger to pleasure and pride. Yet, this enjoyment at her own zinger is undercut by the message's logic problems. Feminists certainly do critique how various domestic responsibilities including cooking can confine or inhibit women. Yet, these critiques illustrate the value of this labour at least partly in order to turn it into a pleasurable and satisfying act rather than a burden; like so many #WAF posts, this one mistakes feminism as the problem when it is actually the remedy.

Accusations and assertions on #WAF like those above do not attempt to create a real debate or bridge the gap between feminists and antifeminists; rather,

FIGURE 10.3 A participant in the #WomenAgainstFeminism campaign cheerfully claims that she enjoys cooking for her fiancé. Author screenshot

they make this gap appear uncrossable. The more incomprehensible antifeminists appear, the less likely feminists may be to communicate with them at all; where there might have been a common ground is instead an abyss. And indeed, many find #WAF posts very upsetting, specifically because they do not appear to make sense or be rational. Part of what makes #WAF so transgressive is the way the women on the site reveal and revel in their incoherence. David Rehorick and Gail Taylor argue that there is a "monolithic insistence on coherence in Western culture" (Rehorick and Taylor 1995, 398). They describe how our very notion of individual autonomy is predicated on the internalization of social constraints, which frame incoherent feelings and feeling incoherent as shameful. Announcing to the world that you strongly believe such willfully incoherent and inane statements is transgressive as it violates boundaries of social acceptability. Yet, not all transgressions lead to positive change. Here, connecting themselves so thoroughly to these illogical beliefs through their physical bodies and handwriting is a transgressive attempt to unify antifeminist women into a coherent collective. For feminists, images like this are powerful and painful specifically because of how difficult it is to reconcile the image of the bodies of these women with the messages they hold.

When I first saw the site, I was confused by its images and messages, but hopeful that the posts were actually deeply and knowingly ironic send-ups of a silly position. One post, which features a woman holding a sign over her face with only her smile visible, states "I don't need feminism because I love masculine men like Christian Grey :-p" (July 17, 2014). Does the smile imply sarcasm, delight, both, or something else entirely? This post actively forgets how the pleasure of the

S&M activities in *Fifty Shades of Grey*, like cooking for your fiancé, is predicated on the feminist insistence that sex be mutually satisfying. While Grey's status as a sex symbol is undeniable, it is difficult for me to imagine someone posting this message as anything other than a parody; the line between absurd and absurdist is often illegible.

#WAF Posts as Multistable Phenomena

To some extent, #WAF posts resemble what Ihde calls "multistable phenomena," which can be experienced in a number of ways, but only one at a time and with some effort. The multistable phenomena that Ihde describes are common two-dimensional trick images, like the drawn outline of a 3D box, which can appear to come toward or go away from the viewer. Ihde also argues that these boxes may appear to some not as boxes at all, but rather as insects or something else entirely depending on the viewer's prior experiences and mindset. Importantly, he also describes how viewers may see the image as an insect, as coming toward them *and* as going away from them, but never both at once.

While the posts on #WAF are much more complex than the puzzle images that Ihde discusses, they are also quite open to interpretation and viewers experience the same vacillations between their experiences of the images. In an article on *Sex, etc.*, a site that includes information, forums, and articles on sex education written primarily by teenagers, Alexandra Yoon-Hendricks stated that when she first heard about #WAF, she assumed it was a parody and found it "hard to believe that so many people . . . could possibly hate a movement that has led to essentially half of the population gaining basic civil rights, inching us closer to total equality regardless of gender" (Yoon-Hendricks 2014). Yoon-Hendricks then describes her emotional reactions to the site from pleasure to anger to confusion as she began to read the posts on the site as earnest critiques of a feminism that she did not recognize. She ends the article by arguing that if feminism was discussed in sex education classes in relation to topics like "healthy relationships and consent," more people "would actually be for feminism and not against it" (Yoon-Hendricks 2014). First, this article illustrates many of the common reactions to #WAF from journalists, academics, and the public at large. While Ihde purposefully chose examples of multistable phenomena that inspire very little to no emotional response at all, those on #WAF often result in a variety of emotional outbursts from humor to disgust. Second, Yoon-Hendricks also illustrates how these outbursts may vacillate as viewers experience them differently from moment to moment. Here, Yoon-Hendricks narrativizes the vacillations as a series of misreadings of the posts that eventually lead to the final, correct experience of the site. Yet, I am invoking Ihde here to suggest that rather than hierarchize these emotional responses, it is far more useful to consider each of them as entirely valid ways of experiencing these posts. Yoon-Hendricks' reactions—from humor to anger to confusion to pity—do not just illustrate a movement from confusion to recognition, but rather show four distinct and common ways of experiencing #WAF and that it is just as reasonable to go from pity to humor as the other way around.

Yet, certain ways of experiencing these women's posts are more common than others and reveal certain assumptions about what types of ideas and behaviors many think women are capable of having and which they are not. A viewer's experience of #WAF may vacillate between seeing them as intelligent women holding ironic signs, ignorant women holding earnest signs, actors holding someone else's signs, or something else entirely. While these are all common ways of experiencing these women, it is significantly harder to experience them as ignorant women holding sarcastic signs, or as intelligent women holding earnest signs, which is ironically, what many assume the dominant reading of this page is supposed to be.

Conclusions, or, Irreconcilable Differences

I still experience the irony of this site but recognize that most read it as sincere and even zealous. Rather than assume these women are intelligent and confident, most critics made fun of them for being ignorant and abject. An article on *Vice* made fun of the women on the site for both fundamentally misunderstanding what feminism is and for continually stating that they do not need feminism because they need men to open jars and lift heavy things for them. Another article in *Total Sorority Move* Magazine featured women responding to specific posts from #WAF by making fun of them in the same selfie format. Their posts, including one that features a woman holding a page on which she has written the dictionary definition of feminism, are an intense form of mean-girl mansplaining. In a condescending way, they explain feminism to these women and assume that they must not have thought about feminism very deeply. They argue that to be against feminism can only be a sign of their inferiority rather than a legitimate position (Jo 2014). Indeed, a surprising number of articles try to refute #WAF's basic assumptions by presenting dictionary definitions of feminism. One article on Bustle.com first present's *Merriam-Webster*'s bland definition of feminism as "the theory of the political, economic, and social equality of the sexes" (Ballou 2014). They then assert that while there may be "some women who call themselves feminists and act more like misandrists," these women are wrong (Bustle). Such arguments give truth to #WAF's claims of feminist bullying and condescension.

In a more extreme case, one annoyed user reacted to the site by starting the Tumblr *Confused Cats Against Feminism*, in which post-it notes near lounging cats state things like, "I don't need feminism because I like it when a man opens the door for me to enter a room. And then leave it again. And enter. And leave. And . . . enter. No wait, leave, definitely leave. Wait, I mean enter . . ." (Cohen 2014). The comparison here between cats and #WAFs rests on a perceived sense that both groups are selfish, manipulative, lazy, and idiotic. This comparison also illustrates how the experience of incoherence on #WAF allows others to dehumanize these women. Others went further by arguing that these women did not appear to express any agency or sense of self at all here. Nina Burleigh described the women involved as "sock puppets of men's rights activists" (Burleigh 2014). This common term for a "planted" campaign or online figure is a suggestive metaphor that presents these women as purposefully simplistic caricatures only capable of relaying the thoughts of others—in this case through the hand of the posts' writers, who are assumed to be these women but may not be. This puppetry rhetoric underscores how difficult it is to actually experience these images as real women expressing real thoughts. Rather, Burleigh frames these women as misogynistic fantasies and refers to them "as nubile and posed in ways that fulfill dirty old men's wildest dreams about pliant young things" (Burleigh 2014). While it is true that many of the posts feature cleavage and some women are topless and use their signs to cover their breasts, these images represent the women not as pliant, but rather as in control of their sexuality. These photos ooze a sense of agency, from the selfie poses, to the cue cards to the commentary below them and their collective placement on this site. Here, incoherence does not negate agency, but rather becomes its most dominant attribute.

While many critics experienced these women as irrational and ignorant, we must keep in mind that such charges have long been directed towards the angry and dispossessed—most notably women and people of color. While rationality and the desire for coherence claims to be a universal good associated with thoughts and people endowed with the power of reason and logic, it is a rhetorical device that shuts down dissent; it props up certain logics and power structures at the expense of others. Those most traumatized by the status quo have the greatest reason to be unreasonable and incoherent.

And indeed, one can sense a great deal of trauma in #WAF and postfeminism more generally. The perceived incoherence may be viewed as a sign of emotional distress. Many posts complain about and/or allude to personal insults and incidents of bullying, harassment, and victimization suffered at the hands of feminists. In addition, there are also signs of displaced anger, denial, hysteria, paranoia, transference, and repetition that all point to a shared traumatic past. In turn, understanding this site as what Anne Cvetkovich has described as an archive of everyday traumas—an archive of feeling—helps to make the irrationality and incoherence of these posts entirely reasonable (Cvetkovich 2003).

Yet, this analytical strategy has its own drawbacks. While experiencing these women as an archive of feeling may be a reconciliatory, reparative move that also addresses the structural problems that make such a site exist, I would assume that these #WAFs would consider it extremely patronizing. Labeling these images as signs of trauma suggests, again, that these women do not understand their own experience, but it does not carry with it the same judgment and blame that many critics level at them. Perhaps the job of the feminist activist when confronting traumatic phenomena like #WAF should be to make its unreasonableness reasonable, to make its incoherence understandable and to take its irrationality seriously.

Works Cited

Abcarian, Robin. 2016. "The Willfully Ignorant Women Who Post on 'Women Against Feminism.'" *Latimes.com*, May 28. Accessed May 28, 2017. http://www.latimes.com/local/abcarian/la-me-ra-women-against-feminism-20140808-column.html.

Ahmed, Sara. 2006. *Queer Phenomenology: Orientations, Objects, Others*. 1st edition. Durham: Duke University Press Books.

Ahmed, Sara. 2010. "Killing Joy: Feminism and the History of Happiness." *Signs* 35 (3): 571–94.

Ahmed, Sara. 2014. *The Cultural Politics of Emotion*. 2nd edition. New York: Routledge.

Ballou, Elizabeth. 2014. "'Women Against Feminism' Facebook Group Is Woefully Misinformed." *Bustle*, July 21. Accessed May 28, 2017. http://www.bustle.com/articles/32509-women-against-feminism-facebook-group-is-woefully-misinformed.

Banet-Weiser, Sarah. 2015. "Popular Misogyny: A Zeitgeist—Culture Digitally." *Culture Digitally*, January 21. Accessed May 28, 2017. http://culturedigitally.org/2015/01/popular-misogyny-a-zeitgeist/.

Beauvoir, Simone de. 1993. *The Second Sex*. Everyman's Library 137. New York: Alfred A. Knopf.

Blyth, Ian, and Susan Sellers. 2004. *Hélène Cixous: Live Theory*. New York; London: Bloomsbury Academic.

Burleigh, Nina. 2014. "Women Against Womyn: First Wave, Second Wave, Third Wave, and Now Three Steps Back." *Observer*, July 30. Accessed May 28, 2017. http://observer.com/2014/07/women-against-womyn-first-wave-second-wave-third-wave-and-now-three-steps-back/.

Cohen, Rebecca. 2014. "'Confused Cats Against Feminism' Is the Purrfect Response to 'Women Against Feminism.'" *Mother Jones*, July 29. Accessed May 28, 2017. http://www.motherjones.com/mixed-media/2014/07/confused-cats-against-feminism-purrfect-anti-feminist-women.

"Coherence, N." 2016. *OED Online*. Oxford University Press. Accessed May 28, 2017. http://www.oed.com/view/Entry/35933.

Cvetkovich, Ann. 2003. *An Archive of Feelings: Trauma, Sexuality, and Lesbian Public Cultures*. Durham, NC: Duke University Press Books.

Elderkin, Beth. 2014. "These Are the 'Women Against Feminism.'" *Daily Dot*, August 3. Accessed May 28, 2017. http://www.dailydot.com/lifestyle/women-against-feminism-tumblr/.

Faludi, Susan. 2006. *Backlash: The Undeclared War against American Women*. New York: Three Rivers Press.

Friedan, Betty, Gail Collins, and Anna Quindlen. 2013. *The Feminine Mystique*. 50th Anniversary edition. New York: W.W. Norton & Company.

Gearan, Anne, Abby Phillip, and Karen Tumulty. 2016. "Clinton: Trump Is 'Dangerously Incoherent,' 'Temperamentally Unfit' to Be President." *Washington Post*, June 2. Accessed May 28, 2017. https://www.washingtonpost.com/politics/clinton-trump-is-dangerously-incoherent-temperamentally-unfit-to-be-president/2016/06/02/577e5174-28db-11e6-b989-4e5479715b54_story.html.

Gill, Rosalind, and Christina Scharff, eds. 2011. *New Femininities: Postfeminism, Neoliberalism and Subjectivity*. London: Palgrave Macmillan.

Hall, Kimberly. 2015. "Selfies and Self-Writing: Cue Card Confessions as Social Media Technologies of the Self." *Television & New Media*, 17 (3): 228–242.

Ihde, Don. 2012. *Experimental Phenomenology, Second Edition: Multistabilities.* 2nd edition. Albany: State University of New York.

Jo, Lucky. 2014. "TSM Responds to 'Women Against Feminism.'" *Total Sorority Move,* July 4. Accessed May 28, 2017. http://totalsororitymove.com/tsm-responds-to-women-against-feminism/.

Knoblauch, C.H. 1979. "Coherence Betrayed: Samuel Johnson and the 'Prose of the World.'" *Boundary* 27 (2): 235–60. doi: 10.2307/303084.

LaFrance, Adrienne. 2016. "Trump's Incoherent Ideas About 'the Cyber'—The Atlantic." *The Atlantic,* September 27.

McRobbie, Angela. 2007. "Postfeminism and Popular Culture: Bridget Jones and the New Gender Regime." In *Interrogating Postfeminism: Gender and the Politics of Popular Culture,* edited by Yvonne Tasker and Diane Negra, 27–39. Durham, N.C.: Duke University Press.

Parton, Heather. 2016. "Trump's Incoherent Greatest Hits: His Stream-of-Nonsense Debate Style Is Tough to Combat." *Salon.com,* September 26. Accessed May 28, 2017. http://www.salon.com/2016/09/26/trumps-incoherent-greatest-hits-his-stream-of-nonsense-debate-style-is-tough-to-combat/.

Radner, Hilary. 2011. *Neo-Feminist Cinema: Girly Films, Chick Flicks and Consumer Culture.* New York: Routledge.

Rehorick, David Allan, and Gail Taylor. 1995. "Thoughtful Incoherence: First Encounters with the Phenomenological-Hermeneutical Domain." *Human Studies* 18 (4): 389–414.

Sobchack, Vivian Carol. 2004. *Carnal Thoughts: Embodiment and Moving Image Culture.* Berkeley: University of California Press. http://www.loc.gov/catdir/bios/ucal052/2004006180.html http://www.loc.gov/catdir/description/ucal051/2004006180.html.

Sokolowski, Robert. 2000. *Introduction to Phenomenology.* Cambridge: Cambridge University Press.

Tasker, Yvonne, and Diane Negra. 2007. "Introduction: Feminist Politics and Postfeminist Culture." In *Interrogating Postfeminism: Gender and the Politics of Popular Culture.* Durham, N.C.: Duke University Press, 1–26.

Valenti, Jessica. 2014. "Feminism Makes Women 'Victims'? I Think You've Mistaken Us for the Sexists." *Guardian,* July 30. Accessed May 28, 2017. http://www.theguardian.com/commentisfree/2014/jul/30/feminism-makes-women-victims-sexist-women-against-feminism.

Yoon-Hendricks, Alexandra. 2014. "Women Against Feminism: Misinformed and Missing the Point." *SexEtc,* August 26. Accessed May 28, 2017. https://sexetc.org/women-against-feminism-misinformed/.

11

LEAN IN OR BEND OVER?

Postfeminism, Neoliberalism, and Hong Kong's *Wonder Women*

Gina Marchetti

In their article "Second Thoughts on the Second Wave," Deborah Rosenfelt and Judith Stacey (1987) use the term "postfeminism" to describe the political malaise of the Reagan–Thatcher years. Almost 30 years later, Catherine Rottenberg (2014) interrogates the rise of "neoliberal feminism," which arguably constitutes the next "wave" of postfeminism marking women's small advances into the world of the financial, political, and military elite since the 1980s. As David Harvey (2005) points out in *A Brief History of Neoliberalism*, Chinese leader Deng Xiaoping worked closely with Reagan and Thatcher to engineer a world economy that would redistribute the world's financial resources on a massive scale to the detriment of those on the bottom rung of the economic ladder, which, of course, includes the preponderance of the world's women. At the edges of Chinese, British, and American political and economic influence, Hong Kong serves as a case study of the ways in which geopolitics and the global economy shape gender hierarchies as well as the feminist response to these changes. Postfeminism, as well as a range of emerging feminisms, compete in the territory with various discourses involving Chinese ethnicity, local identity, gender, and sexuality that emerge at the intersection of what Arjun Appadurai calls the "mediascape" and the "ideoscape" in global modernity (1996, 45–46). Feminism as an ideology and a media image has become part of the fabric of Hong Kong popular culture as women wrestle with the demands of national histories of oppression, diasporic inequities, and local traditions involving gender inequities.

The transformation of Hong Kong from a British colony to a Special Administrative Region (SAR) of the People's Republic of China has prompted the emergence of a new constellation of postcolonial feminisms in the territory which expresses Hong Kong's evolving ideas about gender and sexuality since the 1997 change in sovereignty. In this chapter I explore how the global circulation of

Hollywood entertainment and news reporting from the United States creates an environment in twenty-first-century Hong Kong in which popular American postfeminist discourses rub up against emerging feminisms that reposition ethnic Chinese women in new economic, social, cultural, and political formations. I use Barbara Wong's 2007 film *Wonder Women* as a case study to examine the ways in which this tension is mediated within popular Hong Kong media culture.

In their anthology *New Femininities: Postfeminism, Neoliberalism and Subjectivity*, Rosalind Gill and Christina Scharff (2011) outline the ways in which postfeminism and neoliberalism converge around a set of common ideals, including individualism, the privileging of the responsible, self-regulating and choice-oriented subject, and the gendering of this self-managed and self-disciplined subject as female. In this sense, the freely choosing, independent woman celebrated within postfeminism is also the ideal neoliberal subject, called up to climb the corporate ladder while also raising equally ambitious children. Indeed, this model for female success that Gill and Scharff describe put earlier demands for gender equality to rest and make feminism, as seen in its first and second "waves," passé. From a Western point of view, postfeminism as a sensibility marks upper-class, white, straight, educated women's partial victory to achieve equality with men in the boardroom—if not the bedroom. Working-class, poor, LGBTQ, racial and ethnic minority women did not make the same gains and some actually lost ground as neoliberal reforms redistributed wealth and resources to a small minority at the top of the economic hierarchy (Ehrenreich 2001). The "third" wave, exemplified by riot grrrl, and American feminists like Rebecca Walker and Amy Richards (see Baumgardner and Richards 2000), among others, recognizes the need to consider the women left out of the postfeminist narrative, but it may not fully account for a global sisterhood in which women in Asia, Africa, and Latin America may have very different needs. The feminism that emerges in Hong Kong bears the traces of these conflicts and contradictions between Euro-American postfeminism, third wave feminism, and the postmodern metropolis of Hong Kong. Unsurprisingly, aspirational narratives for women in Asia have limits. In Hong Kong's case, women's lives have been complicated by a British colonial and American-inflected past coming into conflict with a mainland Chinese future. Popular narratives work through these emerging feminist possibilities in stories about Hong Kong's past and present with an eye to a possible future for women who aspire to gender justice and sexual citizenship.

The 1997 financial crisis, intimately linked in time and emotion with Hong Kong's change in sovereignty, put American-style neoliberal feminism as described by Rottenberg (2014) at odds with the fact that macro-economic and geopolitical forces limit any semblance of freedom available to the territory's women. Navigating the gender hierarchy becomes part of the challenge, particularly when global media offer little support. The ideology of "leaning in" and "having it all" obscures the need for collective action and a renewed call for women's liberation from oppressive social norms and cultural expectations. Indeed, neoliberal feminism emphasizes individual responsibility, competition, and material success as privileged wives, mothers, and corporate leaders as the measure of women's "progress" in contemporary society.

Moving away from previous calls for collective political action, women who see feminism in terms of self-help and career development feed into media representations of upwardly mobile professional women in the new global economy as models of gender equality. For example, Facebook COO Sheryl Sandberg promotes this type of feminism in her bestselling book, *Lean In: Women, Work, and the Will to Lead* (2013). In this memoir-cum-self-help volume, Sandberg tells her own inspirational story of managing to juggle family and career to get to the top of a male-dominated corporate pyramid. Although produced before Sandberg's book, Barbara Wong's film *Wonder Women* (2007) illustrates the way in which a woman filmmaker from Hong Kong imagines the lives of the territory's career women through the rhetoric of American corporate attitudes. Like Sandberg, who calls on women in American business to accommodate their behavior to the needs of capitalist enterprise, the women in Wong's film mirror the expectations of the men who have shaped their environment. Looking at Hong Kong in the decade beginning with the Handover to mainland China in 1997 allows Wong to provide contrasting and complementary models of patriarchal organization in transition. As if following Sandberg's advice step-by-step, Wong's "wonder women" continually negotiate terms in their private and professional lives. Powerful men such as entrepreneur George Soros, British colonial Governor Chris Patten, Chinese President Jiang Zemin, Prince Charles, and Hong Kong Chief Executive Donald Tsang shape the environment in which these women live. By alluding to the authority these male leaders exert, *Wonder Women* reveals a geopolitical dimension to the fortunes of the fictional female characters in the film, and the women must bend in order not to break as they navigate changes that go beyond the borders of the territory.

Barbara Wong sees the problems as well as the promise of these successful business women in her film. Interestingly though, she distances herself from feminism as a political strategy. Drawing on postfeminist rhetoric, Wong states that she sees no need for gender equality: "I don't think sex equality is so important. Men and women are from completely two different planets. Why bother to get equality, as A never equals to B. We should all try to 'be ourselves', . . . and go for what we want as an individual instead of always claiming that the world is not equal" (Podvin 2004). However, *Wonder Women* does tacitly acknowledge the fact that women's lives can never be disengaged from the political and economic realities that shape their society. The film captures the contradictory moods of the territory and the gendered nature of these precipitous changes. The narrative relies on melodrama to portray the territory's turn away from old colonial associations, and comedy colors segments that usher in the new regime. This fragmented structure gives the film a hyperbolic, campy quality. This schizophrenic blend of pathos and farce describes the "one country, two systems" agreement between Britain and China, a decade after the Handover, with female protagonists left both laughing and crying.

As the territory continues to struggle for universal suffrage in order to exert control over its identity and destiny, I argue that *Wonder Women* provides an opportunity to consider the role Hong Kong plays in developing political formations—including emerging feminisms—on the global stage. Women in mainland China, Taiwan, Hong Kong, and throughout the Chinese diaspora fight to assert their interests in a global polity. They represent a range of common, complementary, and competing political interests, and the portrayal of women's battle to survive in *Wonder Women* opens a path to understanding how Hong Kong feminism contributes to this struggle. As a female filmmaker, Barbara Wong offers a sometimes comic, often tragic, and not completely convincing story of women's economic assent. Under its melodramatic surface, the film manages to document attitudes about feminism, neoliberalism, and the role globalization plays in the lives of women in Asia.

Hong Kong Feminisms: Between Hollywood and China

Wonder Women draws on Hollywood images of working women to construct its own story of Hong Kong's gender politics. Yet, these politics are fraught due to the unique historical positioning of Hong Kong as a postcolonial cultural and geopolitical hybrid. It is of little surprise that Hollywood films often promote neoliberal feminism as a dominant ideology, which reflects both the hegemonic status of this type of feminism and likely, the demographic makeup of mostly white, middle-class American men and women working in the film industry (Ralph J. Bunche Center for African American Studies 2016; Smith et al. 2016). Indeed, as I discuss in the previous section, neoliberal feminism is intimately related to a particular economic and political history that has shaped Europe and America since the mid-twentieth century.

In contrast, China has a different history of feminist struggles dating back in the modern era to campaigns against footbinding and colonial exploitation of women's bodies during the late-Qing Dynasty, and in support of female suffrage in the Republican Era. After the establishment of the People's Republic of China in 1949, Mao's proclamation that "women hold up half the sky" did not completely erase gender inequities, and, during the Reform Era inaugurated by Deng Xiaoping, women have gained some advances in the marketplace while losing ground in other areas involving personal choice, such as the one-child policy which has only recently been eased (Rofel 2007). Yet, Hong Kong's transformation from a manufacturing powerhouse fueled by cheap refugee labor during the Cold War to a financial giant bridging business interests in Asia and the West in the 1990s has created a climate for the territory's women that is distinct from that of China. For example, women such as the film director Barbara Wong have been educated outside of Asia, and their cosmopolitan views often owe more to American models of gender equity than to the Maoist legacy of state feminism promulgated by the All-China Women's Federation across the border from Hong Kong.

Several Hong Kong female filmmakers, including directors such as Mabel Cheung (Ford 2008), who have attended school in the United States, navigate between American and Chinese cultures through their depiction of gender on the territory's screens. More recently though, a new demographic of younger female Hong Kong filmmakers have emerged as part of what Mirana Szeto and Chen Yun-Chung (2011) have called the "HKSAR New Wave." Many in this younger generation have strong ties to America, having studied in the United States or lived there for extended periods. I am suggesting that their encounter with America had an impact on their development as filmmakers and their vision of women on screen as well. Many of these Hong Kong women filmmakers, including Barbara Wong, continue their conversations with American culture, including feminism, when they return to the HKSAR to make films about Chinese women in the territory.

Barbara Wong studied film production at New York University's Tisch School of the Arts, and although her features deal with Chinese women, her perspective on female sexuality shows the influence of her time spent in the United States. In an interview with *Hong Kong CineMagic*, Wong notes that she has had the opportunity to compare sexual relations in America and China:

> there is a difference between East and West. My experience in New York told me that Americans are actually not that open, but they always 'portray' that they are very open, or want to believe that they are most free-spirited people in the world. While Mainland China is totally opposite. They always portray that they are still traditional, but actually, they will do things that shock you.
>
> *(Podvin 2004)*

Although Wong maintains that she has never encountered sexism in the film industry, she displays a keen sense of gender inequalities in her feature films as well as documentaries such as *Women's Private Parts* (2000), a candid view of Hong Kong women's sex lives.

Arguably, the incorporation of postfeminist discourses lionizing women entrepreneurs, consumer culture, and material wealth as signs of women's assent in the world of men places Barbara Wong's work in conversation with neoliberal feminism, and the writings of Sheryl Sandberg provide the backdrop for looking at how *Wonder Women* nods to American attitudes about gender. As the female protagonists struggle to succeed in a new world of Chinese financial ascendency and political sovereignty after 1997, the competing voices of American and

Chinese policy reverberate. The clashes in 2015 between presidential candidate Hillary Clinton and Chinese president Xi Jinping over the advances for Chinese women since the 1995 United Nations Conference on Women in Beijing, where then-First Lady Clinton claimed that "women's rights are human rights and human rights are women's rights once and for all," highlight the fact that these two superpowers promote very different visions of female empowerment. While Xi sees China leading the world in advancing women's rights in economic terms, Clinton calls him "shameless" for the 2015 detention of five young feminist activists who were agitating for the rights of women to protest violence against women. Although *Wonder Women* was made long before this exchange, the fact that this tension can be felt so keenly in Wong's feature underscores the social and cultural depth of the divisions behind the emergence of a specifically HKSAR feminism.

A Tale of Two Titles

The English title of Wong's film, based on the novel *Waves of the Heart* by Anita Leung Fung-yee, conjures up images of the WW II-era DC Comic Book heroine Wonder Woman, portrayed on American television by Lynda Carter in the 1970s and Gal Gadot in the 2017 reboot.[1] Barbara Wong's "wonder women" have no superpowers; however, the director does have high expectations for her female protagonists, claiming: "That's why it's called *Wonder Women*—it's about how women take control when things go awry, and how they have to put on so many faces nowadays—you have to be tough fielding difficulties in the office, then you go home and your family expect you to be gentle and doting" (Tsui 2007). The English title of the film also connects *Wonder Women* directly to what Molly Haskell has called the "woman's film," a Hollywood staple designed to attract a female audience (1987, 153). Haskell breaks the woman's film down into four main themes—sacrifice, affliction, choice, and competition—and all four make their appearance in *Wonder Women*. The principal protagonist Joy (Gigi Leung) sacrifices her own desires and ambitions for the sake of her family and employer; deals with the affliction of the SARS virus in her household; makes various choices involving men, including the critical one to stay in Hong Kong rather than follow her husband to Singapore to support his career; and her colleague Tung (Fiona Sit) sees herself competing with Joy over the attentions of a conniving boyfriend, Kenny (Jimmy Fu).

The Chinese title, however, brings up very different associations. 女人本色, "The nature of women," bears a marked similarity to the title of John Woo's megahit, 英雄本色 *A Better Tomorrow* (1986), with a Chinese title that roughly translates as the "nature of heroes," a moniker it shares with another classic Hong Kong crime film (Lung Kong's 1967 film *Story of a Discharged Prisoner*). "The nature of women" connotes an essentialist understanding of femininity, but in relation to the earlier iterations of the "nature of heroes" also aligns it with Hong

Kong classics involving traditional values of loyalty and righteousness in the modern metropolis. In several ways, Wong's film provides a female rejoinder to these Hong Kong crime classics by focusing on sisterly bonds among women working together in their own version of the *jiang hu* of multinational corporations, financial transactions, cross-border politics, and the vicissitudes of the stock and real estate markets.[2]

Wonder Women did not garner the same enthusiasm as John Woo's or Lung Kong's films did, however. Produced with Beijing's blessing to celebrate the creation of the HKSAR, Wong's film serves as a tribute to the resilience of Hong Kong during a period of enormous economic, social, and political upheaval. Clearly, the film serves a didactic function, produced under a tight budget, so that product placements vie with archival news footage to provide a skewed portrait of the decade (1997–2007). To be fair, although representatives of mainland China do come to the rescue in dramatic ways in the film, the Hong Kong women manage to succeed largely through their own grit and determination. Their success, however, does come at a price, which can only be measured in the crassest fashion within the consumer marketplace as they display their success through their ability to buy and sell fashionable products. This gives an odd slant to the film's celebration of feminist values. A reviewer from *Far East Films*, Andrew Saroch, complains:

> All the male protagonists are either conniving, cowardly or are simply around to plunge our heroines into more drama. It felt rather uncomfortable to see every representation of my gender come across as, at best, completely selfish, at worst downright unsavoury. There's also that continued message that emanates from so many Hong Kong films, how worthless someone is without money and power. It could be argued that the folly of rampant materialism is shown in the way the economic downturn destroys people, yet without a swaggering financial clout, none of the characters is considered greatly significant.
>
> (Saroch 2015)

Product placements for Mercedes, Samsung, Osim, and Salvatore Ferragamo, among many others, not only help finance the film, but define the characters as well. Commodities take on a moral dimension, and women become consumed within a spectacle that glorifies capitalist excess. The women in the film are "wonders," but also symbols of Hong Kong's empty materialism and moral vacuity. Their ostensibly feminist sisterhood serves the needs of the marketplace first, national unity second, and progress for gender equity as an afterthought. However, within this limited vision of Hong Kong women, political contradictions manage to come to the surface, exaggerated by melodrama and comedy out of proportion to any sense of verisimilitude, and it is in this cinematic world of excess that a nascent feminism struggles to emerge.

Leaning into the Corporate Environment

Wonder Women provides a rich opportunity to examine the ways in which various feminisms are dramatized in relation to particular models of masculinity. Like Sandberg, who calls on women in American business to recognize the reality of the corporate world and accommodate their behavior to the needs of capitalist enterprise, the women in Barbara Wong's film mirror the expectations of the men who have shaped their environment, providing several contrasting and complementary models of patriarchal organization in transition. In the course of the narrative, most men associated with the old colonial regime die, and Wong litters the screen with corpses representing the old order with melodramatic relish. The female protagonists flourish, and the men connected to the rise of the mainland Chinese economy also thrive. The allegorical narrative insists on the death of the old British and the embrace of the new Chinese regime as key to Hong Kong's prosperity. Women allegorize this, and a type of feminist discourse comes into play to support this ideological trajectory.

The film opens with a shot of the exterior of the office building where the fictional corporation, the Lyndon Group, has its headquarters. Drawing on a vaguely American corporate model, the company specializes in hotels, and the standard corporate hierarchy shapes the office culture with an aloof Chairman, a CEO and CFO under him, and a staff of primarily female office workers. The majority of the blue-collar workers appear exclusively during a sequence devoted to a company-wide strike, and most of the film revolves around the relationship between office politics and the domestic life of the managers and their immediate staff. In the first scene, Wong defines her characters through their footwear, and two sets of high heels ascending a staircase introduce the principal female protagonists, junior executive Joy (Gigi Leung) and her assistant Tung (Fiona Sit) (Figure 11.1). Later, when Tung breaks her heel, the close-up signals the character's downfall (Figure 11.2). The high heel shoe provides simply one example of the many commodity fetishes which provide a visual commentary on Hong Kong's material obsessions. In this opening sequence, Joy has a stomachache, as well as suffering the headache of not having any People's Republic of China flags for their Handover banquet on the evening of June 30, 1997. While Tung wants to get medicine for Joy, fear of displeasing the boss, To Lam (George Lam), makes finding the flags more urgent. The needs and desires of men in superior positions take priority over women's bodies and health concerns. While Tung's sisterly attentiveness speaks to a potential feminist subtext, the male-defined business environment precludes taking immediate action, since not having flags for the banquet would give the boss a "heart attack."

The next shot introduces their boss To through a close-up of his shiny formal shoes as he marches toward the camera, clearly in charge. However, unlike the women ascending the staircase, To remains on level ground, and the cut to the shoes of Chairman Chan (Eddie Ko) emerging from his limousine to take charge

FIGURE 11.1 High heels and high ambitions characterize Hong Kong's women on the rise in *Wonder Women*. Author screenshot from *Wonder Women* (Dir. Wong 2007)

FIGURE 11.2 Tung's broken heel signals her failed dreams. Author screenshot from *Wonder Women* (Dir. Wong 2007)

of the event does not bode well for the CEO. Wong intercuts news footage of the Handover ceremony with the banquet in which the Chairman announces a shake-up at Lyndon Group, substituting To with a new CEO, Ching Bit Chung (played by mainland actor, Yuan Nie). Replacing To—played by mustachioed Hong Kong veteran actor George Lam—with a much younger mainland man underlines the allegorical weight of the juxtaposition of the fictional events with the facts of the change in sovereignty. The old guard brought up under British colonialism gives way to the fresh talent brought in by the Chinese.

During the same announcement, the Chairman promotes Joy to Chief Financial Officer and Head of Personnel—a considerable step up from a job defined by finding flags for the banquet. With the ink not yet dry on the stenciled Chinese flags, Hong Kong's corporate elite changes its affiliation with women stepping over their male superiors to get ahead under the new regime. The next sequence reveals that To and Joy are married, and the Chairman has effectively broken up this "power couple" in his company with his surprise dismissal of To. To directly states the political nature of the move when he confirms that his ties to the British government no longer have value and that the need to replace him with someone with stronger connections to the new political order seems clear. Although Joy offers to quit too, her husband does not want to stand in her way, and they make plans for him to get a fresh start in Singapore, while she remains in Hong Kong as CFO.

The regime change opens the way for women's advancement, but not without a price. In fact, the film quickly answers the question To poses after Joy's promotion: "Why would I be jealous of my smart wife?" As Joy's boss and husband, To represents a fading colonial paternal authority in her life. Reluctantly, he accepts the rise of women in the new political economy, since he has few options. For men, "the nature of heroes" calls for loyalty, but the "nature of women" offers the possibility of more flexible allegiances. Paired with To, Joy models the type of "power couple" Sheryl Sandberg and her late husband, Dave Goldberg, appear to be in *Lean In*. Both ambitious with a young family, these couples rely on neoliberal feminism to provide the ideological support for their individual career decisions. This type of feminism, of course, rests on class privileges most women do not enjoy.

In fact, Joy seems to have taken all the advice in Sandberg's book, which acts as a compendium of feminist-inspired wisdom for executive women working in multinational corporations such as Facebook. Sandberg advises women in the global business world to take their rightful "seat" at the table with the male powerbrokers and not feel like "imposters" when they step up for leadership positions. She calls on men to support women as genuine partners rather than as appendages to serve their own ambitions. When called upon, Joy gladly takes her husband's seat "at the table" at the Lyndon Group; she defines her leadership role in relation to her women subordinates and has no difficulty giving orders; she manages motherhood; and, she clearly has her husband on board as a "real partner." Even though *Wonder Women* precedes Sandberg's self-help bestseller, the picture the American executive paints of women in the corporate world finds a stunning parallel in Barbara Wong's film.

Indeed, the similarities between Joy and Sandberg run deep. Both display complicated attitudes toward their female employees. These executive women feel the need to justify their own success and show compassion for those under them, while also rationalizing the elusive qualities of "leadership" in the corporate world. For example, the female domestic workers who make these women's careers possible receive little attention in Sandberg's book and Wong's film. In *Lean In*, Sandberg complains about the "queen bee" syndrome of isolated females in positions of power, while simultaneously criticizing women's awkward attempts to find female "mentors." In *Wonder Women*, Joy takes a number of women under her wing, but no female character in the film proves her equal. Her close associate Tung, for example, never moves up the corporate ladder and even ends up working in a bar when she quits her job at Lyndon. Tung and the eccentric Momo (Kitty Yuen) provide comic relief throughout the film, so when Tung, Momo, and Joy go into business together in the final act, their company name, "Joy Joy," unconditionally announces which character leads the corporation. Indeed, Joy's career trajectory illustrates Sandberg's call for individual leadership rather than collective action: "The shift to a more equal world will happen person by person. We move closer to the larger goal of true equality with each woman who leans in" (2013, 11). Sandberg, of course, fails to see that for every woman who leans in, multitudes bend over.

Moreover, when Joy champions her female subordinates, she does so at little risk to her own career. In one scene, Joy learns that the CEO Ching overturned her endorsement of a second mortgage for the tea lady, Mrs. Lee, who wants to finance her son's MBA with the money. Joy storms into the CEO's office to demand he reconsider his decision but Ching explains calmly that Mrs. Lee poses an unreasonable risk, given the poor condition of the real estate market. However, Joy complains he has undercut her authority. Ching counters by asking: "Why are you arguing with your boss for the sake of a tea lady?" Joy responds, "Human resources are a kind of wealth. Even in the case of a tea lady . . . Otherwise why would anyone keep working so hard for us?" Her logic involving investment in women as "human resources" seems logical. However, while Joy follows Sandberg in arguing for the pecuniary logic of supporting women in the corporation, Ching's libidinous gaze and suggestive grin indicate he is smitten less by his subordinate's business acumen and more by her feminine charms and sex appeal.

Neoliberal feminism provides only one strand of the complex weave that *Wonder Women* utilizes in its narrative of how Hong Kong women chart a course through very different expectations of "success" in the HKSAR. While Sandberg's optimistic view of women in business reads as a manifesto of personal triumph, Wong's film incorporates darker moods and her heroines experience tragic losses, betrayals, humiliations and titanic disappointments as well as moments of hope before the finale. The melodramatic suffering begins as Joy and her husband face the trials of the 1997–98 Asian financial crisis. Losing his job marked the beginning of To's decline economically and emotionally, and Joy struggles to assist her emasculated husband. However, To goes into a deep depression and, drunk, calls

Joy on his cell phone, singing "Joy to the World" to her as a last hurrah before being killed in a car collision. If cell phones and fast cars allegorize Hong Kong's material prosperity, To's death in a car wreck with a phone to his ear provides a fitting visual metaphor for the territory's economic crash.

To's death parallels another in the film to make sure the lesson has been learned. A former neighbor, whom Joy calls Uncle Nine (Shui Hung Hui), cheats her out of half the value of her deceased father's flat. Joy tells him that he "deserves to die," and Nine takes her words to heart. He seals the windows and doors with masking tape and asphyxiates himself by burning charcoal. In this, filmmaker Wong draws on news stories that reported this sort of death as a preferred method of suicide for Hong Kong residents ruined by the financial downturn. The film underscores the fact that another colonial remnant has been eliminated by setting the scene during the Christmas holiday. Decorations line the window frames next to the masking tape and Nine's son, Yim (Kevin Cheng), enjoys an outing at a toy store with Joy's son, while Nine writes his suicide note implicating Joy in his death. When Yim confronts Joy at the hospital, a wall decal, "Joy to the World," provides an ironic commentary on the fact that Joy prefers to give Yim a little "joy" by not telling him that his father had cheated her out of 5 million dollars. The association of all of this with Joy's husband's death and the Christian holiday of Christmas highlights the connection between the remnants of British rule and the decay of male authority in the territory—a point reinforced by repeated shots of Christian crosses in the cemetery during the funeral.

Wonder Women does not spare the younger generation from its clean sweep of colonialism. The film implies that Joy's son Lok is morally bankrupt at a young age because he no longer has a strong patriarchal figure in his life. Lacking any scruples, Luk has taken a classmate's watch in exchange for a homework assignment. When Joy confronts her son, he refuses to return the watch, so Joy threatens to tell his teacher. Lok responds by calling his mother a liar because she has never visited his school in the past. Soon after, Lok contracts a fatal case of SARS and Yim also dies of the disease. With To, Nine, Lok, and Yim all dead, Joy no longer has any intimate connections to colonial Hong Kong. However, her freedom comes at the price of the guilt associated with being a "bad" mother, who spends too much time away from her family. In stark contrast to Sandberg's insistence that corporate women can achieve work–life balance, Joy ends up losing her husband, son, and extended family.

During the Handover, the Chairman kept local women and brought in mainland Chinese men to reflect the new postcolonial reality of the territory. With the Handover, he ushered in another model of "feminism," based on the development of women's rights in the People's Republic of China. The fact that the Chairman does not bring in a woman as CEO—either through internal promotion or from the mainland—speaks volumes about the subordinate role women continue to occupy within Wong's story. Ching's romantic interest in Joy undercuts any possibility that he brings a fresh attitude to gender relations to the Hong Kong work environment. Instead, Ching embodies a tendency in mainland China to move away from discourses of gender equality to a reassertion of male privilege in the post-Mao Reform Era of the 1980s and 1990s, and Wong tacitly critiques the gender politics of the new regime in the narrative.

Chinese women are absent in *Wonder Women*; however, the way in which Hong Kong women position themselves in relation to mainland Chinese men hints at what closer social ties with China may bring. Ching's treatment of his female employees, for instance, gives a clear sense of the inferior position women hold in the office. A Chinese patriot, he grabs every opportunity to display his superior knowledge of China's role in global economics. Hungarian-American George Soros' manipulation of the Thai baht reportedly started the 1997 collapse of the market and sent Hong Kong on a downward spiral for several years. However, Ching blithely ignores Joy's remark that the market is a "dog fight" and maintains confidently that America would never provoke China. Ching's confidence that China's state-controlled version of capitalism can counteract the vicissitudes of the global market makes his Hong Kong colleagues look naïve.

Gradually, Joy comes to trust Ching's judgment, and this precipitates her downfall. Without looking, Joy signs documents that list the employees to be made redundant during the SARS epidemic. While Chairman Chan and Ching conveniently go off on a business trip to the UK at the height of the crisis, Joy must deal with the fallout from the lay-offs. Although Joy manages to reach a compromise with the strikers, not all agree with the plan, and one of the male workers physically assaults Joy on the street. Ching comes to her rescue, and Joy, reduced to tears, confesses to him that she feels "useless" as he tends to her bloody wounds. Admitting her weakness proves to be a mistake, and Ching takes advantage of this when the Chairman demands the termination of the person who fired an employee who subsequently committed suicide. To appease the media decrying the callous treatment of Hong Kong workers by the corporate elite, Ching produces the documents Joy signed so that he can avoid being fired. Joy confronts him, but he simply says, "You know it wasn't easy to get to my position." Wong does not need to elaborate on the sexist implications of Ching's remarks, and the fact that the male character cannot see that Joy likely had a much harder time advancing in the corporate world is made apparent.

Joy's mainland love interest becomes the villain of the film, and this can be seen as part of a geopolitical allegory. Ching's courtship symbolizes the PRC's desire to romance its newly reintegrated territory of Hong Kong. The mainland covets control of Hong Kong, rescues it on more than one occasion, but finally betrays it because it cannot let its "inferior"—feminized—territory usurp the position it has worked so hard to establish in the global marketplace. This part of the film's plot represents Hong Kong's ambivalent relationship to mainland China, and the way this political and dramatic setback is resolved unmasks the difficulty of finding a "happy ending" for any story about the Handover.

After Joy leaves the Lyndon Group, the abstract forces of Chinese sovereignty come to her rescue in a very convoluted way. With the blade poised at her wrist to end it all after losing her job and her son in the same day, Joy interrupts her suicidal plans and pulls herself together to answer the doorbell. Momo appears with the surprising news that her chain of hotpot restaurants in mainland China have turned a profit. Not only has the rise of China's economy directly led to the economic success of these Hong Kong women, but, ironically, their good fortune comes from the increase in consumerism related to the sex trade. Momo's dual hot pot for "lovers," which is more sanitary than using a common cooker, implies that the couple may not mutually trust each other not to have sexually transmissible diseases. Business women in Hong Kong, then, ride high on the fortunes of mistresses, temporary "wives," factory girls moonlighting as prostitutes, and other women working in the commercial sex industry on the mainland.

Joy's investments in her friends' lives and enterprises pay off in miraculous ways, illustrating what Sandberg might call the "jungle gym" of women's career paths. Riding high on hot pots, Joy, Tung, and Momo pool their resources to bid for the OSIM franchise in Hong Kong. A Singapore-based brand, OSIM's massage recliners and other health-related household gadgets dominate the Asian market. The rise of the company reflects an increase in demand by an expanding middle class in the region, and Joy, Tung, and Momo have their fingers on the pulse of Chinese consumerism. Momo's zany business schemes, Tung's investment in counterfeit fashion goods, and Joy's experience as CFO/Director of Personnel with a motley female social network of secretaries, old classmates, and tea ladies now pay off, with their accumulated knowledge of the market increasingly dominated by upwardly mobile women in need of displaying their newly acquired status through conspicuous consumption. They face off in front of a panel of OSIM executives—males on one side of the table and the three female entrepreneurs on the other. Afterwards, lacking confidence, Joy expresses her fear of possible failure, and her thoughts find a striking parallel in Sandberg's book in which the COO admits to feeling like an imposter: "I still face situations that I fear are beyond my capabilities. I still have days when I feel like a fraud. And I still sometimes find myself spoken over and discounted while men sitting next to me are not. But now I know how to take a deep breath and keep my hand up. I have learned to sit at the table" (38). Joy, Tung, and Momo all have "learned to sit at the table," and, like Sandberg, they succeed (Figure 11.3). Joy Joy wins the franchise supposedly because of its superior bid, but more likely because William, the tea lady's son whom Joy had bankrolled, heads the franchise team. Although William recuses himself because of this conflict of interest, the fact that his associates know the boss has a close connection (*guan xi*) with this candidate may have swayed their decision.[3] Because of her compassion for another woman rather than her business training, Joy again succeeds. Later, Joy learns that Ching secretly helped get them started by spotting the fledgling enterprise six months rent on a commercial rental for their first shop.

We have the result.

FIGURE 11.3 Tung, Joy, and Momo wait anxiously for the result of their bid for an OSIM franchise. Author screenshot from *Wonder Women* (Dir. Wong 2007)

Paralleling the opening Handover banquet, the film's concluding scene overlaps a celebration of Joy's company entering the open market with an Initial Public Offering party timed to coincide with the July 1, 2007 festivities. A white American man, Harlan, runs the party venue, and Joy asks him casually how long he has been in Hong Kong. Harlan replies that he has lived in the city for fifteen years, so he can speak Cantonese. When Joy asks whether he can speak Mandarin, too, he answers in the affirmative. With images of PRC-supported stocks, as well as Chinese astronauts on the rise, Hong Kong, America, and the rest of the world tag along and grow rich due to China's good fortune.

As Wong points out in her film, women prove vulnerable to the vicissitudes of the market in ways different from men. Women are last hired and first fired, outsiders in predominantly male business networks, on the margins during shakeups, and continuously on the verge of being passed over or pushed out. If Ching embodies "socialism with Chinese characteristics" in *Wonder Women*, Deng Xiaoping's master plan does not look substantially different from corporate American neoliberalism. Feminist politics take a backseat to profits. Ching sees Joy as a potential romantic conquest, a gullible investor, a weak manager, an expendable colleague, and an investment to be exploited at minimal risk. When Joy literally gets slapped in the face by a violent disgruntled employee, she blames her own weakness—presumably as a woman—rather than a capitalist system that perpetuates gross inequality. Sandberg, of course, in her attempt to get businesswomen to "lean in" ignores the bigger picture of the destructive nature of capitalism.

The fact that the women are turned away by their mainland Chinese bosses and are embraced by the young men of Singapore—another former British colony that is now an independent city-state—may surreptitiously point in a political direction belied by the official celebration of the territory's return to Chinese sovereignty. A competitor as well as an alternative model, Singapore engages in its own struggle to stay afloat in the global business world as it continues to embrace authoritarian Confucianism while wrestling with democratic reforms. Hong Kong's "wonder women" manage to prosper, but their position remains precarious. Eliza W.Y. Lee (2004) writes of her hopes for the development of feminism and democracy in the territory that will:

> open up more discursive space for women activists to articulate a feminist discourse on democratic citizenship as an essential ingredient for the construction of a just polity . . . This involves a direct confrontation with the unjust nature of the existing economic and political institutions and how they have worked integrally with patriarchal structures to reproduce women's subordination.
>
> *(2004, 205)*

Wonder Women's "happy ending" for the independent businesswoman in 2007 may not be as "wonderful" as Hong Kong women deserve, and Lee's vision of Hong Kong feminism points to the emergence of a very different political sensibility. Mainland China has embraced Sandberg's *Lean In* and proudly set up the first "Lean In" circle in Beijing in 2013; however, feminist activists continue to face enormous political pressure in the People's Republic. How Hong Kong's feminists will navigate between corporate models of individual success and wider democratic access for women in the public sphere remains to be seen.

The popular postfeminism with a Hong Kong accent seen in *Wonder Women* incorporates many of the key tenets associated with neoliberal feminist ideologues such as Sheryl Sandberg and embodied by politicians such as Hillary Clinton. However, it emerges in a distinctly different cultural environment and geopolitical position in which mainland China, other "tiger" economies such as Singapore, and the lasting impact of British colonialism play a role in defining women's lives. What appears to be a contradictory mess of cross-class, transnational, and intergenerational feminist possibilities has the potential to empower Hong Kong's women to break new ground in politics as well as popular culture, as seen in singer Denise Ho's commitment to LGBTQ rights and the Umbrella Movement. Feminism does emerge in Hong Kong, and commercial films such as *Wonder Women* offer only a glimpse of the range of voices that contribute to the territory's search for justice.

Acknowledgments

Thanks so much to my research assistant Kasey Man Man Wong for her help in preparing the manuscript. A portion of the research funding for this chapter comes from a General Research Fund award, "Hong Kong Women Filmmakers: Sex, Politics and Cinema Aesthetics, 1997–2010," Research Grants Council, Hong Kong, 2011–15 (HKU 750111H). For more information on Hong Kong women filmmakers, see *Hong Kong Women Filmmakers: Sex, Politics and Cinema Aesthetics, 1997 to the Present*, hosted by the Women's Studies Research Centre and Department of Comparative Literature, University of Hong Kong, https://hkwomenfilmmakers.wordpress.com/.

Notes

1 For more on Wonder Woman, see Lillian Robinson, *Wonder Women: Feminisms and Superheroes* (New York: Routledge, 2004).
2 *Jiang hu* refers to the "rivers and lakes" of the world of outlaws in traditional Chinese culture.
3 For more on *guan xi* in Chinese business and personal relations, see Mayfair Yang, *Gifts, Favors, and Banquets: The Art of Social Relationships in China* (Ithaca, N.Y.: Cornell University Press, 1994).

Works Cited

Appadurai, Arjun. 1996. *Modernity at Large: Cultural Dimensions of Globalization*. Minneapolis, Minn.: University of Minnesota Press.

Baumgardner, Jennifer and Amy Richards. 2000. *Manifesta: Young Women, Feminism, and the Future*. New York: Farrar, Straus and Giroux.

Ehrenreich, Barbara. 2001. *Nickel and Dimed: On (not) Getting by in America*. New York: Metropolitan Books.

Ford, Stacilee. 2008. *Mabel Cheung Yuen-ting's An Autumn's Tale*. Hong Kong: Hong Kong University Press.

Gill, Rosalind and Christina Scharff. 2011. *New Femininities: Postfeminism, Neoliberalism and Subjectivity*. London: Palgrave Macmillan.

Harvey, David. 2005. *A Brief History of Neoliberalism*. Oxford: Oxford University Press.

Haskell, Molly. 1987. *From Reverence to Rape: The Treatment of Women in the Movies*. Chicago: University of Chicago Press.

Lee, Eliza W.Y. 2004. "Prospects for the Development of a Critical Feminist Discourse." In *Gender and Change in Hong Kong: Globalization, Postcolonialism, and Chinese Patriarchy*, edited by Eliza W.Y. Lee, 200–7. Honolulu: University of Hawaii Press.

Podvin, Thomas. 2004. "An Interview with Barbara Wong Chun Chun." *Hong Kong Cinemagic*. Last modified January 24, accessed March 31, 2016. http://www.hkcinemagic.com/en/page.asp?aid=51&page=1.

Ralph J. Bunche Center for African American Studies at UCLA. 2016. "2016 Hollywood Diversity Report: Busine$$ as Usual?" *Ralph J. Bunche Center for African American Studies at UCLA*. Last modified February, accessed September 6, 2017. http://www.bunchecenter.ucla.edu/wp-content/uploads/2016/02/2016-Hollywood-Diversity-Report-2-25-16.pdf.

Robinson, Lillian. 2004. *Wonder Women: Feminisms and Superheroes*. New York: Routledge.

Rofel, Lisa. 2007. *Desiring China: Experiments in Neoliberalism, Sexuality, and Public Culture*. Durham: Duke University Press.

Rosenfelt, Deborah, and Judith Stacey. 1987. "Second Thoughts on the Second Wave." *Feminist Review* 27 (Autumn): 77–95.

Rottenberg, Catherine. 2014. "The Rise of Neoliberal Feminism." *Cultural Studies* 28 (3): 418–37.

Sandberg, Sheryl. 2013. *Lean In: Women, Work, and the Will to Lead.* New York: Alfred A. Knopf.

Saroch, Andrew. 2015. "Wonder Women." *Far East Films.* Last updated June 28, accessed March 31, 2016. http://www.fareastfilms.com/?review_post_type=wonder-women.

Smith, Stacy L., Marc Choueiti and Katherine Pieper. 2016. "Inclusion or Invisibility? Comprehensive Annenberg Report on Diversity in Entertainment." *Institute for Diversity and Empowerment at Annenberg.* Last modified February 22, accessed September 6, 2017. http://annenberg.usc.edu/pages/~/media/MDSCI/CARDReport%20FINAL%2022216.ashx.

Szeto, Mirana and Yun-chung Chen. 2011. "Mainlandization and Neoliberalism with Post-colonial and Chinese Characteristics: Challenges for the Hong Kong Film Industry." In *Global Cinema: Capital, Culture, and Marxist Critique,* edited by Jyotsna Kapur and Keith B. Wagner, 239–60. London: Routledge.

Tsui, Clarence. 2007. "Women on Top." *South China Morning Post.* Last modified July 5, accessed March 31, 2016. http://www.scmp.com/article/599332/women-top.

Yang, Mayfair. 1994. *Gifts, Favors, and Banquets: The Art of Social Relationships in China.* Ithaca, N.Y.: Cornell University Press.

12

@NOTOFEMINISM, #FEMINISTSAREUGLY, AND MISANDRY MEMES

How Social Media Feminist Humor is Calling out Antifeminism

Emilie Lawrence and Jessica Ringrose

In *The Aftermath of Feminism*, Angela McRobbie (2009) defines postfeminism as the *simultaneous* rejection of feminism by critics who argued it was outmoded because it championed a now irrelevant political issue (women's equality), *and* the commodification of feminism through forms of faux feminism or a "post-feminist masquerade" that appropriated feminist rhetoric to sell products. Rosalind Gill's (2007) conceptualization of a "postfeminist sensibility" illustrated by the co-optation of feminism through contemporary advertising and other media demonstrated this dynamic of the market-harnessing feminism. Gill and colleagues have shown how faux feminism and commodity feminism can work in many diverse forms; from aid campaigns where Western women and girls are inculcated to save women and girls in the "third world" from their less empowered forms of femininities (Koffman and Gill 2014), to "Love Your Body" discourses that co-opt fat activism and body positivity in the service of expanding capitalist markets to ever wider nets of consumers (Gill and Elias 2014). Thus, postfeminist media culture has been deemed to be a space where feminism *is either vehemently rejected, or is a form of cultural appropriation* that subverts genuine feminist coalition, solidarity, and politics.

However, recent scholarship suggests that the analytical lens offered by postfeminism may no longer be as useful as it once was. Catherine Driscoll (2016) maintains that postfeminism is a totalizing framework that invokes a temporal frame of before and after feminism that is reductive but also Eurocentric, giving it limited purchase in global contexts. Indeed, some debates about postfeminism seem oblivious to their partiality and location, and fail to engage with an intersectional view of media culture and power relations, falling into a form of neo-colonial feminism (Butler, 2013; see also Moorti, this volume). In this chapter, we continue to be troubled by our own and other feminist media studies' scholars reliance on postfeminism as a concept that describes contemporary media culture when we are faced with ever more visible forms of popular feminisms (Retallack et al. 2016).

Our chapter asks whether we are instead in a period characterized by increasingly intense confrontations between feminists and antifeminists, and between varying forms of feminisms, which indicates renewed political struggle and debate? Have we perhaps moved beyond postfeminism into a post-postfeminist moment (see Gill 2016) or are we in a fourth wave of feminism (Munro 2013)? We need only look at the growth of antifeminism evident through the spread of men's rights activists to see the intensification of vehement antifeminism, particularly evident in the context of social media technologies and innovative participatory communities (Ging 2017). Yet at the same time we see enormous representation of feminist discussion on social media that defend feminism, and reject and mock anti-feminist groups and sentiment. Whilst we do not wish to reject the idea of postfeminism entirely, given that it was developed to analyze mainstream media and corporate appropriations of feminism as part of a dominant media "sensibility" (Gill 2007), we suggest that we need to be careful how we understand the limitations of postfeminism for explaining feminism in a social media landscape post-2010 that is markedly different from the media environment of the mid- to late 2000s, when much of the initial writing on postfeminism was first published. In other words, we may ask how everyday users who self-define as feminists are promoting and proliferating feminisms in multiple and complex ways across digital cultures.

In this chapter we consider how social media platforms have produced new spaces for debates over feminism. The undeniable mass uptake of feminism via social media shows us that self-identified feminists are fighting against antifeminism in ways that enable mass participatory audiences via platforms such as Twitter. In particular, we explore how social media feminist humor and irony are used as rhetorical and debating strategies to challenge problematic arguments against or about feminists by re-staging anti-feminist claims as absurd, ridiculous, and illogical. We argue that humorous posts play a central role in increasing feminist audiences and mobilizing feminist connectivity (Papacharissi 2012), collectivity, and solidarity. To demonstrate this, we explore three different manifestations of social media feminist humor that challenge rejections of feminism or antifeminism. First, we look at the hugely popular Twitter account @NoToFeminism, which posts witty rejoinders to antifeminist discourses, and was created specifically to parody the #WomenAgainstFeminism movement (see Cohn, this volume), and has amassed a large following and popularity beyond social media into the mainstream publishing market. Next, we examine the Twitter hashtag #FeministsAreUgly, interrogating how feminists have intervened into the sexist logic that women are feminists because they are sexually undesirable to men. We explore how hashtags can be co-opted in ways that mutate far outside their original aims, given that the hashtag became a space that reinforced Eurocentric, (hetero)normative beauty norms its founders intended it to interrogate. Finally, we explore "misandry" posts which ironically present female superiority in an attempt to parody anti-feminist claims that feminists are man-hating. This tongue in cheek action can be considered a way of mocking willful misunderstandings of feminism. We also consider whether some of the memes celebrate violence against men in gender binary and essentializing ways. Overall we argue that social media affordances offer women opportunities to engage with and *defend feminism* in novel and exciting ways that complicate claims that our media culture is over- whelmingly postfeminist and that we are living in a moment that marginalizes sustained feminist political dialogue and critique.

Fourth-Wave Digital "Call Out" Culture

Since 2005, both popular and academic writers have argued that we are in a new wave of feminism (Peay 2005; Baumgardner 2011; Cochrane 2013). This "fourth-wave" era is characterized by new media technologies, where digital tools are allowing women to build a resilient, popular, reactive movement online. Ruth Phillips and Viviene Cree (2014, 930) suggest that "we are currently wit- nessing a resurgence of interest in feminism across the world," with their claim that we are experiencing a "fourth wave in the global North that has its birth- place primarily on the Internet." This fourth wave of feminist engagement has been critiqued by those who argue that increased usage of the Internet and new digital media affordances such as social media are not enough to determine a new era of political activism. Nonetheless, it is increasingly evident that the Internet has enabled the creation of a global community of feminists who are challenging misogyny and sexism in new and innovative ways.

It is arguably the immediacy and connectivity of the Internet that have enabled this shift from "third-wave" to "fourth-wave" feminism. Social media sites allow users to interact and create spaces for discussion and what has led to a "call-out" culture, in which problematic behaviour such as misogyny can be identified, "called out," and challenged. This culture is indicative of the continuing influence of the third wave, with its focus on micro-politics and challenging sexism and misogyny insofar as they appear in everyday rhetoric, advertising, film, television, literature, and the media (Munro 2013; Wrye 2009). Feminists are turning to social media sites to make visible marginalized voices and bodies, either through amplifying the stories of others or through drawing attention to their own expe- riences, which has opened up significant spaces for resistance to hegemonic femi- ninities. Indeed, social media sites are so integral to the idea of a new era of feminism that research has positioned them as the birthplace of the fourth wave (Solomon 2009). Jennifer Baumgardner (2011) suggests that movements such as riot grrrl were innovations of the third wave, but the fourth wavers introduced the use of blogs, Twitter campaigns, and online media with names like *Jezebel* and *Feministing* to feminist discourse.

Here we aim to highlight how feminism takes shape and flight through the connective tissues of social media. Feminist activism is asserting itself in new ways via technology and various social media platforms that make it accessible especially for younger generations (see Keller 2015). We see increasing evidence of a desire to tackle the feminist backlash, to seek an equality that demobilizes the power of one gender over another, and to shame sexist and violent behavior wherever it is found (see also Cochrane 2013). What is also significant, however, is how these battles over feminism also provide space for discussing and debating differences between feminisms and debates over inclusive or "intersectional" forms of feminism versus feminisms that are overly simplistic, reproducing forms of "white" entitlement or gender binaries that limit the political potential of these forms of feminist humor. These battles over what it means to be a feminist and what feminism is are being staged through the affective modalities of humor online. We explore how a shared sensibility is cultivated through irony and wit to expose inequality, but also how feminist humor can be misread, transmutes, and even works in ambivalent ways to repeat the sexist, divisive logics it is seeking to challenge.

Researching Digital Feminist Humor

Feminist humor attempts to expose and criticize "the bizarre value systems that have been regarded as 'normal' for so long that it is difficult to see how ridiculous they really are" (Barreca 1991, 185). Social media sites provide a platform for the production and distribution of humor and offer an opportunity to question power dynamics by disrupting traditional, well-established stereotypes, thereby exposing gendered power structures. The use of humor online is relatively unexplored, despite the Internet being a microcosm of society, and providing a new terrain for the construction and dissemination of humor. Limor Shifman and Dafna Lemish (2010) conducted a content analysis of Internet humor and argued that a great majority of Internet humor is sexist. They, and others, suggest that gender representations are rooted in well-entrenched, historical constructions of femininity and masculinity as binary notions, as well as hierarchical oppositions (Van Zoonen 1994) and that Internet humor replicates and reproduces these hegemonic norms. Gallivan suggests that feminist humor in contrast is "humor which reveals and ridicules the absurdity of gender stereotypes and gender based inequalities" (1992, 373).

Our interest in social media feminist humor emerged from a research project on digital feminist activism and responses to rape culture (see Keller et al. 2016). Whilst researching how women were fighting back against the legitimation of sexual violence in rape culture we became increasingly interested in their uses of humor. We took inspiration from Carrie Rentschler's (2015) exploration of the Twitter hashtag #SafetyTipsForWomen, which analyzed the humorous way in which women were rejecting the victim-blaming focus of many rape prevention campaigns. The #SafetyTipsForWomen hashtag worked by shifting attention from the tired trope of women "staying safe" by tweeting nonsensical advice, such as "remove your vagina" or "consider not knowing any men." Tweets from the hashtag were retweeted and widely shared via other platforms, due to how they satirically rebutted the traditional anti-rape rhetoric so commonly doled out to women and approached the issue in an accessible, easily consumable manner.

Considering the enormous affective power of humor to connect and mobilize people to engage in a critique of rape culture (Thrift 2015) we began exploring further examples of "hashtag feminism" (Berridge and Portwood-Spacer 2015) that used humor and irony to deflate antifeminism. We adopted a snowball sampling method to explore hashtags that were calling out antifeminism, and we also found evidence of links to other media content such as Tumblr posts and memes as part of the multi-platform intertextual web of social media. Carrie Rentschler and Samantha Thrift (2015) have further considered the use of humorous memes as a form of digital feminist "warfare" in the network given memes' ability to combine visual and textual references to create inside jokes (see also Kanai 2016).

Snowball methods are part of "cyber-ethnography" (Ashford 2009) where content connects and leads virally to further content (Browne 2005). To keep our search bounded we decided on several "exemplars" of feminist humor that tell us something about current struggles over the status of feminism. Emma Jane (2016) suggests that this type of selective mapping is part of an emerging field of Internet "historiography" and critical histories of the present. We agree that this mapping is valuable in developing a case study approach where we purposefully selected posts that we felt were representative of the account, hashtag, or site in terms of content and structure, while also considering how the digital affordance of the platform enabled different types of interaction.

What is unique to our aim in this chapter is to demonstrate how feminist humor is invoked to critique *antifeminism*. Feminist humor is mobilized as a "weapon" to fight back against the side-lining of feminism as irrelevant, outmoded, or desperate (Rentschler and Thrift 2015). We consider how feminist humor may take on many forms (satire, parody, and irony) as feminists find new ways to engage with sexism and anti-feminist narratives online. We are reluctant to ascribe a specific form of humor to each campaign through fear of essentializing and trivializing the complex ways in which each works to trouble and resist anti-feminist rhetoric but we do discuss how the final example – misandry memes – can be interpreted as veering between humor and anger at times, and how this presents an interesting challenge to researchers when exploring if it condones violence or is merely an effective visual outlet for legitimate anger.

Fighting Antifeminism: @NoToFeminism

Perhaps one of the biggest personal disappointments we have faced in researching this topic is confronting the plethora of women-led, anti-feminist backlashes seen widely on Twitter and other social media platforms (see Cohn, this volume). Whilst anti-feminist rhetoric has existed long before social media sites amplified the discord (Steuter 1992), the platforms give new ways for anti-feminist narratives to be heard. Often tied to a positioning of social media sites as risky for women, this anti-feminist backlash can manifest as trolling, e-bile (Jane 2012; 2014), doxxing (Quodling 2015), and other forms of online harassment.

The women against feminism movement often embodies postfeminist articulations of individualism, arguing that women have achieved equality and that feminism is outdated. Our first example, the @NoToFeminism account on Twitter works to parody anti-feminist ideas and was created in an attempt to mock the #WomenAgainstFeminism hashtag that circulated widely in 2014. Initially anonymous, the @NoToFeminism account uses an avatar of a white, able-bodied woman to signify the lack of diversity it perceived within the #WomenAgainstFeminism movement (Figure 12.1). The account was recently attributed to Bec Shaw, a queer journalist and comedian, who was interviewed by *I-D* magazine in 2016 with the headline "@notofeminism's bec shaw is the internet's favourite feminist troll. Meet the writer taking on the patriarchy, one ridiculous internet statement at a time." The account is now so popular that a book is being published of the tweets. Whilst a book negates the participatory power of social media responsiveness, it offers an opportunity to spread awareness of this type of campaign beyond Twitter and provides financial compensation to Shaw. It also demonstrates the transcendence of online/offline boundaries in interpreting and internalizing this kind of humor and thinking, showing an impact beyond the immediacy and transience of social media forms of feminism.

The @NoToFeminism account produces content that refutes the claims that feminism is no longer needed by humorously drawing attention to instances of sexism and racism. This works to highlight how inequality is still an issue in society, and how feminism needs to be inclusive as it moves forward in order

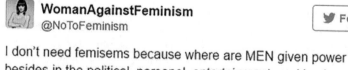

WomanAgainstFeminism
@NoToFeminism

🐦 Follow

I don't need femisems because where are MEN given power besides in the political, personal, entertainment, and business industries?????????

3:24 AM - 11 Aug 2014

↩ ⟲ 522 ♥ 742

FIGURE 12.1 The Twitter account @NoToFeminism parodies anti-feminist ideas. Author screenshot from Twitter

to challenge injustice, yet utilizes a playful manner to make the content witty, ironic, and clever, encouraging a buy-in to the message. What is interesting is that the account appears to embrace what we may call an implicit "intersectional" approach dominant in self-proclaimed fourth-wave feminism (Munro 2013) which critiques feminism operating from positions of privilege that fail to consider intersecting forces such as race, ability, or sexuality on how an individual experiences and moves through society. Tweets such as "why didn't she turn into a white man?" following the abusive, racialized harassment that actress Leslie Jones faced on Twitter manages to incorporate the need for feminism to work to tackle racial inequality whilst identifying how white men are the most privileged in society (Figure 12.2). In addition, a tweet suggesting that men who are white, rich, good at sports etc. are able to avoid punishment for sexual crimes sheds light on the very real issues within the justice system that enable and uphold male privilege such as low conviction and sentencing rates for instances of domestic and sexual violence (Figure 12.3).

The account uses humor to introduce intersectional feminist issues such as racialized power dynamics, male dominance of public spaces, and political policies that aim to limit access to abortion or birth control. Tweets such as "I don't

WomanAgainstFeminism @NoToFeminism · Jul 19
I don't need femisms if Leslie Jones didn't want to receive horrendous abuse why didn't she simply transform into a white man?? Suspicious

🔁 2.6K   ❤ 5.1K   •••

FIGURE 12.2 Author screenshot from Twitter

WomanAgainstFeminism @NoToFeminism · Jun 20
I don't need fimsms because men who abuse women are always SEVERELY PUNISHED!! unless they are famous or rich or white or good at sport or

🔁 3K   ❤ 5K   •••

FIGURE 12.3 Author screenshot from Twitter

need feminism because women are well represented on tv and in movies there is thin and white, thin and more white, thin and whitest" or "I don't need feminis i love seeing lively debate online!!!! between one woman on twitter & hundreds of men threatening to rape and kill her" are important examples of the way the site parodies anti-feminist articulations by drawing attention to social inequalities such as the lack of diversity in media and the prevalence of online abuse levied at women. By making the tweets humorous they encourage critical thinking by inviting audiences to be part of a complex set of understandings about power and privilege. They also spread an intersectional feminist sensibility since they become part of the collective consciousness associated with the account and others like it as they get retweeted and liked.

Some of the tweets deliberately misspell words including misspellings of feminism (as in "feminis" above) in an attempt, we suggest, to parody the anger and haste with which trolls may type online, so incensed and enraged that there is no time to spellcheck. Another reading of this mocking, however, could be of classism as it is perhaps suggesting that the angry individuals who spout these anti-feminist views are illiterate and uneducated. Again it creates insider/outsider dynamics of being part of a clever, intersectional feminist sensibility that has the power to "correctly" read the tweets. Indeed, the Internet has produced new ways of communicating (Crystal 2001), from emojis to shorthand styles which are often employed by specific communities to demonstrate collective thinking or identity which both include insiders and exclude those not considered part of the group (McLeese 2015; Danesi 2016).

The account draws attention to instances of systematic inequality and injustice through humor rather than anger, frustration, or the sadness characteristic of being a "victim" of sexism. In doing so it offers participants new, potentially empowering, ways to understand and engage with topics like the wage gap and sexual violence. We find a potentially therapeutic element to this practice or form of self-care, which deserves further academic attention, perhaps through work that could explore the affective experience of using humor to deal with social injustices.

Debating Dominant Beauty Ideals: #FeministsAreUgly

The #FeministsAreUgly hashtag was initially created in 2014 by two American feminists of color, Christine Yang and Lily Boulourian (on Twitter at @cheuya and @LilyBoulourian), who wanted to create a space where people of color could speak back to cultural privilege and dominant beauty norms, and challenge perceptions of what counts as attractive (Figure 12.4).

Yang and Boulourian started #FeministsAreUgly as a way to trouble those "absolutely silly and completely unattainable" standards under which "every single woman is [considered] ugly, especially if you're a woman of colour," Boulourian told online news site (Dickson, 2014). She continued, "I wanted to find

Follow

Hi,   and I started #FeministsAreUgly last summer as satire and used it to post sexy selfies of WOC.

9:46 PM - 26 Apr 2015

↩   ⟲ 75   ♥ 86

FIGURE 12.4 The hashtag #FeministsAreUgly challenges dominant beauty norms from an intersectional feminist perspective. Author screenshot from Twitter

a way to change the narrative on that and thought I could help inspire others to reclaim that narrative and define for ourselves what 'beautiful' or 'ugly' mean."

Despite the hashtag being created to satirize the notion that feminists are unattractive and to provide a space for people of color to trouble dominant beauty norms, it changed shape in 2015 following a Twitter software update that saw headlines, hashtags, and images from the site's users pulled and collated on its homepage. #FeministsAreUgly was featured on the Twitter homepage and gained considerable attention when it was falsely attributed as being developed by misogynists and MRAs (men's rights activists). With its resurgence, the hashtag became a space for feminists to upload and share selfies, to validate each other's experiences with trolls and to collectively convene to counter anti-feminist attacks. Yet some of the uses of the hashtag ran counter to the explicitly politicized critique the founders used to reject heteropatriarchal and white beauty norms. Instead the hashtag became a way of talking back to trolls who relied on e-bile (Jane 2012) in the form of hurtful, appearance-related judgments which fall back on narrow beauty norms and sexual shaming. In doing so, posters sometimes reinforced problematic Eurocentric feminine beauty norms (Figure 12.5).

Many of the posters using the hashtag were outraged at the idea they would be considered unattractive and they protest and defend themselves by using the hashtag to share selfies, affirmations of "self-love," and pictures of attractive celebrity feminists. In each case, however, the women defend their own attractiveness without directly critiquing the hegemonic beauty norms through which these judgments are actually being made. Founder, @LilyBoulourian responded by tweeting, "Proximity to whiteness means safety, upward mobility, opportunity, etc., but proximity also plays a major factor in who is deemed beautiful." She continues, "If white women were here for abolishing them, they'd be long gone. But they're still here because those standards still benefit whiteness."

An intersectional view helps us to understand white-centric globalized beauty ideals which are also racialized, culture specific, and classed in varying contexts

(Sastre 2014). The speed with which users were quick to upload images of globally recognized white feminist celebrities such as Emma Watson to refute suggestions that feminists are ugly demonstrates the validity of Boulourian's arguments (Figure 12.6).

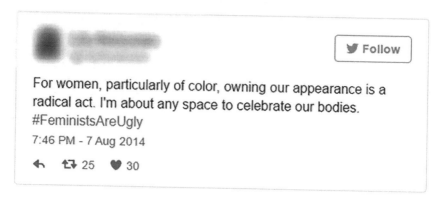

For women, particularly of color, owning our appearance is a radical act. I'm about any space to celebrate our bodies. #FeministsAreUgly

7:46 PM - 7 Aug 2014

25   30

FIGURE 12.5 Author screenshot from Twitter

#FeministsAreUgly YEAH SORRY I CAN'T HEAR U

11:19 PM - 7 Aug 2014

1,474   1,609

FIGURE 12.6 Self-proclaimed "feminist" celebrities began to be featured with the hashtag #FeministsAreUgly. Author screenshot from Twitter

Widespread circulation of images of Watson (Figure 12.7) rather than non-celebrity selfies indicates the hashtag aligning with commodified feminism and a reproductive logic rather than the possibility for disruption of the dominant postfeminist media economy theorized by Rosalind Gill (2007).

We have chosen to highlight tweets featuring Emma Watson as particularly interesting because individuals have chosen to draw attention to a normatively attractive celebrity rather than post selfies which could potentially disrupt normative beauty conventions (see Lawrence 2016). The degree to which writings on postfeminism remain a useful lens with which to critique celebrity appropriations of feminism is perhaps evident here as Watson could be seen as a paradoxical postfeminist figure who both embodies commercial beauty ideals but presents an edgy confident side by proclaiming herself to be a feminist. Here, we see the slide of feminism into corporate salability. Indeed Watson was chosen to be the

Feminist @ItsFeminism · Aug 6
#FeministsAreUgly uhhhh if they are ugly can i please be ugly too

598   1.6K   •••

FIGURE 12.7 Actress Emma Watson appears with the hashtag #FeministsAreUgly, representing a form of commodified feminism. Author screenshot from Twitter

face of *Elle* magazine's "rebranding of feminism" in 2014 (Keller and Ringrose 2015). But the version of feminism Watson sells (both on magazine covers and to the UN Assembly) has been called into question as a problematic form of celebrity feminism because it positions itself as non-threatening and appealing to men. Watson's #HeForShe campaigning is about constructing a form of palatable feminism that placates men, assuring them women present no threat, rather than offering hardline challenges that would highlight the enormous scale of structural change needed to equalize gendered (racialized and classed) power relations.

Whilst images of non-white celebrities were included, focus was concentrated on and limited to mixed-race stars such as Beyoncé, Nicki Minaj, and Rihanna, all of whom may be racially mobile as they perform whitened forms of blackness (Sastre 2014; see also Thompson, this volume). The repeated celebrity feminist postings under the hashtag thus shows us not only corporate appropriation of feminist discourse, but how widespread women's own buy-in to this message is, again affirming the utility of Gill's concept of a dominant "postfeminist sensibility" and McRobbie's "postfeminist masquerade," the idea that identifying as a feminist is only acceptable if you also align with dominant hegemonic white feminine beauty norms. Thus, this viral uptake of the hashtag worked in the reverse of the creator's intentions, re-valuing Eurocentric norms as the epitome of beauty.

We could critique the hashtag in a number of ways; it is body centric and reduces users to their appearance; it is exclusive and denies access to people who are already maligned in mainstream depictions of beauty; it drew a lot of negative attention from trolls who systematically trawled the hashtag sending hostile comments to users; it misinterpreted the original aims, missing the irony of the hashtag originators by positioning men's opinions on women's beauty as paramount. Nonetheless, it is important to consider the process of viral spread and mutation of the hashtag and ensuing debates that took place through the #FeminstsAreUgly hashtag, which is part of a larger movement that is changing the normative relations of power (such as racialized hierarchies of feminine beauty or sexiness) through humor – its playful and satirical functions as well as misinterpretation are part of a wider, complex, shifting, and sometimes ambivalent assemblage of social media feminist humor.

Mocking Misandry

As noted, feminism has long been associated with man-hating and anger (Scharff 2010; Moi 2006) and the introduction of social media has heightened the visibility of feminist anger towards men. As a result of social media sites providing a platform for women to share their experiences of sexism and sexual violence and to call out instances of both, feminists have been accused of promoting "misandry." Defined as the hatred of men, the term is utilized particularly by some MRAs who use the label to construct all feminist resistance as "man hating."

Rachel Schmitz and Emily Kazyak suggest that, "The growth and dissemination of MRA ideology is highly dependent on vast social networks of men connecting with other men" (2016, 1). Debbie Ging (2017) has termed these networks the "manosphere," offering a complex mapping of the online collection of various MRA websites which promote extreme, misogynistic viewpoints that blame women, particularly feminists, for the downfall of society.

The upsurge of the use of the word "misandry" by the MRAs has led to responses from feminists, who have ironically embraced the term (Figure 12.8). There is limited academic research into pro-misandry discourses as an online feminist tool against misogyny and sexism, yet popular commentators suggest it is a way of sticking a tongue out at a school yard bully (Summers 2015) and protesting the fact that white men still hold the majority of political, social, and economic power in society (Valenti 2015). In this section, we will attempt to theorize ironic misandry comedy as a way of allowing women the space and tools necessary to be angry, while also questioning the potential limitations of some of these approaches.

Popular writer Amanda Hess suggests that, "ironic misandry is more than just a sarcastic retort to the haters; it's an in-joke that like-minded feminists tell even when their critics aren't looking, as a way to build solidarity within the group" (Hess 2014). Tweets like Figure 12.9 draw on this idea.

These tweets work to decenter male comfort and refute notions of women being accommodating and passive by simply tolerating instances of sexism. They also aim to draw attention to how patriarchy and sexism harm men as well as women. For example, the tweet above tells men to blame misogyny instead of misandry for them seeing ballet as off limits to themselves (Figure 12.9). Often the gender binaries placed on toys, activities, careers, and subject choices are the result of long-held gendered norms being internalized and positioned as natural, and tweets such as telling men to blame misogyny for ballet being considered a

> **Follow**
>
> #INeedMisandryBecause apparently, any activity done by a group of women that doesn't place men at the very center qualifies as misandry
>
> 3:26 AM - 1 Sep 2014
>
> 15   33

FIGURE 12.8 The hashtag #INeedMisandry works as a form of "ironic misandry." Author screenshot from Twitter

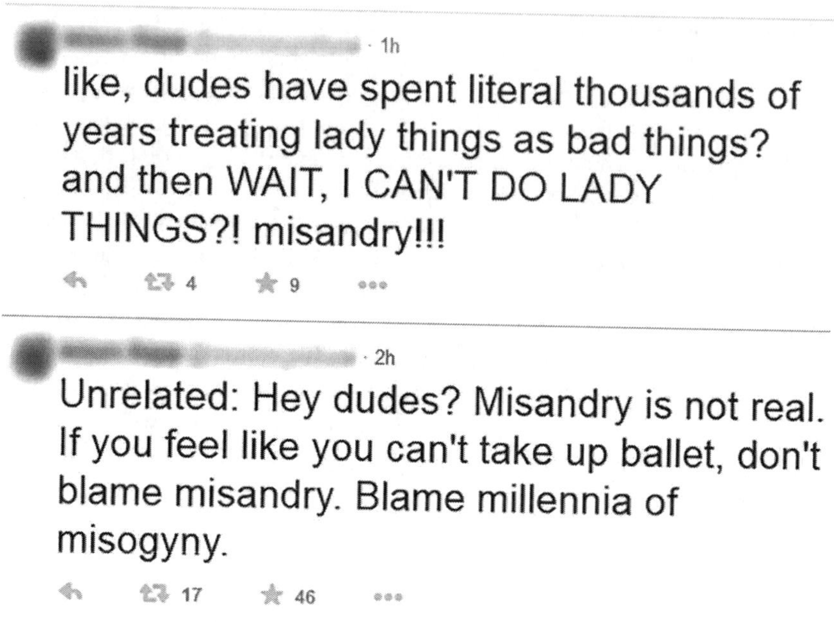

· 1h

like, dudes have spent literal thousands of
years treating lady things as bad things?
and then WAIT, I CAN'T DO LADY
THINGS?! misandry!!!

↩ ⟲ 4 ★ 9 •••

· 2h

Unrelated: Hey dudes? Misandry is not real.
If you feel like you can't take up ballet, don't
blame misandry. Blame millennia of
misogyny.

↩ ⟲ 17 ★ 46 •••

FIGURE 12.9 Author screenshot from Twitter

feminine pastime are important in that they aim to destabilize these norms by
drawing attention to their absurdity. The purpose of some of these misandry
tweets is to highlight structural and systematic misogyny by pointing out how
the term is often deployed when women create discussion or collectively share
negative experiences of sexism. They are also intent on suggesting that misogyny
is a structural and systematic form of discrimination against women, whereas misandry does not have the same power, it is not "real" in the same ways. Therefore,
it attempts to deflate the claim that feminism is about hating men rather than
challenging inequality.

Going beyond textual hashtags or images on Twitter, the development of misandry memes on Tumblr combines visual images with textual slogans to create
symbols of feminist humor (Figure 12.10). Carrie Rentschler (2015) and Samantha Thrift (2014) both argue that the construction, use and distribution of memes
depict new forms of feminist communication and open up avenues of community
and consciousness raising. Indeed, they suggest feminists are "deploying humor
as a weapon of cultural critique," which creates new models of political agency
for doing feminism in the network (Rentschler and Thrift 2015: 331). Similarly, Akane Kanai (2016, 2) explores the gendered, raced, and classed nature of
meme culture in constructing teen feminine subcultures, exploring how "shared
literacies" can be developed through the digital relationships to social media arti-
facts. She argues memes can be circulated and repeated and create new forms of

"spectatorial girlfriendship." Sarah Connelly (2015, 24) has researched Tumblr communities that have cultivated knowledge of "misandry" noting the phenomenon emerged as a satirical response to notions that feminists must be man haters and goes on to claim that "the Tumblr feminist community . . . participates in an ironic exaggeration of those stereotypes." A meme can reference a shared feminist literacy without the poster having to articulate or spell out the views themselves. Memes that originate on Tumblr can also migrate to Twitter or other social media platforms showing inter-platform contagion. Thus misandry memes present new mimetic and viral communicative tools for women to use online to express their anger and frustration at male dominance.

FIGURE 12.10 Misandry memes are often humorous while engaging in feminist cultural critique. Author screenshot from Tumblr

Memes that jokingly claim that "men are temporary; cats are forever" open up space rejecting women's reliance on men for value and esteem, and offer new ways of celebrating objects coded as feminine and cute (cats).

The memes from the Tumblr site "Misandry Mermaid" such as "bathing in male tears" illustrate the mocking of the implication that feminism harms or upsets men (Figure 12.11). These memes also play with long-held notions of subservience and passivity to male sexual fantasies (the mythology of mermaids). Women may choose to visibly engage with misandry via circulating memes such as these to perform exaggerated displays of disregard for men's feelings. As per Kanai's "spectatorial girlfriendship," users can "bond" over shared antagonism towards male supremacy, playing into the man–hating stereotype. Jillian Horowitz (2013) writing about a misandrist meme that says women should have eyeliner wings "so sharp they can kill a man" argues that "all of these sites of misandry trade on the bizarre assumption that women who hate men are necessarily unfeminine; thus, the consciously cartoonish expressions of femininity (like a mermaid bathing in male tears) function as both an in-joke and a strategic manoeuvre." When paired with articulations of ironic violence or earnest rage "misandry" is not only emptied of the meaning ascribed to it by men's rights activists, but simultaneously weaponizes feminist

FIGURE 12.11 Author screenshot from "Misandry Mermaid" Tumblr

anger and the devalued trappings of femininity. It also operates as a type of fantasy space of reversal that feminists are capable of inflicting injury and tears upon men in retribution for injustices against women.

This fantasy of control is apparent again in the misandry memes (Figures 12.12 and 12.13) that showcase extreme anger and violence. A (white) religious icon fights against female heterosexist rivalry and men's rights activists, underscoring women's potential for aggressive retaliation against dominant or coercive masculinity. This form of misandry meme is the most reactive, defensive, and binary driven of all the tactics, pitting "women" against "men". As Emma Jane (2016, 12) has argued about some forms of feminist Internet conflict, it is embroiled in a binary of "adversary/enemy" and "antagonism" rather than sparking room for debate, critical change and transformation. This

FIGURE 12.12 Some misandry memes are more violent than cute. Author screenshot from Tumblr

FIGURE 12.13 Author screenshot from Tumblr

critique is applicable to some of these misandry memes, which re–inscribe sexual difference and essential male/female. These memes employ a logic of reversal, a space to contain feminine rage, but we wonder about the intersectional appeal of these reversals and their limited purchase to challenge male violence through the promotion of female violence. If creating a violent white goddess for feminism is funny, for whom is it humorous? When responding to "two girls fighting over a boy" or confronting an MRA troll, a misandrist meme may seem an appropriate response but how useful are they if deployed in discussions of sexual violence or domestic abuse or the wage gap, which is differentiated by race, class, citizenship, and other axes of structural privilege and disadvantage? Whilst women may use a meme as a tool for expressing boredom or indifference at something a man may say to them online as a way of shutting down discussion, this could arguably be demonstrative of the privilege the woman in question has in her ability and relative safety to dismiss a man outright, in her refusal to engage with men online, and to reduce discussion to anti-male violence.

Conclusions: New Shared Digital Feminist Literacies?

In this chapter we have explored examples of how Twitter and Tumblr offer digital spaces for those who identify with various forms of feminism to connect and defend their views against anti-feminist positions through the use of humor. These new forms of feminist interaction and engagement draw on digital tools and new methods of feminist activism that were inconceivable when postfeminist media culture was initially written about. Rather than a postfeminist moment, then, we ask whether are we in a period defined by ever more extreme pro- and antifeminism hastened by the continuing spread of MRAs and the alt-right via social media (Ging 2017; Marwick and Lewis 2017). Those of us interested in contributing to theories of postfeminism need to take such questions about anti-feminism very seriously.

Our chapter has demonstrated how feminist debate and dialogue against MRA discourses is gaining strength and employing the tools of intersectional thinking to challenge antifeminism as deluded and absurd (Gallivan 1992). The @NoTo-Feminism account for example, has gathered an extensive following because it humorously explores the contradictions of denying the intersectional structural and discursive conditions that underpin sexism such as gender pay gaps or widespread violence against women. We showed why the account works as a new form of social media feminist literacy widely understood and celebrated because it cleverly exposes the absurdity and ignorance of anti-feminist views to highlight the "facts" and evidence that feminism is still needed.

We also argued discussions of postfeminism need to open up to thinking about the rising power of new forms of digital and fourth-wave feminist activism for younger generations of girls and women enabling them to join in to widespread online conversations critiquing idealized beauty norms, but how critical feminist discourses can easily be co-opted into familiar postfeminist tropes of femininity defined through good "looks," which we found in our analysis of the hashtag #FeministsAreUgly. Similarly, our exploration of the mocking humor of Tumblr misandry memes demonstrates a shared feminist literacy (Kanai 2016) created through the circulation of memes that humorously exaggerate man-hating. However, we argued the simplistic knee-jerk violence in memes like "cut the fucker in half" accompanied by a white female religious icon operates through binary gender and white privilege in ways that fail to adequately consider *which* women and *which* men are being hailed by such memes. Whilst using humor and sarcasm to articulate female rage is a critical component for feminism (Austin 2005), we think the claims of pro-misandry violence may be limited for whom it may compel into political action given it is not attending to complex intersectional power relations in how misogyny articulates itself in the public sphere through structural sexism combined with racism and classism, as evident in examples like larger wage gaps facing women of color. Failing to account for the complexities of violence amongst and *between* women enlivened through histories of colonization and racism makes the anger in the misandry memes exclusionary and defensive rather than inclusive, potentially delimiting their appeal. What is clear, however, is that social media provides an unrivalled space for redefining, debating, and defending emergent feminisms against widespread detractors and for using humor to galvanize new audiences, discussions, and debates about what feminisms are at stake.

Works Cited

Ashford, Chris. 2009. "Queer Theory, Cyber-ethnographies and Researching Online Sex Environments." *Information & Communications Technology Law* 18 (3): 297–314.

Austin, Sue. 2005. *Women's Aggressive Fantasies.* New York: Routledge.

Barreca, Gina. 1991. *They Used to Call me Snow White . . . but I Drifted: Women's Strategic Use of Humor.* New York: Viking.

Baumgardner, Jennifer. 2011. *F'em!: Goo Goo, Gaga, and Some Thoughts on Balls.* Berkeley, CA: Seal Press.

Berridge, Susan and Laura Portwood-Stacer. 2015. "Introduction: Feminism, Hashtags and Violence Against Women and Girls." *Feminist Media Studies*: 15 (2): 341.

Browne, Kath. 2005. "Snowball Sampling: Using Social Networks to Research Non-heterosexual Women. *International Journal of Social Research Methodology* 8 (1): 47–60.

Butler, J. 2013. "For White Girls Only? Postfeminism and the Politics of Inclusion, *Feminist Formations* 25 (1): 35–58.

Cochrane, Kira. 2013. *All the Rebel Women: The Rise of the Fourth Wave of Feminism* 8. London: Guardian Books.

Connelly, Sarah. 2015. "'Welcome to the FEMINIST CULT': Building a Feminist Community of Practice on Tumblr." Student Publications, April 1. Accessed on January 17, 2017. http://cupola.gettysburg.edu/student_scholarship/328.

Crystal, David. 2001. *Language and the Internet.* Cambridge: Cambridge University Press.

Danesi, Marcel. 2016. *The Semiotics of Emoji: The Rise of Visual Language in the Age of the Internet.* London: Bloomsbury Publishing.

Dickson, E. J. 2014. "*Feminists Are Ugly.*" Last modified December 11. Accessed on January 17, 2017. http://www.dailydot.com/irl/feminists-are-ugly-hashtag/.

Driscoll, Catherine. 2016. "Nowhere To Go, Nothing To Do: Place, Desire, and Country Girlhood." In *Girlhood and the Politics of Place*, edited by Claudia Mitchell and Carrie Rentschler, 51–67. New York: Berghahn Books.

Gallivan, Joanne. 1992. "Group Differences in Appreciation of Feminist Humor." *Humor* 5 (4): 369–374.

Gill, Rosalind. 2007. "Postfeminist Media Culture: Elements of a Sensibility." *European Journal of Cultural Studies* 10 (2): 147–166.

Gill, Rosalind. 2016. "Post-postfeminism? New Feminist Visibilities in Postfeminist Times." *Feminist Media Studies* 16 (4): 610–630.

Gill, Rosalind, and Ana Sofia Elias. 2014. "'AWAKEN Your Incredible': Love Your Body Discourses and Postfeminist Contradictions." *International Journal of Media & Cultural Politics* 10 (2): 179–188.

Ging, Debie. 2017. "Alphas, Betas, and Incels: Theorizing the Masculinities of the Manosphere." *Men and Masculinities*. doi: 10.1177/1097184X17706401.

Hess, Amanda. 2014. 'The Rise of The Ironic Man-Hater.' *Slate.com*. Accessed January 15, 2017. http://www.slate.com/blogs/xx_factor/2014/08/08/ironic_misandry_why_femi nists_joke_about_drinking_male_tears_and_banning.htm.

Horowitz, Jillian. 2013. 'Collecting Male Tears: Misandry and Weaponized Femininity on the Internet." *Digital America*. Accessed October 30, 2017. http://www.digitalamerica.org/collecting-male-tears-misandry-and-weaponized-femininity-on-the-internet-jillian-horowitz/.

Jane, Emma. 2012. "'You're a Ugly Whorish Slut': Understanding E-bile." *Feminist Media Studies* 14 (4): 531–546.

Jane, Emma. 2014. "'Back to the Kitchen, Cunt: Speaking the Unspeakable about Online Misogyny." *Continuum: Journal of Media and Cultural Studies* 28 (4): 558–570.

Jane, Emma. 2016. "'Dude . . . Stop the spread': Antagonism, Agonism, and #Manspreading on Social Media." *International Journal of Cultural Studies* 19 (2): 1–17.

Kanai, Akane. 2016. "Sociality and Classification: Reading Gender, Race and Class in a Humorous Meme." *Social Media & Society* 2 (4): 1–12. doi: 2056305116672884.

Keller, Jessalynn. 2015. *Girls' Feminist Blogging in a Postfeminist Age*. New York: Routledge.

Keller, Jessalynn and Jessica Ringrose. 2015. "'But then Feminism Goes out the Window!': Exploring Teenage Girls' Critical Response to Celebrity Feminism." *Celebrity Studies* 6 (1): 132–135.

Keller, Jessalynn, Kaitlynn Mendes and Jessica Ringrose. 2016. "Speaking 'Unspeakable Things': Documenting Digital Feminist Responses to Rape Culture." *Journal of Gender Studies* 27 (1): 22–36.

Koffman, Ofra, and Rosalind Gill. 2014. "'I Matter and So Does She': Girl Power, (Post) Feminism and The Girl Effect." In *Youth Cultures in the Age of Global Media* 242–257. Basingstoke: Palgrave Macmillan UK.

Lawrence, Emilie. 2016. "Nudes, Food and Changing Attitudes?" Paper presented at Mediated Feminisms: Activism and Resistance to Gender and Sexual Violence in the Digital Age, UCL Institute of Education, London. May 6.

Marwick, A. and Lewis, R. 2017. "Media Manipulation and Disinformation Online." Report prepared for Data and Society Online. Accessed August 15, 2017. https://datasociety.net/output/media-manipulation-and-disinfo-online/.

McLeese, Nora. 2015. "How 'Selfie' Got Into the Dictionary: An Examination of Internet Linguistics and Language Change Online." Accessed November 8, 2017. http://dare.uva.nl/cgi/arno/show.cgi?fid=606586.

McRobbie, Angela. 2009. *The Aftermath of Feminism: Gender, Culture and Social Change*. London: Sage.

Moi, Toril. 2006. "'I Am Not a Feminist, But . . .': How Feminism Became the F-Word." *pmla* 121 (5): 1735–1741.

Munro, Ealasaid. 2013. "Feminism: A Fourth Wave?" *Political Insight* 4 (2): 22–25.

Papacharissi, Zizi. 2012. "Without You, I'm Nothing: Performances of the Self on Twitter." *International Journal of Communication* 6: 1989–2006.

Peay, Pythia. 2005. "Feminism's Fourth Wave." *UTNE reader* 128: 59.

Phillips, Ruth, and Viviene E. Cree. 2014. "What does the 'Fourth Wave' Mean for Teaching Feminism in Twenty-First Century Social Work?" *Social Work Education* 33 (7): 930–943.

Quodling, Andrew. 2015. "Doxxing, Swatting and the New Trends in Online Harassment." *The Conversation*. Accessed January 17, 2017. http://theconversation.com/doxxing-swatting-and-the-new-trends-in-online-harassment-40234.

Rentschler, Carrie. 2015. "#Safetytipsforladies: Feminist Twitter Takedowns of Victim Blaming." *Feminist Media Studies* 15 (2): 353–356.

Rentschler, Carrie, and Samantha Thrift. 2015. "Doing Feminism in the Network: Networked Laughter and the 'Binders Full of Women' Meme." *Feminist Theory* 16 (3): 329–359.

Retallack, Hanna, Jessica Ringrose, and Emilie Lawrence. 2016. "'Fuck Your Body Image': Teen Girls' Twitter and Instagram Feminism In and Around School." In *Learning Bodies*: 85–103. Singapore: Springer.

Sastre, A. 2014. "Hottentot in the Age of Reality TV: Sexuality, Race, and Kim Kardashian's Visible Body." *Celebrity Studies* 5 (1–2): 123–137. doi: 10.1080/1939 2397.2013.810838.

Scharff, Christina. 2010. "Young Women's Negotiations of Heterosexual Conventions: Theorizing Sexuality in Constructions of 'the Feminist'." *Sociology* 44 (5): 827–842.

Schmitz, Rachel M., and Emily Kazyak. 2016. "Masculinities in Cyberspace: An Analysis of Portrayals of Manhood in Men's Rights Activist Websites." *Social Sciences* 5 (2): 1–16.

Shifman, Limor, and Dafna Lemish. 2010. "Between Feminism and Fun(ny)mism: Analysing Gender in Popular Internet Humor." *Information, Communication & Society* 13 (6): 870–891.

Solomon, Deborah. 2009 "Fourth-Wave Feminism." *New York Times* 13: 285–327.

Steuter, Erin. 1992. "Women Against Feminism: An Examination of Feminist Social Movements and Anti-Feminist Countermovement's." *Canadian Review of Sociology/ Revue canadienne de sociologie* 29 (3): 288–306.

Summers, Chelsea. 2015. "The Year in Male Tears." *Vice.com.* Accessed November 8, 2017. https://www.vice.com/en_us/article/the-year-in-male-tears.

Thrift, Samantha. 2014. "#YesAllWomen as Feminist Meme Event." *Feminist Media Studies* 14 (6): 1090–1092.

Valenti, Jessica. 2015. "Feminists Don't Hate Men: But It Wouldn't Matter if We Did." *Guardian.com.* Accessed November 8, 2017. https://www.theguardian.com/comment isfree/2015/mar/13/feminists-do-not-hate-men.

Van Zoonen, Liesbet. 1994. *Feminist Media Studies.* London: Sage.

Wrye, Harriet Kimble. 2009. "The Fourth Wave of Feminism: Psychoanalytic Perspectives Introductory Remarks." *Studies in Gender and Sexuality* 10 (4): 185–189.

INDEX